The Teacher

ZVI KOLITZ

THE TEACHER

An Existential Approach
to the Bible

CROSSROAD · NEW YORK

To Mathilde

1982

The Crossroad Publishing Company
575 Lexington Avenue, New York, NY 10022

Printed in the United States of America

Unless otherwise indicated, quotations from the Biblical
text are in accordance with either the King James version
or the Hebrew Family Bible, London, 1882.

Library of Congress Cataloging in Publication Data

Kolitz, Zvi, 1916–
The teacher: an existential approach to the
Bible.

Includes index.
1. Bible   O.T.—Criticism, interpretation,
etc.—Addresses, essays, lectures.   I. Title.
BS1171.2.K64   1982   221.6   82-13114
ISBN 0-8245-0507-7

Contents

1

La'Assoth

The teacher, Ariel Halevi, was one with his thought. No publicity
preceded his classes in Jerusalem, and this was typical of the man:
He shunned publicity not from excessive humility, but from an inor-
dinate fear of futility. Though he was an author, teacher, and lecturer
of note, his fear of a day's passing without his having acquired some ad-
ditional knowledge was even greater than his fear of a day's passing
without his having imparted any. When he quietly decided to impart
his knowledge of a subject with which he was most at home—the Bible—to others in form of a series, it appeared as if the knowledge he imparted and that he acquired were simultaneously enhancing each
other. This he achieved by a kind of dialogue he developed with members of his audience and by the freedom he gave them to choose biblical
questions at random. It was a totally unprecedented way of teaching
the Bible, yet eminently reasonable. If the Bible was indeed written in
code, as the teacher, a student of Kabbalah, maintained, more than a
lifetime would be needed to decode it chronologically. The teacher, in
his late fifties, had indeed dedicated most of his life to the work of de-
coding it. He was helped in this task by a special mixture of Lithuanian
Mussarist and talmudic training and existentialist philosophy studied at
the Hebrew University and the Sorbonne.

The audience was more of the spiritually restless than the religiously
settled kind. That was also why Ariel Halevi elicited such a responsive
chord from his audience: A religious man who happens to be learned as
well is likely to regard a kabbalistic revelation as an interpretation. A
nonreligious man, however, provided he is a seeker after ultimate
meanings, is likely to regard a kabbalistic interpretation as a revelation.

1

At eight o'clock in the evening the teacher, with a book and some notes under his arm, stepped up to the small platform. Speaking in a low, clear voice he began by saying that at the previous week's lecture a question had been raised as to what attitude one should assume toward the Bible to understand it properly, and he had replied, "the eternally contemporary." The eternally contemporary, Ariel Halevi went on, was a definition he had borrowed from Paul Valery: "The exalted man . . . does not miss the old because he himself is old, nor the new because he himself is new; but he consults something in himself which is the eternally contemporary."

The teacher began to illustrate the concept of the Bible as eternally contemporary.

La'Assoth

The teacher quoted from the second chapter in Genesis: — "And God blessed the seventh day and sanctified it, because in it He had rested from all His work which God created . . . *La'Assoth*." Now, the teacher asked, what does the word *la'assoth* mean in simple Hebrew?

"*La'assoth* is *la'assoth*," was the laconic answer here and there. "To do."

— Now, to whom does the word "to do" apply here, to God or to His creation?

No answer.

Untroubled, the teacher continued. — The Kabbalah speaks of three worlds of creation: the world of *Beriah*, which is the highest and is the exclusive domain of the Creator, as it is written, "At the beginning God created *Barah* — heaven and earth"; then the world of *Yetzirah*, another exclusivity of the Godhead, as it is written "*Vayitzer elohim*" — "And God created man"; and then the world of *Assiyah* — doing, which is applied in the Bible to the doings of both God and man. Now, in that passage in Genesis reference is made to two kinds of creation, *Beriah* and *Assiya*, as it is written "For on that day God rested from all His work which God created — *Barah*. To whom, then, does the word *la'assoth* apply here: to God or to man?

"To both?" someone asked.

— Yes, the teacher said, but before he could continue, someone in the audience objected. "That is not how the word *la'assoth* is usually translated. In the King James version of the Bible, which I have in front of me, *la'assoth* appears *in addition* to the word 'created'; it says 'Which God created and made.'"

The teacher nodded. — The crucial word is almost universally mistranslated.

"But what difference does it make?" someone asked.

— All the difference in the world, the teacher replied. If *la'assoth* stands for a kind of doing that can be equally effected by God and man, then creation was not completed with the creation of man. Man is here to complete creation.

"But what does such a message mean to me personally?" asked another student.

— It means, the teacher replied, that you are here *to help God.*

"I don't understand," responded the same student after a moment's pause.

— I shall try to explain, the teacher replied.

First, the Contemporary

— *La'assoth* may be a code word for a basic biblical tenet that can illustrate the very "eternally contemporary" nature of which I have spoken. Let me take the liberty of referring to the "contemporary" to explain the "eternally."

— When I studied in France, and became acquainted with the works of Albert Camus, I was struck by the fact that Camus's antipathy for religion was based on the conviction that human helplessness in this world was a notion basic and indispensable to Christianity. Now, said the teacher emphatically, there is nothing I wish less than to introduce theology into our discussions. To me, the Bible is ontology, not theology. But if I must for a moment mention certain theological speculations, it is only in order to explain what this word *la'assoth* was really all about.

— According to Camus, Christianity, lacking a social stance, preaches an accommodation of sorts with a world of injustice that is anyway, *a priori*, consigned to the devil. Camus argues that Christianity has thereby created a climate of indifference to human suffering; it keeps man from total involvement in his time and from regarding the agony of the human experiment as an invitation to action, to change, not merely to pious and noncommittal pronouncements. Camus saw here an attempt to emasculate human creativity and to hamstring human responsibility by divine sanction, as it were. Such a God, argued Camus, must be dethroned. And some radical Christian theologians, like Professor Harvey Cox of Harvard Divinity School, agree with him — on biblical grounds!

— The central question that faces us, according to Professor Cox, is what are the sources of meaning and value by which we live our lives? Are they precreated and imposed *a priori* by God, or does man detect and develop them himself? This question is particularly critical, in Professor Cox's view, as we realize that the urban secular person of to-day perceives himself as the source of whatever significance the human enterprise holds. But the question immediately arises whether we can accept this grandiose assessment of man's place in the universe without at the same time limiting or degrading God.

— Cox's answer, the teacher continued, sounds to some extent like one the Kabbalists might have given. He says that the trouble with Camus's atheism, as with Christian theism, is that both arise from a concept of God that is *not* biblical, but essentially Platonic or Aristo-telian. Generations of biblical scholars, charmed by the spell of Greek philosophy, have simply overlooked the astonishing fact that creation is not completed by God in the Bible until after man is formed and begins to work as a partner of the Creator in bringing order to the chaos and giving form to the formless. Thus, an authentically biblical doctrine of God not only survives the view that man himself is the source of cultural meanings, but actually supports and encourages such a view.

— The Kabbalah itself goes even further. Man is not only the source of his cultural meanings, but the cause of supernatural reverberations that affect the whole universe. At the beginning, the Bible tells us, the earth was "without form and void": God's creative activity expressed itself in separating and naming. Then, after man is created, the Creator actually enlists him in His creative work; He enlists him "to do" along with Him, to create. The world does not come to us already finished and ordered. Far from it. Man, the unfinished, must either continue creation or, *ipso facto*, engage in decreation. The world, in other words, receives its significance from man, while man receives his significance from the significance he gives himself as a creature cre-

ated in God's image. The Bible tells us that man—not God, but man
—was the one to give names to all the living things the Creator made
for his sake, as it is written, "Whatever man called every living creature, that was his name." Man gives names to all living creatures as
God gives names to all celestial bodies, as it is written in Psalms,
"And He gives them all names." God, in other words, does not simply
insert man into a world filled with creatures that are already named
in relationships and meaning-patterns already established by decree,
nor does He insert man into a universe that "knows him not," as Sartre
says. Rather, man, by being called on, from the beginning of time,
to regard creation as a demand to create, to fashion the world himself, actually *originates* meaning. He does not simply discover a ready-
made meaning; he is called on by his Creator to discover it for himself.

— Now, said the teacher, I would like to explain what the Kabbalah
means when it says that we are the source of cosmic reverberations. In
the Kabbalah lie the knowledge and the cognizance—the two do not
always go together—that there are other spheres, *sefiroth*, aside from
those we perceive with our senses, and that those spheres, ten in
number, which the Kabbalah can name, are affected, for better or
worse, by the most minute things we do here below. Since those
spheres are affected by our doings, we, in turn, are affected by the
way those spheres are affected by our doings. Here is an ordinary example. In the world press we read about the damage done to the
ozone layer in the outer atmosphere by the hair spray women use with
no immediate ill effects to themselves. Scientific authorities tell us,
however, that the damage to the ozone layer exposes our earth increasingly to the deadly force of unfiltered solar radiation. Since
everything that has been created in the physical world has its counter-
part in the spiritual, as it is written in Ecclesiastes, "And one as
against the other He created them," certain things we do here below,
certain mental "sprays" that we use not on what grows *on* our heads
but on what develops *inside* them, may damage the upper, supernatural layers that protect us against the deadly radiations of a metaphysical evil. If absolutely nothing is lost in the world of matter, as
science assures us, neither is anything lost in the world of the spirit, as
we are assured by Kabbalah. But if nothing is lost in the world of the
spirit, man is up against a powerful force of metaphysical evil that is

constantly fed by the psychic evil in each and every one of us. The idea that man's psychic imperfections cause metaphysical imperfections above is Kabbalah. So is the thought that the spread of the metaphysical imperfections weakens the power of God.

"Did you say 'weakens the power of God?'" someone asked incredulously.

Thou Hast Weakened the Rock That Begot Thee

—Isaiah said this, the teacher replied: "Thou has weakened the Rock that begot thee." This amazing thought occurs very frequently in the Zohar, as in the statement "The sins of man cause imperfections above." When the sins of man cause imperfections above, we weaken the Rock that begot us. The area of the *sitrah aharah,* the dark and impure, increases only at the expense of the *sitrah dikedusha,* the bright and holy. There are no no-man's-lands in between. We are constantly called on to take sides. The tension is immense. The area from which our *sitrah* is forced out is immediately occupied by the other and is used by it as a launching ground for further conquests. The slightest character improvement, say the Lithuanian Mussarists, the slightest improvement even in the midst of the worst degeneration, creates worlds. Conversely, the slightest neglect of one's *midess*—measures of behavior, character training—even in the midst of the most stringent piety, destroys worlds. Only the Lithuanian Mussarists, the greatest metaethicists in history, could have come up with a motto like "Any toleration of a defect or sparing of oneself is the destruction of whole worlds." Or "Man's every deed is eternity." If a person does not totally identify with his friend, Mussar teaches, he must be considered among the shedders of blood. Just like that! A shadow of a good thought in the mind, the slightest manifestation of kindness, the quiet pouring out of the heart in solitude, the passionate study of the Torah in groups—all these, by fortifying our souls, add strength to the Creator.

Again came an astonished query from somewhere in the room.

Give Ye Strength Unto the Lord

—This verse in the Psalms, replied the teacher, confounded every school of biblical thought down through the ages, except for the

school of Kabbalah, which saw in it another way of saying something
at least as baffling that appears in Isaiah: "And the Lord God is raised
—vayigbah—through justice." This word "raised" is usually translated
"exalted." But vayigbah, the teacher exclaimed, is not exalted, but
raised! Does God need our raising Him? Does He need the strength we
can give Him? Yes, He does! The Almighty endowed human partnership in the process of ongoing creation with the awesome power to affect the degree to which His power is manifested in the world!

— Rabbi Haim of Volozhin, the teacher went on, the inspired Kabbalist and disciple of the Gaon of Vilna, dedicated the first chapter of
his master thesis, Nefesh Hahayim, to the interpretation of the
biblical passage "And in the image of God He created man." The
heart of his kabbalistic argument, which raises man to unparalleled
heights of spiritual grandeur, rests on a unique interpretation of an
adage in The Chapters of the Fathers: "And know what is above you."
In Rabbi Haim's interpretation it reads, "And know [that] what is
above [is from] you."

— The repercussions of this basic tenet of Kabbalah are indeed
awesome. What it means, in the words of the Rav—Rabbi Yoseph Ber
Soloveitchik of Boston—is that creation, the creation that is for us to
pursue and perfect, means our bringing down the power of transcendence into the coarse, profane, material world we live in. Man, as
the Rav puts it, symbolizes, on the one hand, the most perfect form of
Being-in-this-world as expressed in his divine image, but, on the
other, the most horrible state of chaos that reigns in this world. The
whole clash that takes place in the macrocosmos between the onetic
glory and the monster of nothingness is mirrored in the microcosm of
man, who stores up in himself both the perfections of creativity and
the disfigurations of chaos; the light and the darkness; the abyss and
the Law; the beast and the divine image; the coarse, base reality and
the lucidity of transcendence. Man, says the Rav, stands before a terrible choice: divine image or beast of prey; glory of creation or
monster of decreation; the chosen among creatures or the most corrupt of all living things. Man, he says, must create himself; that is the
heart of the matter, and that is an idea Judaism brought down to this
world.

There was a long pause. A student spoke. "It seems to me that such
a clear-cut existentialist interpretation of the biblical concept of man

justifies a query I have concerning a word — a term — a state — that has become almost sacrosanct in philosophy generally and particularly in existential philosophy, the word 'being.' Why has the Bible no word for 'being'? Did it not first appear in Greek philosophy?"

— No, the teacher replied. The Bible tells us that on the occasion of God's first revelation to Moses at the burning bush, Moses raises the question, "When the children of Israel shall inquire of me: Who is the God who has sent you to us? And what is His name?" God answers him thus: "I AM has sent me to you."

— To this, my friends, the teacher went on, Hermann Cohen remarks that there is probably no greater miracle in the history of the human spirit than that revealed in this verse. For here a primeval language, as yet without any philosophy, emerges and haltingly pronounces the most profound word of all philosophy: The name of God is: *I AM* that which *I AM* — He is the "I" who denotes "Being." Being, moreover, the teacher continued, is not presented as a neuter, but as the personal pronoun "I": Being is *I Am*. I derive my knowledge that I am, that is to say, the knowledge of my being, out of my knowledge that *He is*. He makes it possible for me to know that I am, as I make it possible for Him to make it possible for me. I help Him help me.

Someone remarked that while the idea of man helping God was clearly kabbalistic, it had counterparts in other esoteric creeds. "Jung," he said, "tells the story of a chief of the Pueblo Indians in Mexico who believed he was helping the sun to rise at dawn."

I Will Awaken the Dawn

— Exactly! the teacher exclaimed. Did you assume for a moment that the countless sparks of an introspective, all-embracing method and vision that, by definition, aim at reality itself and the depths of man can be confined to a circumscribed area? I am glad you mentioned Jung. Jung was no mystic, but he reached kabbalistic conclusions by means of poetic knowledge. In his later years, Jung tried to find a myth for modern man that would be as transcendent and vital as the one about the chief of the Pueblo Indians. After years of work, Jung came up with a statement that, as he thought, summarized all his spiritual labors: "Man," he said, "is needed to illuminate the obscurity of the Creator." That is only another way of saying, or believing, that we are here to help the sun rise, or to make creation a phenomenon that is eternally contemporary.

—Jung began to gain a true cosmogonic insight into consciousness in the mid-twenties on a visit to a great game preserve in Kenya. Of this experience he wrote—and the teacher looked down to find his notes—

> To the very brink of the horizon we saw gigantic herds of animals: gazelle, antelope, gnu, zebra, warthog, and so on. Grazing, heads nodding, the herds moved forward like slow rivers. There was scarcely any sound save the melancholy cry of a bird of prey. This was the stillness of the eternal beginning, the world as it had always been, in the state of non-being; for until then no one had been present to know that it was this world . . . .
> There the cosmic meaning of consciousness became overwhelmingly clear to me . . . . Man, in an invisible act of creation, put the stamp of perfection on the world by giving it objective existence. This act we usually ascribe to the Creator alone without considering that in so doing we view life as a machine calculated down to the last detail, which, along with predetermined rules, runs on endlessly, obeying foreknown and predetermined rules. In such a cheerless clockwork fantasy there is no drama of man, world, and God; there is no "new day" leading to "new shores," but only the dreariness of calculated processes . . . . But man is indispensable for the completion of creation . . . in fact, he, himself, is the second creator of the world, who alone has given to the world its objective existence—without which, unheard, unseen, silently eating, giving birth, dying, heads nodding, through hundreds of millions of years, it would have gone on in the profoundest night of nonbeing down to its unknown end.

Looking up, the teacher remarked, —The chief of the Pueblo Indians may have been an idolater when he thought he was helping the sun rise. But King David was not. Yet he had a similar feeling, a similar sensation of cosmogonic consciousness. It must have been a moment aglow with poetic vision and prophetic insight when the great king intoned those memorable words we read in the one hundred eighth psalm:

"Awake, O psaltery and violin!
I will awaken dawn."

The joyful image reverberated through the attentive classroom. Suddenly, someone struck a different tone altogether. "Do you agree," he asked the teacher, "that there can be no ethics without God, or, to quote Dostoevsky, that if there is no God murder is permissible?"

— You mean, the teacher smiled, to quote Abraham?

"Abraham?"

No Ethics Without God, or Abraham and Dostoevsky

— Abraham, the teacher repeated. I am familiar, of course, with the famous line by Dostoevsky and I think he was right. What surprises me is that nobody, as far as I know, not even Dostoevsky himself, noticed that Patriarch Abraham had made the selfsame observation, couched in almost the same words, about four and one-half thousand years ago. Abraham, the Bible tells us in Genesis, pays a first visit to idolatrous Egypt, accompanied by his wife, Sarah. "Verily," he declares, "there is no God in this place and whoever finds me may slay me." It is as simple as that: If there is no God — no fear of God — murder is inconsequential. But what is so amazing about this statement, the teacher continued, is not only what it says, but *when* it was said! Others, before and after Dostoevsky, came to the same conclusion. Immanuel Kant observes in his *Critique of Pure Reason* that, while it is true that the existence of God cannot be demonstrated, without a belief in God, which of course implies free will and the immortality of the soul, there can be no valid and true morality. Why even Sartre, the explicitly godless existentialist, admits that morality without God is hardly a tenable position. But these great men, like many others, have come to this conclusion as a result of observing the dissolution of all values in the centuries we call modern. Abraham, however, forty-five centuries ago, that is to say only fifteen centuries after the beginning of recorded history, stood up, as the first Hebrew on earth, and made a statement — a prophetic statement — that is probably one of the most eternally contemporary in the Bible.

The Poison and the Burden: Telling Forth

A student rose to his feet. "Is there a reason," he asked, "why you have refrained from touching on that aspect of biblical prophecy which deals with foretelling things?" The teacher replied: — Contrary to the popular view, the greatness of biblical prophecy does not lie in foretelling things — Nostradamus also foretold events to come — but in *forth*telling them. The Bible comes to life, of course, when we can relate recent history to ancient prophecy, but *we* come to life when we relate ourselves to the Bible personally.

The teacher continued. — I am no "End of Days" speculator. In fact, the sages of the Talmud have harsh words for such speculators. But I will mention one observation that was very acute. I have been struck by the fact that in the furor over Jerusalem, we overlook the view of biblical prophecy that a growing furor over Jerusalem would be an eschatological sign. The prophets use two words in particular, words that have lately been used to describe how friend and foe feel about us. The late General Brown, a former chairman of the Joint Chiefs of Staff of the United States, said that Israel was fast becoming a "burden" to America. At the same time, the Saudi Arabian representative to the United Nations declared that the question of Jerusalem, unless the old city is returned to Arab rule, would continue to "poison" the international atmosphere. Now those two critical words — "burden" and "poison" — are used by a prophet of old to describe exactly how the nations will feel about Jerusalem at the end of the days. I refer to a passage in the twelfth chapter of —

"Zechariah," a voice from the class supplied.

— That is right, the teacher responded. Let me read to you what he says: "The burden of the word of the Lord for Israel: Thus saith the Lord who stretcheth forth the heavens and layeth the foundation of the earth, and formeth the spirit of man within him . . . . Behold, I will make Jerusalem a *threshold of poison* unto all the people round about, and also unto Judah when he shall be in the siege against Jerusalem . . . . And in that day I will make Jerusalem a *burdensome stone* for all people; all that *burden* themselves with it shall be badly bruised, though all the people in the world be gathered together against it."

Someone asked, "But doesn't the reference to the ancient animosity between Jerusalem and Judah render this prophecy somehow dated?"

The teacher replied, — The prophecy obviously deals with both the "dated" and the "dateless," as prophecies often do. The main thing is this: By no stretch of the human imagination could Jerusalem have been described in the days of Zechariah—about two and a half thousand years ago—as a "burden" or a "poison" to the nations. Jerusalem in those days of the Babylonian onslaught was either a contested or a conquered city. The very terms "burden" and "poison," when used to describe a political attitude, are, so to speak, "modern."

2

King David and Being Oneself

The Truth Shall Grow Forth from the Earth

The next class was, as they say in theatrical lingo, "standing room only." The teacher, punctual as usual, opened by saying that he would tackle two questions that had been put to him at the end of a previous class, one dealing with truth, the other with untruth, with masks.

—We read in the eighty-fifth psalm, he began, reading from the text before him, "Truth shall grow forth from the earth and righteousness shall look down from heaven." The question was, if I may remind you, how we are to understand a statement to the effect that truth grows from the earth at a time when we are all aware that the earth is full of lies. Can there be a kind of truth that grows out from the earth?

—Let me offer first a Talmudic commentary to the passage in question. "When the Holy One, blessed be He, came to create Adam, the ministering angels formed themselves into two opposing groups. Some said, 'Let him be created,' whilst others said, 'Let him not be created.' Love said, 'Let him be created for he will dispense acts of loving kindness.' Truth said, 'Let him not be created for he will be compounded of falsehood.' Righteousness said, 'Let him be created because he will perform good deeds.' Peace said, 'Let him not be created because he will be full of strife.' So what did the Creator do? He took truth and cast it to the ground. Said the ministering angels, 'Lord of the universe, let the truth spring forth from the ground.' Hence it is written, 'The truth shall grow forth from the earth.'"

—This interpretation, the teacher went on, requires an interpretation of its own. What does it mean to say "He took the truth and cast it to the ground?" Since it could not possibly have been meant as a punishment, we must assume that it was thrown as a *seed*. To the question what kind of seed, what kind of plant, of growth, can be identified with truth, the *Malbim*, of blessed memory, provides this amazingly simple answer: The creative partnership that exists between God and man can be deduced from the fact that growth as such —and we mean the growth of things on which human life depends—is incomplete until man completes it. What good would there be in fields full of wheat if there were no person to harvest them? The wheat depends on the harvest as much as the harvest depends on the wheat. The fact that one depends on the other bears testimony to the most important truth of our existence, namely, that God made it not only possible but *indispensable* for man to complete creation.

The teacher led slowly into the existential heart of the matter. —Do not forget, he said, that a dialogic relationship with nature was depicted by the sages of all ages as the equivalent of, or at least the condition for, a dialogic relationship with the Creator. When the Talmud says of some of its greatest figures that they knew the language of birds, trees, plants, and leaves of grass, the implication is that here were men who had reached the summit of perfection. The same is true of the great pillars of Kabbalah, Hasidism, and the Mussar movement of Lithuania. That "awesome man of God," as he is often called, the Holy Ari of Safed, sought in the woody green hills around Safed that final touch of communion with the nameless powers that alone made it possible for him to give expression to his kabbalistic teachings. The same is true of Israel Baal-Shem-Tov, the founder of the Hasidic movement, who emerged with all the vigor of his winged thought after years of isolation in the depths, or heights, of the densely wooded Carpathian Mountains. It is also true of the saintly Rabbi Zundel of Salant, the teacher of Rabbi Israel Salanter who later founded the Mussar movement. Rabbi Zundel lived in a hut he built himself in the pine wood forests around Salant, and Rabbi Israel, as a young man, one day followed him there. Rabbi Zundel, aware of who was following him, then told his God-thirsty follower the three words that changed his life: "Study Mussar, Israel!"

Here the teacher related an experience he had had after a lecture he had given at the Brandeis Institute near Los Angeles on the subject of biblical existentialism. In his lecture he had ventured the thought that since nature is a manifestation of what is divine, alienation from nature usually signifies a state of alienation from oneself. After the lecture, a tall, handsome, middle-aged man approached and asked to speak with him privately. As they walked together on the beautiful wooded paths the man introduced himself. He said he was a very successful theatrical agent, representing some of the great names in the movies, television, and the theater. He was successful in a glamorous business, and his entire life, including, of course, his social life, revolved around this glamor and glitter. A few months earlier, the man told him, he had been stricken with cardiac arrest. He spent four weeks in the hospital and another three weeks at home. The man's Beverly Hills' home, which the teacher later visited, was replete with every imaginable luxury—swimming pool, sauna, outdoor bar, and the like. The day he was brought home, the man told him, he went out for a little stroll in the garden, and suddenly discovered something that had always been there, but that he had hardly noticed before: the flowers. "I never really knew I had flowers in my backyard," said the man with tears in his eyes.

— Now, what did this mean? the teacher asked. "I never really knew I had flowers in my backyard!" Of course he knew he had flowers in his backyard, but he knew them as an ornament, not as a truth. The flowers he had hardly noticed in his busy-busy surface life stood for a side of himself he had never come to grips with. Suffering had made him receptive to truth. Since this man's recovery, he has gone to the Brandeis Institute, with its green hills, tall trees, and beautiful flowers to seek spiritual nourishment.

— "The truth shall grow forth from the earth" repeated the teacher. — Does not this formerly enigmatic passage now make existential sense?

Losing Oneself on a Country Lane

— In this connection, said the teacher, Heidegger speaks of the terribly busy, highly successful businessman who goes to the country for a weekend. He plays golf and tennis, entertains his guests lavishly, but briefly; has a gag for one, a drink with another, a game with a few, all on a split-second schedule. At the end of the weekend he goes back to the city without once having had the occasion or the desire to lose himself walking down a country lane. Such a man, we rightly say, is marvelously organized and really knows how to manage things and manipulate people. He has, as Heidegger puts it, mastery over beings, but not over Being with a capital *B*. He never really comes in contact with Being. He does not even know it exists in him as a potentiality any more than the theatrical agent in Los Angeles knew that the flowers in his backyard existed as an actuality indicative of such a potentiality! That potentiality, my friends and fellow students, we sometimes discover as we discover the truth that grows forth from the ground.

Mask Gods

There was a short pause before the teacher continued. —The first question dealt with the truth of flowers. The second deals with the untruth of masks. There is a commandment in Exodus 34 that says "And thou shall not make a molten god unto yourself." The Hebrew word *masseha* in that passage is almost universally translated "molten." The question, as I recall, was what new ground does this law break? What does it say about idolatry that has not been said before? What does it say that was not covered by the law against idolatry in the Ten Commandments? Why does it proscribe making a *molten* god? Does this mean that a god of stone or wood or an animal god would be permissible? What is the special kind of idol worship one is warned against in this biblical law?

The class listened expectantly. —The sages of the Talmud, began the teacher, like most other commentators, interpret this law to mean that one is not supposed to make for himself molten replicas even of the ornaments of the holy Temple in Jerusalem. This is the prevailing interpretation. But the strange word *masseha*, "mask," in this instance points toward other interpretations, too. Biblical words can often be understood differently as time passes. Let me give you an example.

Damim

—The word *damim*, the teacher went on, means in Hebrew both "blood" and "money." Thus the verse in Psalms, "Save me from *damim,* O Lord," which is usually translated to mean "Save me from blood, O God," was reinterpreted by a Hasidic master to mean "Save me from a money-god!" That is to say, "Save me from people whose money is their god." Not one iota of that passage in Psalms has to be changed to accommodate the newer meaning. By the same token, the biblical injunction against making for oneself *Elohei masseha,* "molten gods," as it is usually translated, also lends itself to a more timely, or perhaps more timeless, interpretation: "Thou shall not make mask-gods unto yourself." That is to say, thou shall not be a human-image worshiper, a human-image maker, or worse, a false-image bearer, the bearer of an image that you put on like a mask, which is not the *you* you are supposed to be. Rabbi Mendel of Kotzk would often burst into the assembly of his Hasidim, probably the most humble and God-fearing lot Hasidism has ever known, and cry out, "Masks, where are your faces?"

"Go thee" or "Go to thee"

The teacher took the thought further: — The injunction against worshiping the masks others wear, or are, he pointed out, is also a stern warning against the grave danger of our becoming masks ourselves and the consequent belief that we are or should be the masks we wear. A mask in this case stands for the opposite not of sincerity but of inwardness. It stands, in other words, for the soulless surface life driven to a point of ejection of the self into the exterior. In such a state of exteriorization, the mask disconnects itself from whatever is left of the inner self and, contrary to what one may expect, there is not even a clash between the two. Whatever is left of the inner self is there to serve the mask, to make the mask feel more comfortable in its disconnectedness. I truly believe, the teacher exclaimed, that we live in an era of mask-gods. Every statement made by a politician in a totalitarian state, and to a large degree even in the West, is made by a mask. The whole tone and tenor of social life in Western society is set by masks. The celebrity, as he is called, is a mask, plain and simple. "The beautiful people," as they are referred to in America, are, at best, beautiful masks.

— Actually, the teacher went on to say, the interpretation of masks as manifestations of disconnectedness is found implied in the usual interpretation of the biblical injunction against making "molten gods" unto oneself. If to make a molten replica of even the most sacred Temple ornament amounts to idol worship, it is simply because the thing thus worshiped is disconnected from the sacred whole of which it was only a part. The ornament may be sacred as a *part* of the whole, but to worship it in its disconnectedness *from* the whole is idol worship, the worship of a mask-god. Thus, to worship a mask, as to wear a mask one wants others to worship, is to live in a fragment of reality that is the dwelling place of the nonself. The mask, in fact, is the nonself incarnate, because it demands that the mask wearer make a fetish of the fragment represented by the mask. The warning against mask-gods is, in other words, a call to inwardness, to wholeness, to selfhood, an attempt to tell man that above all—

"'To thy own self be true'?" someone volunteered.

—No, no, no! the teacher cried. That is not at all what I was about to say. The Shakespearean line you just quoted assumes that there is an a priori, inborn, ready-made self one should and could be true to. But what if the self is a criminal self, an idiotic self, a stupid, ignorant self? You cannot—nay, you must not—be true to yourself, we say, *unless there is a self to be true to!* The self in yourself must first be created—and *you* must create it! It is a long, arduous road. The longest road, in fact, is that which leads from yourself to yourself. And that, too, my friends, is indicated in the Bible. The holy Zohar, the Book of Splendor, interprets thus the divine order issued to Abraham that he leave his land, his family—everything, and proceed to the land of promise: "*Lech lecha,*" God tells Abraham, and the two words are usually interpreted to mean "Go thee." But *Lech lecha,* says the Zohar, also means "Go *to* thee." And Abraham, as the Bible tells us, has to go a very long way in order to comply with the mysterious divine order. Abraham gets the order to go to *himself,* and he goes. He leaves everything behind and goes, no questions asked. The eternally contemporary moral of the story is that in order for you to get to yourself you must leave everything behind and embark on a long journey over untrodden roads leading to unknown shores, accompanied, however, by the divine promise that there is self-fulfillment at the end of the road.

King David and Being Oneself

Someone in the class asked the teacher whether there was a case in the Bible where a state of not-being-oneself, of not being one's true, realized self, is depicted as a sin as grave as the worship of masks. "To me it seems," the man said, "that the whole concept of being or not being oneself is of a much more recent vintage."

— Not so, the teacher replied. Leafing through his Bible, he said he would read parts of 2 Samuel 6:14.

> And David leaped about before the Lord with great might; and David was girded with a linen *efod* . . . . So David and all the house of Israel brought up the ark of the Lord with trumpet blast and with the sound of the *shofar* . . . . And as the ark of the Lord came into the city of David, Michal, Saul's daughter, looked through the window and saw King David dancing and leaping before the Lord, and she despised him in her heart . . . . Then David returned to bless his household, and Michal, the daughter of Saul, came out to meet David and said, 'How glorious was the king of Israel today in that he uncovered himself today before the eyes of the handmaids of his servants as one of the low fellows shamelessly uncovers himself!' . . . And David said to Michal, 'It was before the Lord who chose me before thy father and all his house to appoint me prince over the people of the Lord, over Israel; therefore will I play before the Lord, and I will be yet more lightly esteemed than this holding myself lowly . . . . And of the maidservants thou has spoken of, of them shall I be had in honour.' And Michal, the daughter of Saul, had no child to the day of her death.
>
> And it came to pass that night, that the word of the Lord came to Nathan saying, 'Now, therefore, so shall thou say to my servant, David, thus says the Lord of Hosts . . . . And when thy days are complete and thou shall lie with thy fathers, I shall set up thy seed after thee, and establish his kingdom . . . . My covenant of love shall not depart away from thee, as I took it from Saul, whom I put away before thee . . . . And thy house and thy kingdom shall be established forever before thee; thy throne shall be firm forever.'

Replacing the Bible on the podium before him, the teacher commented: — To understand this remarkable story one must first see King David as the unique historical phenomenon he was. King David ruled at a time when kings were gods, but as late as the eighteenth century in France, some of France's grandees declared their kings gods. And how can human beings, even exceptional ones, play gods

without pretense? Thus kings were always trained to be masters of
pretense. E. P. Whipple said a century ago that Napoleon and Lord
Chatham were as much actors as Garrick or Talma, two of the greatest British actors of that time. An imposing air, Whipple said, should
always be taken as evidence of imposition; majesty is often a veil between us and the real truth of things.

— But not so David's majesty! the teacher exclaimed. Having gone
through trials enough to shake and shape his soul, David is armed
from the very outset of his rulership with both the ability to transform
a nation and the power to be himself. As a king he knew the meaning
and indeed the importance of decorum, but he also knew the power of
simplicity and the sincerity of true passion. It was this latter that overwhelmed the king as he wore the *ephod* and marched to the sound of
the *shofar* before the holy ark. Discarding false dignity the king
danced in true ecstasy before the Lord.

— Michal greatly resented this sight. Considering the socially rooted
image of the king more important than the public revelation of the
fire in his soul, she despised him in her heart, as the Bible says. She
understood neither the spiritual necessity nor the mask-destroying
spontaneity involved in the king's fiery demonstration. She knew not
the holy simplicity from which all great art proceeds. Her loyalty was
to a man-made image, to a mask-god called king, to a king whose
power lay not in what he was, but in the way he appeared to others.
For Michal appearance was everything, while the king strove for essence even at the expense of appearance. The king, the teacher went
on, who knew at times what Kierkegaard calls the despair at being
oneself, also knew the *glory* of being oneself. Michal, having associated glory with glamor, knew only the despair at not being — or looking — glorious, and the simplicity of expression that comes to man when
he touches the very bareness of his being — as bare as the style of the
Bible — eluded her completely. By mocking the king's joyful dance, she
rendered herself, significantly enough, sterile. The king's simple joy
before the Lord, by everlasting contrast, perpetuated his creativity.

At the Beginning

An old man rose. "I have come across a thought in Hasidic literature," he said, "that supports the kabbalistic thesis that man, as seen

by the Bible, is here to complete creation. The verse with which the Bible begins—'At the beginning, God created heaven and earth,'—was interpreted by a Hasidic master to mean not only that *at* the beginning God created heaven and earth, but that God created the beginning, what He created was beginnings. The rest he left to man."

The teacher nodded and added that the interpretation was attributed to Rabbi Mendel of Kotzk, Hasidic existentialist par excellence. —There was, so went the story, a very learned and pious man in the Kotzker's days, by the name of Rabbi Shlomo Eger. He was not a follower of Hasidism, but he decided to go to Kotzk to find out whether Reb Mendel was really as great as his followers claimed. Returning from his first visit with the famed Hasidic master, Rabbi Shlomo said the first thing he had learned in Kotzk was, "At the beginning, God created." Did a renowned scholar, he was asked, need to travel to a Hasidic master to learn the first verse of the Bible, which everybody knows by heart? "I learned," Reb Shlomo replied, "that God created only the beginnings; everything else is up to man."

—This idea of man's decisive part in and decisive responsibility for creation, the teacher went on, is tremendously important. A remarkable passage in the Talmud deals with this question in a manner that is nothing short of astounding. Turnus Rufus, the Roman general, asked Rabbi Akiba which was more useful or more beautiful in the world: the works of God or the works of man. Holding some stalks of grain in one hand and a loaf of bread in the other, the great sage told the astonished pagan that the works of man were quite often more useful—or beautiful (the Hebrew word *naeh* stands for both)—than those of his Creator! What could the natural process alone, the work of God, achieve without the completion supplied by man? Rabbi Akiba proceeded to explain, in the same vein, the biblical commandment about circumcision: Could not man have been created circumcised? Why did a male child have to undergo surgery eight days after birth? But that, said Rabbi Akiba, was the whole point. Both world and man were created incomplete, "uncircumcised," so to speak. The Bible, moreover, speaks not only of uncircumcised bodies, but, yes, of uncircumcised hearts! *Orlat lev,* the "uncircumcision of the heart," stands in the Bible for a certain coarseness of spirit, an insensitivity, a lack of feeling in man that it is his task to alter, to change, to mend. Man, the created creator, must, in imitation of his Creator, apply the

life-giving scapel of his creative power to life as a whole: his environment, his body, his heart.

And They Lusted After a Lust

There were now some questions from the audience, which the
teacher, as was his habit, noted down. But he did choose to reply immediately to one of these questions. It concerned Moses' baffling reactions to transgressions of the Israelites in the desert. The questioner
was referring specifically to the way Moses reacted to the cardinal sin
of the "golden calf" — this most blatant idolatry — and his even angrier
reaction to the Israelites' lusting after the fleshpots of Egypt. "Why
did lusting after fleshpots surpass even the sin of idolatry?"

The teacher replied that there was one aspect of the question that
he felt he should deal with right away. — In the one hundred and sixth
psalm, he said, the seemingly minor second transgression is shown not
simply as a desire for Egyptian fleshpots but as a lust after lust itself.
Vayitavu ta' avah, the psalmist says — "They lusted after a lust." The
expression is unique in the Bible. Its story is eternally contemporary.
It explains not only what happened in the desert three and one-half
millennia ago, but also what happens in technological society today.

— During a visit to the United States, I had a chance to learn firsthand about how technological society needs not merely to satisfy con-
sumers' demands, but to create *new* demands. Coca Cola, for example. There is such a powerful publicity campaign going on all the time
that people are simply brainwashed into thinking that they really have
a need for the beverage.

— In other, more complex and more intimate areas of life, artifi-
cially created needs are infinitely more damaging. The commerciali-
zation of sex, for example, turns it into an easily accessible commodity, but this easy accessibility makes the need for new sensations insatiable. Whether or not the new sexuality destroys morality, the teacher
went on, is another question. What we want to point out is that it
trivializes sexuality to the point of inducing people not simply to
lust — lusting, after all, is human — *but to lust after new lusts,* since the
"old" ones were dulled by easy availability and predictability. You
see, the teacher went on, it is one thing to have normal needs — physical, material, sensual — and to seek to satisfy them. But to be told

what kind of *new* needs one should have and what kind of new satisfactions one should seek is degrading and dehumanizing. We have enough problems as we try to cope with our legitimate needs and normal lusts, but to tell us, as purveyors of new products constantly do, that there are other lusts we can acquire and other needs we can experience is to encourage lust after lust—a cardinal sin in the Bible.

— The sages tell us, said the teacher, that the *manna* that the Israelites ate in the desert possessed the miraculous quality of satisfying everybody's nutritional needs. Yet when they got used to the food from heaven, they began to yield to the temptation of needing new needs. Not that their lusts were not taken care of, but they began to lust after new lusts, and not only those confined to food but, as the term "fleshpots" suggests, for flesh. The golden calf, as the Rav points out, was a case of a temporary madness, an idolatrous seizure—too sudden, too brazen, to atrocious to last. Lusting after lust, however, was worse, for it suggested a state of paganism that can exist perpetually, like hedonism. It is an eternally contemporary description of a state of human fallenness embraced by an uninspired or rebellious generation as a "turn on." We witness this phenomenon today.

3

Satan in Jonestown:
A Biblical View

When the world was shocked by the mass suicide at Jonestown, there was, that evening, a particular spiritual intensity about the teacher alternating with moments of quiet dismay. He began softly: — The neatest trick Satan played upon us, Baudelaire said, was to convince us that he did not exist. Now I am fully aware of the reserve with which rationalists have treated the very notion of Satan, and perhaps I ought therefore to be a little more circumspect in what I am about to say. But observing the saturnalia of hate and violence that is sweeping the world, for which even the cynics among us find no description more appropriate than "satanic," shall we not conclude that Satan is more than just a poetic creation, a romantic symbol, or a theological scarecrow, that he is rather a formidable protagonist of history?

— Historians and psychologists have explained how the concept of the devil developed, he continued. They dismiss it as an ancient "myth." And indeed it is. Denis de Rougemont rightly remarks that if anybody says that Satan is a myth and therefore does not exist, his answer is, yes, Satan is a myth and therefore does exist! For what is a myth but the revealed depth of a hidden structure of reality? Psychology especially has been quite adept at explaining things away, but not at explaining them. What psychology actually does is to tell us a great deal about externals, the forms and symptoms that phenomena reveal. Therefore we learn both sense and nonsense about the way people regard Satan, but very little about the way Satan manipulates peo-

24

ple, not only without their knowing who and what manipulates them, but quite often with their settled conviction that it is God Himself who is pulling the strings. Satan is thus a protagonist of history as he is able to underplay his role as an antagonist of God. Satan is a deceiver or a seducer not necessarily because he tells people that God does not exist, but because he manages to substitute for the seas of God the abyss of chaos, his habitat. The seas and the abyss, as seen by Hebrew thought, are of necessity, neighbors. The relationship between the Divine and the Satanic is quite often depicted in Kabbalah like that of the negative to the positive in electricity—both are required to produce energy. As the sages of the Talmud express themselves, the separation between good and evil, or heaven and hell, is as thin as a *dinar*, a coin. Nowhere in Hebrew thought is there any suggestion that a profession of faith as such can render one eligible for grace, that is to say, immune to the Satanic in man. Nor should one strive fully to attain such a state, for saintliness—immunity to Satan—may easily mean stale virtue, as bad as stale vice.

—The very proximity of what the Kabbalah calls the *sitrah aharah,* literally "The Other Side," he continued, to the *sitrah dikedusha,* "The Holy Side," creates the dialectical tension without which creativity is well nigh impossible. Yet this proximity is also responsible for the marked tilt toward evil in the world. This tilt toward evil results from increased intoxication with Satan, while Satan himself sees to it that he remains an unmentionable in the company of the so-called enlightened. Surprisingly, some of the most enlightened among the enlightened had firsthand knowledge of Satan and did not hesitate to admit it. Thus, André Gide declares that no work of art can be complete without some participation by Satan, and Jean Genet, that genius of evil, makes the amazing statement, "Suffice it to know that the devil in us doesn't have the last word."

—The question, however, is not whether the devil in us has or does not have the last word, but whether we can know with absolute certainty whose word we hear. Once this is established, the aim, the highest possible aim of man in this world, is to use the energy generated by Satan to launch the divine word. Nietzsche, great, unhappy, and much misunderstood, described an ideal power of rightness imbued with the energy generated by murder. The sages of the Talmud not only say "The greater the man, the greater his evil urge," but "A man should strive to serve his creator with *both* his urges, the good and the evil." We can only understand this maxim to mean that the energy generated by the evil urge — Satan — should be used to launch the good in us. But in our contemporary world, "The best," as Yeats writes, "lack all conviction while the worst are full of passionate intensity."

— The central problem here is that while the Divine can act only out of fullness, the Satanic thrives on the void. The void itself, in fact, has its own mysticism, "nihilistic mysticism" as Gershom Scholem calls it. Once infected by this state of mind, man can reveal the most terrifying symptoms of the *sitrah aharah*, which is the power of defilement, and regard it as divinely inspired. Not pathology, but only demonology in its bottomless depth — for the depth of demonology can be as great as that of Divinity — can explain the fact that Hitler, for example, believed in God and was convinced, as he told Mussolini in 1942, that Providence was on his side. What kind of God must Adolph Hitler have believed in? Yet he believed in one! This incredible deception, which allows the ultimate in evil to appear as a task undertaken for the greater glory of God, is Satanism at its most manifest. Yet, when you tell people it is Satanism, they will deny it. Well, "Judging from the vehemence with which you deny my existence," says the devil to Dostoevsky's Ivan Karamazov, "I am convinced you believe in me." Every day we witness Satanism at work. Mindless nihilism poses as ideological purity, as love for the wretched of the earth. Executioners affect the language of martyrs; bright young people switch easily from the rage at human injustice to the most horrendous acts of inhuman justice; people everywhere crave for God but embrace idols.

— But who or what are these idols that seduce people? What, I ask, is the primary characteristic of someone who makes himself a human idol? The Bible, as we all know, speaks of pride as a cardinal sin. But it also uses the same word, *toevah*, "abomination," to denote both idolatry and pride. The sages of the Talmud made it a point to equate idolatry with pride, as in the typical maxim of Rabbi Shimon bar Yochai that "pride and idolatry are one and the same thing." Rabbi Ahron the Great, the nineteenth-century Hasidic master, imbues this old equation with a frightful contemporary relevance: "Melancholy," he says, "results from pride." The kind of pride that typified Jim Jones and was subsequently responsible for the suicide and murder of a thousand idol worshipers at Jonestown was melancholy pride.

— What is the primeval source of pride? Pride makes its biblical debut with the seductive promise of the Edenic serpent to Eve: "And ye shall be like gods." With these few words, rebellion against God made its entry into history through the gates of pride. This pride later assumed a thousand faces but the one we are interested in at the moment is the pride that leads to idolatrous derangement, the derangement of mind of the human idol in his greed for absolute power. He confuses it, of course, with the omnipotence that accompanies absolute knowledge and is trying to assert it through *decreation*, which he regards as the ultimate manifestation as well as justification of his power. Thus Livia, the Roman Empress and murderess, orders her son, as she dies, to declare her posthumously a goddess, "for only gods can commit such crimes." The idea behind this remarkable testament is that the divinity that must be the ultimate in pride is also bound to be the ultimate in permissiveness. Two millennia later, on the day the Allies were about to enter Paris, Hilter repeatedly demanded from his aides an answer to the question whether Paris was burning, as he had ordered. It is a matter of ultimate pride to the idol-tyrant to think that nothing survives him.

— The Reverend Mr. Jones, as a melancholy idol in flight from civilization, orchestrated the mass suicide as a tribute to his idolatry. The diabolic logic behind this act is simple: If a god is accountable to no one, there is no crime he cannot commit. The first thing that the Edenic reptile, the unmistakable archetype of Satanism, tells the first humans is that they will be like gods, "knowing good and evil." "Did not the first human beings know good and evil even before this?" the Seer of Lublin asks, in Buber's rendition.

> They knew concerning things that were bidden and things forbidden, those concerning which the Holy One, Blessed be He, desired that they come to pass, and those which He desired that they do not come to pass. Hence they did know good and evil even as a human being in his merely human manifestations does know them. The serpent, however, said that not until man becomes as God would he know good and evil. This, then, is clearly another kind of knowing from the merely human knowing. For it is written: "He who makes peace and creates evil." If He, Himself, creates it, it cannot be something concerning which He desires that it be not. It must be another kind of "evil" than that which Adam and Eve

knew. One can only know this other kind of evil if one *creates* it.
Consequently, the serpent meant: you will know good and evil like
one who creates it.

— In view of this interpretation, the Jonestown horror appears as an
evil *created*, that is to say *invented*, by a demonically possessed man,
who believed what the serpent told him, namely, that he could be like
a god. It thus came as no surprise to me to read in today's newspapers
that one of Mr. Jones's former disciples who managed to escape the
jungle inferno described him as follows: "He was a slithering reptile
who passed himself off as a saintly person." Giovanni Pappini, the
Italian author who turned from communism to Catholic mysticism,
writes that the serpent is the most subtle animal because it is also the
most wretched, the least fortunate. The Creator, writes Pappini, was
"tightfisted" with the serpent, denying it the agility granted to other
animals. The snake has no wings, no fins, no feathers. It has no arms
or legs or hands. It must therefore concentrate all its defensive and of-
fensive powers in the intelligence of its flat brain. And because the serpent drags its body in the dust and mud of the earth, it is also the only
animal that can, so to speak, enclose and clasp the earth within a single compass, as does intelligence itself.

— While it is true, of course, that the primordial serpent cannot
easily be reduced to purely human elements, its traits are precisely
those we encounter in satanically possessed men. To begin with,
fascination. Who can deny that the fame of the snake lies in its ability
to deceive, to bewitch? "A rabbit fascinated by a snake" is proverbial.
There is something deceiving, if not disgustingly bewitching, about
the very physical appearance of the snake. It drags itself through the
mud more than any other animal, yet manages to convey an impression of glistening cleanliness enhanced by an ability to shed its skin.
On a metaphysical level, however, the serpent embodies the loathsome purity of Satan himself, the purity of the defiled.

Another quality attributed to the Edenic serpent was eloquence.
The deceptive power of the serpent, as is evident from the biblical
story, is concentrated in its tongue. Is that why, one is tempted to ask,
in its great warning against the misuse of speech, the Bible tells us that
"life and death are in the *hand* of the tongue"? Why *hand*? Since when
does the tongue have a hand? The serpent's tongue, a forked little

thing, indeed looks like a tiny hand. It stings and wounds, hits and hurts like a hand, but it also seduces and poisons, fascinates, and kills.

— And, lest we forget, the serpent is also a soothsayer. The Hebrew word *nahash*, "snake," also stands for soothsaying or sorcery. Let us look at one example from the Bible, the story of Balaam. Balaam, the great heathen prophet whom the sages say was as great among the gentiles as Moses among the Hebrews, is sent by Balak, king of Moab, to curse the Israelites. Instead of cursing them, however, Balaam is compelled, as it were, not just to bless them, but to bless them in a manner so lofty, so beautiful, that some of his words still form part of our daily prayers. What was the greatest compliment Balaam offered to the Israelites? ("There is no *nahash* in Jacob," that is to say, no black magic, no idolatry, no soothsaying.) When Balaam felt compelled to bless the Israelites, the Bible tells us, "he went not after the *nehashim*"—sorcerers—that is to say, he was not in the domain of Satan. Later, however, we learn that Balaam did indeed return to *nahash*, to sorcery and Satanism, but then, as we find out, he could only curse, not bless.

The most casual look at Jonestown is enough to convince us that there was something of the dark soothsayer about the person of Reverend Jim Jones, something of the *nahash* in him, and about him, and not only because it takes a soothsayer of diabolic proportions to bring a thousand followers to a caldron of poison and convince them of the goodness of dying with him. Jim Jones himself, undoubtedly, was as captivated by death as by sex and must have regarded his fascination with the two as feathers in his idol-crown, on the one hand, and as a means to intoxicate his followers, on the other. At Jonestown death presented a temptation as strong as sin, a satanic death appeal that is a terminal case of fascination with the abyss. The sages of the Talmud probed the very depths of demonology when they said, "Satan, the evil urge, and the angel of death are one and the same thing." This amazing thought is already prefigured in the Bible where the word *toevah*, "abomination" or "obscenity," is used to describe not only pride and idolatry, but sorcery, soothsaying, and communicating with the angel of death. The fact that there were sex orgies at Jonestown, presided over by Jim Jones, bears testimony to his depravity as well as to his idolatry. The third stage of the ritual—human sacrifice—was inevitable. Immorality, whether in the guise of depravity, idolatry, or death, is thus to the religion of Satan what purity of heart is to the religion of God. The Bible speaks of this process in its summary of the Balaam story. When Balaam finally succumbs to the urgings of King Balak to curse the Israelites, he advises the king first to let the daughters of Moab seduce them *en masse*. The well-planned sexual mass seduction succeeds, the Bible tells us, and inevitably leads the Israelites to idolatry and then, equally inevitably, to death.

—Jonestown succumbed, then, to this unholy threesome. But how did it begin? What caused people from every walk of life to join the possessed pastor in the first place? What were they running away from? Why did they become such easy prey for mental seduction? I believe that they were running from the spiritual void that is swallowing up technological society. They fell into the abyss of the metaphysical void, where salvation and damnation become interchangeable.

> *We need a theme? Then let that be our theme:*
> *that we, poor grovelers between faith and doubt,*
> *the sun and north star lost, and compass out,*
> *the heart's weak engine all but stopped, the time*
> *timeless in this chaos of our wills*
> *that we must ask a theme, something to think,*
> *something to say between dawn and dark,*
> *something to hold to, something to love.*

—These memorable lines by Conrad Aiken tell us about the desperate need of aimless people, adrift in a sea of alienation, to hold on to something. But that great need—even the need for love, even the need for God—can be turned, in the hands of a black magician, a dark mesmerizer, into an accepted invitation to madness and death. Biblical prophecy speaks of this eschatological state. In a prophecy that confounded other ages and clearly describes our own, the prophet Amos says:

> —Behold, the days come, saith the Lord, that I will send a famine in the land, not a famine for bread nor a thirst for water, but for the hearing of the word of the Lord.... And they shall wander from sea to sea and from north even to the east, they shall run to and fro to seek the word of the Lord and will not find it ... *in that day shall the fair maidens and the young men faint for thirst*—they

that swear by the sins of Samaria and say "Thy god, O Dan,
liveth," and "Long live the road to Beer Sheba"; even they shall fall
and never rise up again.

— The fair maidens and young men in this startling prophecy began their search for meaning, as the prophet tells us, with a hunger
for God's word fed by their wrath at the injustices of Samaria. Yet in
no time we find them singing the praises of idols: "Thy god, O Dan,
liveth!" and "Long live the road to Beer Sheba!" clearly imply, as the
sages tell us, idolatry, and that the first phrase does so is apparent.
But to what does the second phrase refer? Why is this road a banner
for the confused at the end of the days?

— The prophet speaks here, not without mockery, of how the hunger for God's word may lead not to the bread of purity but to the
witches' brew of defilement. The hunger for God's word per se is no
guarantee that it will be found. This hunger may subvert the search.
Coming in the wake of bankrupt reason and a dying optimism about
man's ability to work out his own salvation, this hunger makes it possible for militant obscurantists, pernicious cultists, and promoters of
facile mysticisms to take over. A slogan like "Long live the road to
Beer Sheba!" really means "Long live anything we can hold on to as
long as it promises to lead us somewhere, anywhere, no matter
where!" The road to Beer Sheba leads, geographically speaking, to
the desert, to aridity, to nothingness, but it is at least a road. The void
cries for a road even if it leads to the desert. Is it accidental, one is
tempted to ask, that the Reverend Mr. Jones took his followers to the
jungle? That is the first stage of the search for meaning. Zefania
speaks of a second messianic stage that is marked — yes! — by *an end to
confusion*. "For then," the prophet says in the name of God, "I will
turn to the people a clear language." *A clear language!* These three
marvelously simple words define redemption, or the true beginning
thereof, as a condition of clarity. The human mind, until then a re-
pository of the confused, the bitter, the defiled, the chaotic, will finally see a break in the clouds. There will be clarity and, with clarity, an
end to the muddled thought and word that typified man before he
saw the clear light. After this second stage, the third and final stage of
redemption will come to pass. Isaiah speaks of it: "The earth will be
filled with the wisdom of the Lord like the waters that fill the sea."

The audience sat still for a long while; then there were a few questions. The first question concerned the biblical Balaam. "How is it possible," someone asked, "how are we to understand that that man, Balaam, who spoke some of the most prophetic and poetic utterances in the Bible, was at the same time rotten to the core?"

— Not at the same time, the teacher interrupted.

"I don't understand," the student said.

— Please continue your question.

"How could a man endowed with prophecy attempt at the end to destroy the very nation he felt compelled — divinely compelled, as he himself said — to bless? If Balaam knew the truth of God, how could he pursue the idolatrous lie of Baal-Peor?"

Pausing as if to turn the pages of an unseen book, the teacher finally quoted: — Rabbi Yohanan ben Zakkai asks: "What has Balaam seen that compelled him to bless the Israelites when he had initially come to curse them? He had seen *that the doors of the tents of the Israelites did not face each other.*" He had seen, in other words, something that bore witness to moral purity, discretion, and chastity. That sight, unheard of and unseen anywhere else in those days, rendered him incapable of cursing. At the same time it also rendered the *seer* in him capable of seeing things, at least temporarily, in the light of pure prophecy. The manifest purity of the Israelites brought out the best in Balaam while the equally manifest impurity of idolatrous, incestuous Moab brought out the worst in him. Balaam's oscillating between the Divine and the Satanic depended, in other words, on the company he kept. It is as simple as that, and that is true of other great men down the ages. Even the knowledge, the absolute knowledge, mind you, that it is God, not Satan, who has the last word did not prevent him from behaving as if it were Satan's. That is the power of evil!

The next question came from a young soldier and it concerned Massada. "I am aware how misleading analogies can be," he began somehow tentatively. "But can you tell us about the difference between Jonestown and . . ."

The listeners stirred.

— I expected this, the teacher said.

"The nine hundred and sixty Jews who committed suicide at Massada almost two millennia ago," the soldier continued, "belonged to a religious cult, too — the Zealots. I think the similarities between Mas-

sada and Jonestown are obvious—even the numbers of people involved are almost the same. Yet we feel there is a difference, or is
there?".

—The Zealots of Massada, the teacher began, were followers of
what Josephus Flavius calls "The Fourth Philosophy," the other three
being those of the Pharisees, the Saducees, and the Essenes. The
fourth philosophy was based on a unique and unprecedented interpretation of the the holy word "ONE" in the eternal declaration of the
Hebrew faith: *"Hear, O Israel, the Lord our God, the Lord is ONE."*
This *Oneness*, as interpreted by the Zealots of Massada, meant that
the domain of God was not confined to the spiritual realm. The very
idea that God was restricted, so to speak, in His spheres of influence
and that the social and political realm was not His business was heresy
to them. The God of the Zealots was, in fact, the God of the Bible,
and there is little doubt that their philosophy would have found many
more adherents had they not stained it with innocent blood, something that Eliezer ben Yair deeply regretted as we learn from his last
great oration to the besieged garrison. Ben Yair's philosophy of *Oneness* was all-embracing. For the Zealots it was either God *or* Caesar.
Caesar was an idol, and if you give anything to an idol, you take everything from God. That is why I think, the teacher concluded, that we
can say without hesitation that while at Massada people died, or killed
themselves, in a war *against* idolatry, at Jonestown they died, or killed
themselves, *for* idolatry. Jonestown, in other words, can be regarded,
if you will, as the *sitrah aharah*—the other, the dark side—of Massada.

With urgency another student addressed the teacher. "If the divid-
ing line between God and Satan is so thin, if people can die for one
with the same zeal as for the other, how do we know in advance whether
even Massada isn't on the road to Beer Sheba, so to speak? How can
we know with any degree of certainty, in the confusion that surrounds
us, where the road to Satan ends and the road to God begins? How do
we know?"

—What you are actually asking, the teacher replied quietly, is how
do we know what is right? That, of course, is a momentous question,
and all I would say at this point is that anyone who tries to answer it
with a formula, a system, a shortcut to a truth, a promise of easy solu-
tions, is a deceiver and, quite often, a serpentine deceiver. The thing

to remember in this confusion is that the acquisition of *understanding* is the end of confusion. This understanding, my friend, cannot be handed to you in a capsule nor can it be given to you as the bottom line of someone else's lifelong pursuit of understanding. Understanding — *hohmah*, in biblical Hebrew, the understanding required to discern what is right — can be gained only when prophecy, history, and personal experience begin to shed light on one another.

4

Teach Us to Count Our Days

Teach Us to Count Our Days

The question to be addressed at the next class concerned a well-known passage in the ninetieth psalm: "Teach us to count our days so that we shall bring forth a heart of wisdom." What did it mean to be thought to "count our days," and what was the connection between this and the bringing forth of "a heart of wisdom?"

The teacher began his reply in an atypically light, even humorous vein: — In order to understand the meaning of "a heart of wisdom," we must first acquaint ourselves with a heart of foolishness, a foolish heart. I came across a few such hearts during a lecture tour of some major U.S. cities. There is a Hollywood in Florida, only a half-hour drive from Miami, and it is built in a manner that tells a story. The growing city consists of long lines of high-rise condominiums situated on one side of a river and masses of small, lovely garden villas on the other side. The much-coveted condominium apartments are mostly owned by the retired or semiretired leisure class, wealthy elderly people who have come to Florida for good, or middle-aged couples who live up north or in the Midwest and come down to Florida for the winter season. The villas on the other side of the river are mostly occupied by young professionals, especially doctors.

—The heavy concentration of so many doctors is understandable in view of the exceedingly health-conscious, mostly elderly condominium population whose main topics of conversation, I learned, are health and wealth. Though some of these condominiums are the last word in luxury, even equipped with oxygen tanks on every floor, this conve-

nience did not lessen the frequency of ambulance arrivals and depar-
tures. Ambulances come and go to rush the heart-stricken to hospi-
tals, while inside, in the sumptuous play rooms, card-stricken men
and women, totally oblivious of what is happening around them, try
desperately "to kill time."

The action in those rooms is feverish. It starts right after breakfast,
is interrupted for lunch, and goes on till dinner time. There the
thought occurred to me that this cast of characters would have to be
declared insane. I witnessed a clash, totally unconscious, between the
frantic desire to prolong life and equally frantic desire to kill time, between the fear of death and the fear of boredom. It seemed to me that
the fear of boredom was stronger than the fear of death, or else how
can one explain the phenomenon of people who have come from all
over to prolong their life in the sun making such desperate efforts to
kill time? Do they not realize that you cannot possibly kill time without shortening life? Do they not ask themselves what kind of life is it
whose main problem consists of killing time?

My Time Is In Thy Hands

—I would like to tell another story dealing with cards and with
hearts, but illustrating a situation antithetical to that of the foolish
hearts. It concerns two sages of Israel, Rabbi Akiba Eiger and his son-
in-law, the *Hatam Sofer*, as he was called after his magnum opus. The
time was the middle of the nineteenth century and the place was Ei-
senstadt, in Germany, where Rabbi Akiba served as rabbi of the community. One evening a complaint reached the two luminaries that
there was noisy gambling going on in the house of a certain rich member of the community. They played cards there for high stakes, the
rabbis were told, day in and day out, gambling away money when
there is so much misery in town. In addition, these gamblers, so the
rabbis were told, were the same people from whom nobody could get
anything for charity. The two great men arose and went to face the
gamblers.

—It was late at night. Reb Yekel, the old beadle, lighted their way
with a lantern. The gambler's house was beaming with bright lights
and resounding with loud, gay voices. Rabbi Akiba, without first
knocking, turned the handle of the door and the two sages entered.

The gamblers, of course, knew who they were. Their fame was as compelling as their appearance. A few among the gamblers tried to edge their way out. Someone snatched up the cards and stuck them in his pocket; he upset a wineglass in the process. In the center of the table there stood a plate with a lot of money in it. Rabbi Akiba Eiger drew close to it and, finally breaking the uneasy silence, spoke: "Forgive me, gentlemen," he said quietly, "for interrupting your amusement. We have come, I am afraid, about something less, much less amusing . We have a poor widow in town with five little children and no bread in the house. We were wondering whether we could find a few charitable souls in town and were directed to you. We shall be grateful for your help."

—Silence. No one spoke. No one moved. The gamblers expected rebuke, reprimand, admonition, but instead they heard a plea for charity. It was somehow disarming. Rabbi Akiba went on after a moment. "We have come to the right place, it seems. The children of Israel are known for compassion. When we arrived here, we heard from behind the door someone crying out, 'Heart is trumps!' Now, gentlemen, that is truly Jewish. The heart, the charitable Jewish heart, is indeed always trumps. What did wise King Solomon say? 'Above all that you guard, keep your heart, for out of it are the issues of life.' Indeed, gentlemen, heart is trumps. I see you have anticipated me in this regard: You had that plate on the table with the money in it—a considerable amount, I can see—prepared, I assume, for the good cause we have come for. That is most kind of you, I must say." Stung and stunned by the great man's bitter irony as well as by his unmerciful directness, the gamblers watched in perplexity as Rabbi Akiba began to count the money in the plate. He did it slowly, deliberately, loudly: "One . . . three . . . five . . . ten . . . twenty . . . thirty . . . forty . . . fifty . . . sixty gulden. Wonderful! Can you imagine what sixty gulden can do for the poor widow and her children? It can save them—save them, gentlemen, isn't that something?"

—Nobody moved. Nobody spoke. Then, suddenly, a very wealthy, very important man in the community pulled a ten-gulden coin out of his pocket and put it on the table without a word. He was followed by the others. Seeing this, Rabbi Akiba Eiger felt compelled, as it were, to change his tune. "This time," he said, "your gambling has done some good, my friends, but it will not always be so. Do you know what the Mishna says of dicing and gaming? Those who indulge in it, the sages of the Mishna say, are unfit to be witness before a court of law and unfit for social honors and community responsibilities. Do you know that?"

— The very wealthy, very important man, a community leader, spoke up: "Don't — don't misunderstand us, Rabbi. We play only occasionally, really. You know, to kill time."

Tremors shook Rabbi Akiba Eiger's body. "To kill time!" he cried out bitterly. "What a dreadful thing to say! *Ribono shel olam*, Creator of the universe — what is more precious than time, and you want to *kill* it? Look, gentlemen, when someone says, 'I have no time!' he is right. He hasn't got any. The psalmist says, 'My time is in Thy hands.' He owns our time, not we. How, then, can a Jew who has acquired, as I must assume, some knowledge of the Torah and is familiar, as he must be, with the psalms, wish to kill time? Let me tell you something that happened last year in Posen, gentlemen. There was, as you know, a cholera epidemic in Posen. I was there. We did all we could for the victims, but hundreds died. We fought for each life — the doctors with their skills, we with our prayers. And you know, gentlemen, what we prayed for? For *time!* For one more day of life, one more hour, one more minute. It would make all the difference. And you, gentlemen, safe and sound as you are, you want to kill time? The only thing I can say in your defense is that you haven't thought about what you were saying."

— There was a shamefaced hush. No one spoke. No one moved. The two great men said goodnight and left. Soon afterward, the lights in the gambler's house were put out. There were no more gambling parties held there, no more games to kill time.

— What struck me particularly, said the teacher, in this true account of the power of spiritual leadership is the seemingly unimportant detail of Rabbi Akiba Eiger's loud and deliberate counting of the guldens in the plate. Rabbi Akiba, saintly soul that he was, could not possibly have done it just out of mockery. A little bitter irony, yes, but no pointless mockery. He was too great and compassionate a man for that. So why this loud counting of the guldens in the plate? Would it not have been enough if he had simply said that whatever was in the plate would go for charity? But no! The sage decided to count slowly and deliberately the gold coins he confiscated, as it were, for charity, because the very act of *counting* demonstrated a reaction to the idea of killing time.

— You see, counting, as we all know, is a cumulative process. If you say one, you are bound to say two and three and four, and so forth. Each succeeding number must supersede the previous one. That is counting. At least that is counting money. But what of counting days? For that is what *counting* our days is, or should be, all about — to make each day be more — count more — than the one that preceded it. This is not done merely by adding days to our lives; we must add *understanding* to our days. The question we must ask ourselves, in other words, is this: Have we learned each day something we did not know the day before, something that can add to our understanding of ourselves and of the world? Only if we count our days in such a manner can we make our days count, while to kill time is the surest way to make sure that our days *do not* count. Wisdom, the end product of understanding, emerges as the sum total of a life whose days were counted cumulatively, like money. This, my friends, is the meaning of the words of the psalmist, "Teach us to *count* our days so that we can bring forth a heart of wisdom."

A Heart of Wisdom

A gentleman in the front row who identified himself as a clinical psychologist remarked that his experience with elderly patients, from all kinds of backgrounds and degrees of knowledge, led him to think that senility rarely if ever strikes the wise of heart. "And I say," he stressed, "the wise of heart, not the clever of mind."

— That is a very wise observation. The teacher nodded. — And it is implied in the Bible.

"Implied in the Bible?" the man asked.

— Implied in the Bible, the teacher repeated. There is indeed a crying need to understand the difference between cleverness, or even intelligence, and wisdom. One of the great tragedies of old age today is that the vast majority of people face it with a heart *empty* of wisdom, no matter how clever and smart they are. The very cleverness of which they were sure, which served them well in younger years, turns against them in old age. The reason is very simple: Cleverness is a way of manipulating immediate things. The temporary, the dated, the transitory, the tangible, and the accessible depend, for their success, on cleverness or smartness. When a lifetime is spent on the exclusive pursuit of this smartness and on the enjoyment of its success, old age, when this smartness is no more relevant, may become a curse.

— Intelligence alone, the teacher went on, cannot protect us from it, for it is usually associated with the kind of rationality that is indistinguishable from materialism. If wisdom is our instrument for seeking the truth, intelligence is but our means of manipulating people and things. This kind of intelligence hardly provides any exercise for the mind even in middle age. For the mind — the whole of it — must be exercised, like the body, if it is not to atrophy. William H. Sheldon, the eminent American psychologist, had a term for the kind of atrophy afflicting the unexercised mind. He called it the "dying back of the brain." He said, in essence, that while the days of youth teem with fragments of living knowledge, daring philosophies, and morning dreams, the human mind at forty is commonly vulgar, smug, and deadened, and wastes its hours. Everywhere, he said, adult brains seem to resemble blighted trees that have died in the upper branches, but yet cling to a struggling green wisp of life about the lower trunk.

— What Sheldon had in mind, the teacher continued, is quite obvious: At the beginning of maturity there is an attempt to involve the whole mind in a process of growth. Then, slowly, under the impact of the prevailing rationality-equals-materialism syndrome, only one part of the mind, which may be its smallest, is regularly exercised while all the other parts are left to atrophy. The small, well-exercised part of it is irrelevant to old age. Senility, in other words, may very well be nothing but the decaying of the intelligence in one-dimensional man.

But the Bible says of Moses, the great lawgiver, that old age sapped neither his mental nor his physical strength. "And Moses," says the end of Deuteronomy, "was a hundred and twenty years old when he died; his eye was not dim, nor his natural forces abated." This was not a reward, but rather clearly the result of a life in which the whole man was used, and filled to the brim with a humanity centered in Divinity. The psalmist makes the point clearly, speaking of the truly righteous "firmly planted in the house of the Lord and flourishing in his courts." The end of the ninety-second Psalm states, "They will bear fruit in old age, they will remain full of sap and vigor forever." The sages of the Talmud too make a statement, and theirs spells it out both ways: "The wise men, the older they get, the wiser; the ignoramuses, the older they get, the more stupid."

—If we are not the embodiment of the spirit, we are doomed to become caricatures of our selves.

Thou Givest Truth to Jacob

"I have been wondering about this last verse in Micah," remarked a student. "Why was patriarch Jacob singled out as the carrier of truth at the very time when he was involved in lying to his blind father, Isaac, about his identity? And also, since when is truth given? Isn't truth, of all things, never given, but rather gotten, acquired, fought for?"

In his reply, the teacher spoke at length of the general tendency to confuse truth with facts. —A truth, he said, is not necessarily a fact, and a fact is not always the truth. It is a fact, not a truth, that "man to man is a wolf," and it is a truth, not a fact, that "you are your brother's keeper." When a newspaperman, for example, says he is in the business of truth, he is not telling the truth. He is in the business of facts, not of truth, and quite often of ugly, mean, lying facts. Even science is not in the business of truth, for being morally neutral, it is not, it cannot possibly be, in the business of truth, but only of verifications. Truth is bound to have an existential, not just an informative dimension. Tale-bearing, even if true, is the spreading of lies and is branded a sin by the Bible. The serpent of Eden told the first human couple a "truth" when he said that they would not die if they ate from the forbidden tree, but it was a lying truth, a damning and damaging one. Conversely, we have a case in the Bible where God Himself, so as not to create bad blood between two of His favorite human beings, resorts, as it were, to an untruth . . .

"To a—what?" someone cried out.

—An untruth, the teacher repeated. Please open your Bibles to Genesis 19:ll, 12, 13. The text before us says: "Now Abraham and Sarah were old and well stricken with age; and it ceased to be with Sarah after the manner of women. . . . Therefore Sarah laughed within herself saying, 'After I am old shall I have pleasure? And my master is old!' . . . And the Lord said unto Abraham, 'Wherefore did Sarah laugh saying, Shall I of a surety bear a child, and I am old?'" But there is something wrong in here, isn't there, the teacher asked. Sarah did not tell God that *she* was old, but that *Abraham* was. But that is not what God tells Abraham; He tells him that Sarah said *she* was old. Just look!

These passages in the Bible, with which we had all been familiar since childhood, suddenly appeared as incredible as they were simple and revelatory. "Incredible!" someone exclaimed. "Unbelievable!" said another. "I never noticed it!" someone else admitted.

— The sages of old drew some vital existential, moral, and domestic conclusions from the way God resorted to an "untruth," so to speak, in order not to hurt Abraham and his relationship with his wife. Thus Rabbi Levi said, "Great is peace for [even] the Holy One, blessed be He, digressed from it for peace's sake, as it is written, 'And He said, Why did Sarah laugh saying, "Shall I of surety bear a child and *I* am old?"'

The second part of the question, dealing with the possible "givenness" of a truth, the teacher answered by invoking a Hasidic story.

— A Hasid came to Rabbi Moshe of Kobryn and told him the reason for his coming: His late master, he said, had often told him that it was his sacred duty to get to know the Rabbi of Kobryn because he spoke the truth that was in his heart. And so, the Hasid said, he had come in the hope that the rabbi might teach him how to attain to truth. And this was the rabbi's answer: "Truth," he said, "is not something that can be attained. God looks at a man who has devoted his whole life time to attaining the truth — and suddenly he gives him a free gift of it." We will come back to this.

Before the teacher tackled the only remaining question of the evening, he wanted to return briefly to a passage he had mentioned at the end of his Jonestown talk: "And I shall give unto the nations a clear language."

— Pure prophecy, my friends, sometimes sounds so simple that we do not suspect its underlying insight into the futuristic depths of history. The prophetic mating of redemption at the end of the days with such a seemingly simple thing as clarity of language is typical; for it suggests that the human discourse, up to that hoped-for period, will be conducted in an increasingly *muddled* language. And let us understand what we mean by a "muddled language," the teacher continued. It is not that this or the other language is in a bad way. It may be, but that is not what we are talking about. The disaster area of language is that of the human discourse. George Orwell invented a term for muddled language, "Newspeak." Remember? Newspeak is the extreme opposite of "a clear language." What Orwell tried to say was that when politics is decaying, language tends to decay, too. In Newspeak, words like "truth" and "freedom" are anything but truth and freedom. When Russian dissidents, like Solzhenitsyn, protest the repression of their mother tongue, they mean precisely this: that when there is no more clear language, the twisting of a term like "insane," for example, comes to mean any thought that departs from the party line. By the same token, a term like "revolutionary justice," or "people's justice," easily comes to mean, in the idiom of hostage takers, for example, legitimized murder. The word "progressive" is now used as the official label of regimes that have regressed into the darkest of ages. The word "people" is certainly the most cruelly mocked and muddled in Newspeak, for in its name one can destroy absolutely everything, including, of course, the people, as long as one does it in its name. Political language, Orwell said, is designed to make lies sound truthful and murder respectable and give an appearance of stability to pure wind. Orwell speaks of the need to simplify one's language so as to think more clearly. But there is an even higher state than that, ladies and gentlemen: to possess the clarity of thought that is *conducive* to the simplicity of language. That is what we feel when we come across a prophetic line like "a clear language." A momentous prophecy about the unmuddling of the human discourse at the end of the days was expressed in so few and so simple words: "And I shall give unto the nations a clear language."

The Sons of Belial

Someone asked the teacher for the meaning of the biblical epithet *b'nei Belial* in referring to a sect of evildoers or apostates. "The King James version," said the man, "translates *b'nei Belial* simply as 'the sons of Belial.' But what does 'Belial' mean?"

—Among the many interpretations I have come across, the one by the saintly Hafetz Hayim, tells a timeless story. In his interpretation the word *Belial* actually consists of a merger of two words, *beli*, which means "without," and *Al* or *Ol*, which means "yoke," that is to say, the yoke of the kingdom of heaven. *Belial* thus means "those without a yoke" or "the sons of no yoke." In some translations, *Belial* comes to mean "evil" or "wicked," but to me it seems to be more a matter of an ideological or psychological lawlessness that approaches what is meant by the term "anomie." Anomie is a kind of lawlessness that cancels the seriousness of both belief and unbelief. In a book titled *Varieties of Unbelief*, the author, Martin Marty, describes this malaise as the disease of the postcivilized, occurring only in the overorganized life. The negative of nihilism and the positive of the will to power may be its only intrinsic value.

— "And slime had they for mortar." The anomic person is not at home in the universe. He is leaderless and valueless, but above all, rootless and faithless. He thus drifts into normlessness and slow spiritual death. In brief, anomie is a state in which man has thrown off the "yoke" of the guiding spiritual principle without realizing that he has become a slave of nothingness. It is interesting that in Chronicles *b'nei Belial* is paired with *rekim*, empty or vacuous creatures. The connection between yokelessness and lawlessness, the teacher concluded, is quite obvious. Less obvious is the connection between the shedding of the kingdom of heaven's yoke and the epidemic spread of anxiety and alienation in the world today. We shall discuss it, God willing, the next time we meet.

5

Biblical Dialectics:
The Freeing Yoke

The Brass Serpent

Before Ariel Halevi could start his promised elaboration on the connection between the overthrow of the *Ol* and some forms of anxiety and neurosis, a question about the biblical snake was put to him again. It concerned a passage in the Bible in which the serpent appears, for the first and only time, as endowed by the Creator with the power to do good: the baffling passage in Numbers 21 according to which a distraught Moses is told by God that in order to stop an on slaught of fiery serpents in the desert, which had already caused many Israelites to perish, he should make a serpent of brass and put it on a pole. "And it came to pass that if a serpent had bitten any man, when he beheld the serpent of brass, he lived." How was this to be understood?

—This has indeed baffled commentators in the Jewish tradition down the ages and some of their commentaries are as baffling as the text itself, the teacher replied. The only exception is Nachmanides, eleventh-century sage and Kabbalist, whose intimation of an answer can be called prophetic. While it does not explain the whole story as scripture relates, it does contain a startlingly apropos illustration using the maxim from Ecclesiastes: "One as against the other He created them," that is, in the metaphysical world there exist laws similar to those that govern the physical one. In Spain, more than six centuries before Edward Jenner discovered the principle and method of vaccination, this giant, Rabenu Moshe Ben Nachman, reached the same

45

principle, in spiritual terms, as he tried to answer the question how it was possible that a snake, a serpent, was used by divine order to counteract the deadly effect of its own venomous sting.

— The Mishnah, the teacher continued, offers a metaphoric explanation, namely, that anyone among the bitten Israelites in the desert who lifted his eyes to see the brass serpent, held high on a standard, would in fact be lifting his eyes to heaven and from heaven would come his recovery. This explanation is far from satisfying. The enigma of the biblical account grows, moreover, as we read in Second Kings that Hezekiah, a saintly king known as a smasher of idols, an iconoclast, who lived about seven hundred years after the incident in the desert, destroyed the brass serpent! Are we to infer from this that for seven hundred years the brass serpent was kept intact? the teacher asked. And what kind of cure, once again, did it offer to the snakebitten Israelites in the desert? To these questions I have no clear-cut answer, only a clue. But before I disclose this, let us return for a moment to Edward Jenner, the British country doctor to whom goes the credit for the discovery, first reported in 1798, that infectious material from lesions of cowpox, for example, could be inoculated artifically into the skin of a man and thus induce immunity against smallpox. Louis Pasteur and others, as we all know, applied the same principle to the prophylaxis of other bacteria. Now, having said this, let me read to you the exact word that Nachmanides used to explain the phenomenon of the brass serpent in the desert. "We learn from it," the master Kabbalist said, "that the ways of the Torah are such that all its happenings are a miracle within a miracle, for it repairs the damage by that which causes it, and cures the sickness with what makes one sick!" Is the connection to our modern practice of vaccination not obvious?

— While the biblical story is still veiled in mystery, I feel free to interpret the plague of poisonous snakes in the desert — a plague that followed an earlier punishment of the Israelites for their temporary loss of faith in God and in Moses — as a double plague: The Israelites are physically stung by snakes after being spiritually stung by what the snake stands for — the demonically seductive power of sorcery and black magic. The very name of the place that the Israelites had to cross immediately following the mysterious onslaught of fiery serpents hints at an equally mysterious story. *Oboth,* plural for *Ob,* the place in the desert where the snakes were violently active, was seemingly and fittingly close to another place called *Oboth*. As you know, *Ob* or *Oboth* stands in the Bible for necromancy and black magic. It was, after all, the Witch of Endor, referred to in the Bible as a *Baalath Ob*, a practitioner of *Ob*, sorcery, to whom a desperate King Saul went centuries later on his last tragic night to seek illegitimate contact with the hereafter. The first words with which the unhappy king addresses her are: "I pray thee, divine unto me by the spirit of *Ob* and bring me up *Him* whom I shall name unto thee."

Ol and *Al*

The teacher now returned to the question of why the Bible placed so much importance on the *Ol*, "yoke" — that it branded those who did not have it, or overthrew it, *b'nei Belial*.

— Like faith, the teacher explained, whose antithesis is not faithlessness, but idolatry, the alternative to the *Ol*, the yoke of the kingdom of heaven, is not permissiveness, but *slavery*. The philosopher Nicholas Berdyaev, that great, lonely Russian soul of our time, said that the crisis of our culture, subverted by false freedoms and genuine tyrannies, cannot be surmounted by its own exclusive means, shaken as it is to its very foundations. We must of necessity turn to much deeper sources. Berdyaev indeed went to those sources like a desert wanderer to an oasis and came back with a thought for this confused age, a thought so eternally contemporary that it may be called a summary of the biblical world view:

— "Man is so made," the teacher read from a note before him, "that he lives by faith in God or else by faith in idols. When he loses his faith in God, he falls into idolatry. The cult of idols is found today in all areas: in science, in art, in the political, national, and social forms of life. Thus Communism, for instance, is an extreme form of social idolatry."

— Berdyaev's either/or proposition is highly biblical, the teacher went on. Either we submit ourselves to the experience of an *Ol* as an anchor in the *Al*, the "*Above*" — these are two vitally interconnected and interchangeable biblical word-concepts — or we become idol worshipers, anxiety-stricken, alienated slaves of idolatry. Most people today, are in fact, idol worshipers.

"In what sense?" someone asked.

— In the sense that people today worship what they themselves have created, and this is not only blasphemous, but sickening in the clinical sense, for man cannot tolerate for long gods of his own making and remain sane.

— We shall not be able to feel the depth of the biblical outcry against idolatry unless we understand the timelessness of its thrust and threat. The biblical message consists of two parts, Ariel Halevi went on, the belief in one invisible God as the source of all truth, and the rejection of idolatry as the source of the lived lie. The belief in one invisible God as the source of truth demands the destruction of idols, and indeed the struggle against idolatry is the most typical trait of biblical Judaism down the ages, for Judaism always suspected that the professed belief in one invisible God could very well go hand in hand with idol worship. Today, this is more than a suspicion; it is a reality whose manifestations we prefer to ignore.

— Technological society, be it in its Western or Eastern versions, is both an *idol-consuming* and *idolatry-consumed* society. In the so-called revolutionary regimes, people are capable of the wildest cruelties to dramatize their fidelity to such idolized stereotypes as "progress," "revolutionary justice," "the people's will," "equality." Such idolized stereotypes have nothing whatsoever to do with improved human relationships; they reflect the unholy life of a mighty Baal that demands human sacrifice. In a consumer society we get the impression that man is made for the product, not the product for the man. In a consumer society, the product created by man becomes, as it were, a creator. The promise is that the splendor of the Rolls Royce will rub off on its owner and he will be judged as a man by the grandeur of the machine he can afford. Ultimate importance is attached to what meets the eye, to a one-dimensionality of man that technology has helped to extend sensually. Blake called this idolatry "one vision" and warned against it. The audiovisual extension of our senses induces people to think that only what can be seen or heard is real. It is a mighty and constant helpmate to idolatry. Sooner or later it alienates us from the spiritual dimension, which insists, on the contrary, that the only true reality is precisely that which transcends the easily perceptible.

They That Make Them Shall Be Like Them

Continuing, the teacher spoke of verses in the Psalms as interpreted by Marshall McLuhan, regarded as the finest diagnostician of the media: — "In an idolatrous age," McLuhan maintains, "men become what they behold: extensions and expediters of the sense life. Any medium at once affects the entire field of the senses." If the medium is the idol, we the onlookers become *its* extensions. In this context, McLuhan quotes from Psalm 115:

> *Their idols are silver and gold,*
> *The work of man's hands.*
> *They have mouths, but they speak not;*
> *Eyes they have, but they see not;*
> *They have ears, but they hear not;*
> *Noses they have, but they smell not;*
> *Hands they have, but they handle not;*
> *Feet they have, but they walk not;*
> *Neither speak they through their throat.*
> *They that make them shall be like unto them;*
> *Yea, everyone that trusteth in them.*

— To this McLuhan remarks that the concept of "idol" for the psalmist is much like that of Narcissus in the Greek myth. For the psalmist insists that the beholding of idols, like the use of technology, conforms man to them: "They that make them shall be like unto them." People become what they behold, are built by the "bricks" they fashion in their image, an image they then refer to as a deity.

— Blake, in his inspired poem "Jerusalem," explains that the reason men become what they have beheld "is the spectre of the reasoning power in man," which has become fragmented and separated from imagination "and enclosing itself as in steel." Blake, in other words, sees in the dominance of technology the self-amputation of some of our vital organs, primarily those of perception. Rationalism, for Blake, our self-enclosure in a fragment, becomes the amputation of perception. Each amputated organ of the mind then becomes "a closed system of great new intensity and hurls man into martyrdom and wars." This is precisely the frightening intensity of idolatry. The men formed by such systems becomes slaves who, in their total lack of "the courage to be," choose slavery over everything else. Thus the choice is not between the *Ol* of heaven and free thinking, but between God and Baal. Man is either built by the *Al*, the "Above", or is a builder of Baal, which is the Below.

The Man Who Was Built by the Yoke

— One of the greatest biblical figures speaks of himself, before his death, as a man who was raised, or literally "built," by submission to a yoke. This refers, the teacher continued, to King David's mighty last words as recorded at the outset of the twenty-third chapter of Second Samuel, which contains a solemn declaration of *dependence* on the *Ol*: "So speaks the man who was *built* [*hukam*] by the *Ol*—or*Al*." (The usual translation is "Thus spoke the man who was raised up on High.")

Biblical Dialectics: The Freeing Yoke

To further explain the biblical notion of *Ol*, a yoke or obedience, as a builder of man, the teacher introduced the term "biblical dialectics."

— Biblical dialectics, he said, makes its first appearance, appropriately enough, with the idea of freedom. Moses tells Pharaoh to let his people go so that they can serve God in the desert. The biblical word for the status of the Hebrews in Egypt is *avadim*, "slaves." Yet Moses uses a derivative of the very same word, *vya'avduni*, "And they shall *serve* me," to delineate obedience to, that is, the yoke of the Lord God Jahweh. Jacques Ellul, French sociologist and theologian, here poses the question whether these two themes were not contradictory. Does God liberate merely in order to reduce to slavery again? Did the Jews leave one bondage only to enter another? No, says Ellul. The Bible says that at this point God, having liberated His people, controls them and guides them, but with the initiative and independence of His people. The people must constantly take up the conditions of their liberation again, and that is what they do. If we have been set free by God, then this means for our future. Hence we must accept control and management from God at the same time we accept this access to freedom.

In Ellul's own words,

> This is hard to grasp intellectually; but at the same time it is something that can be lived with concretely. Intellectually, it is the great problem posed by Karl Barth. Barth said that, on the one hand, there is the freedom of God and, on the other hand, the freedom that God gives to human beings. The goal is to live the human freedom within the freedom of God. Thus, logically the two cannot be reconciled. But dialectically one can live them.

— This is of central importance for us, said the teacher. As we try to understand the Bible existentially, our purpose is to put the stress on truths that can and must be lived *whether or not* we can grasp them intellectually. The biblical concept of the *Ol*—the freeing yoke, the healing obedience—has been vindicated in our day and age, not only as a religious truth but as a paradigmatic psychological insight. Think of Kierkegaard's famous definition of anxiety as "the dizziness of freedom." Such a dizziness, a mental and spiritual dizziness, occurs when a misconstrued concept of freedom cuts man's lonely boat free from its moorings in the *Ol*. The dizziness of freedom is a dizziness of feeling—and being—adrift. For a couple of centuries the "progressive" idea prevailed that we cannot really regard ourselves as free as long as we are tied to the moorings of a restraining *Ol*. Only recently has a growing body of thought made the connection between the severing of our inner moorings to the *Ol* and our sense of being cut adrift, which we feel as a sense of anxiety and futility.

A member of the class nodded. While living in New York, he said, he had joined the Society of Ethical Culture, founded a century ago by Felix Adler, who believed, in typical nineteenth-century fashion, that there was such a thing as autonomous ethics and that man could be trusted to work out his own salvation. He had joined that society, as he now realized, because in his ignorance he had sought to *escape* the restraints of the *Ol*.

Someone else asked whether, speaking of futility, the first words in Ecclesiastes, *hevel havalim*, often translated "vanity of vanities," did not really mean "futility of futilities." The teacher agreed. —And a remedy for futility is suggested in the same book, he said.

A Biblical Definition of Futility

The teacher quoted from the beginning of the twelfth chapter of Ecclesiastes:

— "And be mindful of thy creator in the days of thy youth, while the troubled days come not, nor the years draw nigh when you shall say, 'I have no pleasure in them.'"

In his ensuing commentary, Ariel Halevi first tried to establish whether the word "pleasure" conveyed the real meaning of the Hebrew *hefetz*. — When Ecclesiastes makes the famous statement "To everything there is a season and a time to every *hefetz*" — *hefetz* is usually translated as "purpose." It may actually mean both pleasure and purpose, for the beginning of pleasure, of contentment, is to have a purpose in life. Futility takes over when there is no pleasure in purpose and no purpose in pleasure. Such are "the troubled days," as Ecclesiastes sees them, which are bound to haunt adulthood if there was no mindfulness of the Creator, no submission to the *Ol*, in the days of youth. I am aware, the teacher went on, that Nachmanides, like some other Kabbalistic commentators, interpreted "the troubled days" eschatologically, that is to say, as a reference to the state of the world at the end of days. But I believe that certain passages in the Bible, like certain words we have mentioned — *damim*, for example, which means both "blood" and "money" — are sometimes there precisely in order to stimulate various interpretations. Let us look also at the passage that follows.

When "The Clouds Return After the Rain"

— Ecclesiastes, the teacher went on, using the metaphor of clouds and rain, speaks of that most painful aspect of futility which we feel as existential loneliness if we feel, with Sartre, that "we are thrown into a universe that knows us not." We experience loneliness not only as a social but as a cosmic phenomenon. Even nature loses its luster because it appears blind to us. What can be more blind, more absurdly blind, after all, than clouds, for example, returning after rain? So Ecclesiastes invokes this metaphor as a warning. Things will seem absurd to us, meaningless, accidental, unless we are mindful of the Creator in the days of our youth: "While the sun or the light or the stars be not darkened *nor the clouds return after the rain.*"

Peaks and Valleys

"What," asked someone in the audience, "is the meaning of Ecclesiastes in general? How were we to understand passages in that marvelously wise, wonderfully sad little book, part and parcel of the Holy Writ, that can be easily construed as heretical? What can we make of the statement 'There is neither work nor invention nor knowledge nor wisdom in the *sheol*—the grave—toward which you are going'?"

The teacher's reply was surprising in its candor. He remarked that while there were many answers to this question, he, for one, had not yet found an entirely satisfactory explanation. —Ecclesiastes, like man himself, is full of contradictions. We find statements like "But the dead do not know anything," and, on the other hand, warnings that "God shall bring every work into judgment, even everything hidden, whether it be good or bad," or that "the spirit—*ruah*—will return to God whence it has come." Perhaps Ecclesiastes was the archetypal torn man, who recorded in his master thesis both his "peak" and his "valley" experiences. The term "peak" is borrowed specifically from Abraham Maslow, but he was echoing an archetypal image, for peaks have belonged to the spirit since Mount Sinai and Mount Moriah, Mount Zion and the Mount of Olives, Mount Olympus and Mount Patmos. The peak experience is a way of describing the spirit in search of itself, and approaching its object. The *vale* experience, by contradistinction, depicts a depressed emotional and spiritual state; it is the psalmist's "valley of the shadow," the world regarded as a place of sorrow and weeping, as the scene of the mortal, the lowly, the lonely, the earthly.

—The person, the real person, the teacher continued, unless he has attained to saintliness, is torn between the peaks and valleys of existence. When a Hasidic master said "There is nothing as whole as a broken heart," he actually put the seal of highest spirituality on the torn man.

And I Said in my Haste All Men Are Liars

"Can biblical man," asked someone in the class, "in any way be described as 'torn'?" —Yes, said the teacher. The psalmist was the torn man par excellence, but that did not diminish—indeed it enhanced— the power of his faith. Listen to what the Rav, Rabbi Yoseph Ber Soloveitchik of Boston, has said on the psalmist's strange words. "I said in my haste all men are liars." He asks, what kind of lie did the psalmist have in mind when he hurled this serious accusation at man in general? Did he have in mind the lie that the I tells the Thou? Was he referring to the everyday social lie? Did he have in mind the commercial lie of the dishonest businessman, the political lie of the faithless ruler, the judicial lie of the perjurer? In a word, did he speak of the profitable, immoral lie? Does man constantly engage in immoral lying? the Rav asks. And he replies, By no means! The psalmist, he says, is concerned with a different kind of lie, the existential lie that man tells not to others, but to himself. Man, says the Rav, is indeed a liar, for he is involved in an unresolvable contradiction, in an absolute dialectic, because he is caught, like Abraham's ram, in the thicket of antinomies and dichotomies. He swings like a pendulum between two poles: the thesis and the antithesis, the affirmation and the negation, identifying himself either with both of them or with neither. He *must* lie, so to speak, the Rav states, but this inevitable lie is rooted in man's uniqueness and is a *moral lie*, for it is the wellspring of human creativity. If agony accompanies the process of creativity, this is because it is the torn man who is the creator.

In the Days of Thy Youth

Again there was a question concerning the much-discussed passage in Ecclesiastes: "Be mindful of thy Creator in the days of thy youth." Why "in the days of thy *youth*"? Why not "Be mindful of your Creator all the days of your *life*?"

The teacher replied: — There is a profound psychological meaning in the emphasis on youth, that is to say, on the mind-forming years as the ideal time for acquiring a mindfulness of the Creator that will be, at the same time, *memorable*. The Hebrew word for being mindful here is *zehor*, imperative also for "remember." The accent here seems to be on a memorable paradigmatic experience one can fall back on in times of crisis. It is like the Greek concept of entelechy, the idea that the ultimate form is contained in the seed, and the tree, like the human being, grows toward this form, twisted or blasted though it may be in the process.

— We live in an era that has seen the emergence of a generation of men and women whose "youthful souls did not know" the kind of seed that shapes form. There comes to my mind a lecture I read some time ago, "Psychiatry and the Sacred" by Jacob Needleman, who teaches philosophy at San Francisco State University. He said, in essence, that when I am in trouble it is not the psychotherapist or the spiritual leader I turn to. It is something in myself that I turn to first. Some ideas, some memories, some habits of thinking, some emotional associations, some spiritual insights. In the moment when life becomes unbearable, it may seem that I take any hand that is offered, but this is not so. I have an "inner guide," Professor Needleman writes, that gets me through the night, and by the "inner guide", he says, we mean a "sacred tradition" radiating from the past, which quite often makes it possible for psychiatry to work.

— In this light, continued the teacher, "the days of thy youth" in that passage in Ecclesiastes assumes a special meaning. It emphasizes that no matter what course a person may eventually chart for his own life, it should be the purpose of education or at least of the family to implant in him, during the formative years of his life, something to serve him as a lighthouse in the stormy waters of adulthood. That "something" which Professor Needleman defines with inspired precision as "the something" that starts with being mindful of the Creator in one's youth, is the real process of growth. It may be a painful process, but there is one that is even more painful — to oneself and to others: the process of *non*growth.

Haruth and Heruth

"How," asked a listener, "are we to understand the word, the state, the range of being 'mindful' of the Creator?"

— To the biblical passage about "the Law engraved — *haruth* — on the tablets," the sages say, "Do not read *haruth* — engraved, but *heruth*, liberty." The sages of the Talmud were suggesting seventeen centuries ago the revolutionary idea that *obedience* — the Law — and liberty are predicated on each other. To be mindful of the Creator in one's youth can thus mean only to be ultimately mindful of obedience and liberty as a dialectical process that lends meaning to existence.

But being mindful of the Creator, since it suggests a panacea for troubled days, means something else, too: It means that those without obedience are not only without liberty but, quite often, without sanity. It is highly significant that in the Psalms, lawlessness, the lack of an *Ol*, is depicted as existential stupidity, a stupidity, however, that has all the characteristics of a mental sickness. I cite Simone Weil reluctantly—since her total ignorance of Judaism, though she was Jewish herself, was as great as her intimate familiarity with the whole range of the human predicament—to the effect that since obedience is a necessary tool of the soul, whoever is deprived of it is ill. Thus any body politic governed by a sovereign ruler accountable to nobody, is in the hands of a sick man. Any number of signs show that the people of our age have for a long time been starved for obedience. But advantage has been take of this fact—to give them slavery.

Sin Its Own Punishment

"To what kind of stupidity does the Bible ascribe the characteristics of mental sickness?" asked a participant. —The stupidity of sin, the teacher replied.

"But isn't sin in the Bible depicted as *evil?*"

—Evil, even more than sin, the teacher countered, is depicted in the Bible as insanity.

"Where in the Bible?"

—In many places, the teacher replied. The whole powerful Psalm 107 deals with it in an awesomely grand manner. But you must remember the basic biblical tenet that man is not punished *for* his sins, but *by* them.

"How so?"

—Sin, the teacher responded, is depicted in the Bible as its own punishment. Thus, from a biblical viewpoint, if anxiety, for example, is the sickening sensation of "free floating," this floating, in turn, is inherent in the very act of cutting oneself loose from the moorings.

His Own Iniquities Shall Catch the Wicked

Ariel Halevi quoted here from Proverbs 5:22: "His own iniquities shall surely catch the wicked, and with the cord of his transgressions he will be held firmly."

—We read a paradigmatic biblical passage like this one as we read others, without realizing that it suggests something revolutionary in our whole approach to mental sickness. Man may be the "catcher" of his iniquities, but he is also the one who is caught *by* them and, what is more, held by them firmly, as in a prison of his own making. Thus the Ralbag, Rabenu Levi Ben Gershon, interprets this passage to mean just that: that our sins are *themselves* the means we unconsciously use to lead ourselves down the road to perdition. A great disservice was rendered both to the cause of truth and to our understanding of the Bible as existential truth by describing punishment, as depicted in the Bible, as something that is brought upon man by a God who is angry at his transgressions, rather than something man brings upon himself by a psyche diseased in the very act of transgressing.

The Reprimand of the Wise and The Song of the Fools

The teacher concluded the class on a homiletic note, taking for his theme a passage from Ecclesiastes: "It is better to listen to the reprimand of a wise man than to a man who hears the song of the fools."

— Something seems to be wrong with the wording of this passage, the teacher said, for all it had to say to make its point was "It is better to listen to the word of the wise than to the song of the fools." Why say "than to a *man* who hears the song of the fools"? "A man" here seems superfluous. The late Rabbi Y. L. Maimon quotes a nineteenth-century sage who explained the passage to mean that "it is better to hear the reprimand of the wise *from* a man who listens to the song of the fools." Thus wise words, if they are to have the desired impact, must emanate from a person who has his ears attuned to every possible melody of his time, even the silly ones, like "the song of the fools." Not one letter in the Hebrew text need be changed to accommodate this wise interpretation, for the Hebrew letter *m* can mean both "from" and "than."

A participant spoke up. "Since it is quite obvious from this class that it is all a matter of how the Bible is taught, what, in your opinion, are the things that qualify one to teach the Bible?"

— Let me first tell you what would disqualify one from teaching it, the teacher countered. — Overexposure to the song of the fools.

"Can you mention one such 'song,' sir?"

— Yes, rationalism, was the answer.

6

Light Is Sown
for the Righteous

Job and His Friends

Though there was immediate interest in the comment about rationalism when the class next met, the teacher deferred a development of it. Instead, he turned not to "the song of the fools" but to what seemed to be the reprimand of the wise. — Three wise friends, the Bible tells us, come to be at Job's side and console him in his affliction. The sorely tried man, however, rejects their reasoning and invokes the great bitter "Why?" His pious friends reprimand the stricken man, reminding him that there is no suffering without sin. Somewhere, somehow, he must have transgressed if God, whose ways are always just, has brought down such punishment on him. Job cries out against this justification with the same vehemence. The afflicted man also talks back to God, and his friends, though they understand his bitterness, are appalled by his impudence. But Job is undaunted. At the end, God speaks to Job "out of the darkness" and tells him that He is "sore displeased" with these friends who have justified God's ways to Job. Are we then to think that God prefers the terrible questions to the pious amen-sayings?

— Yes, said the teacher. God is asking man to wrestle with Him. That is part of the message conveyed by the book of Job. But let me first make something clear, the teacher went on. Two great sages of the Mishnah, Rabbi Akiba and Rabbi Ishmael, conducted a lifelong discussion on the question whether it was fitting for man to let audacity replace subordination to God's will. Rabbi Akiba held that man, even when subjected to and consumed by utter darkness, ought to receive suffering lovingly. To complain against God under any circumstance was impudent. Rabbi Akiba, as we all know, lived this faith right up to his bitter death at the unmerciful hands of the Romans. Rabbi Ishmael, to the contrary, refused to consent to the suffering of his people without remonstrating. He even dared to challenge the Almighty with the audacious words "Who sees the abashment of His people and remains silent!" Rabbi Ishmael too was executed by the Romans, and the dispute between the two sages seems to have remained unresolved. But it was resolved, so to speak, by celestial rather than human beings. The sages of the Talmud, speaking of the uproar caused in heaven when the ten sages of Israel, among them Rabbi Akiba and Rabbi Ishmael, were put to death, tell us that the angels—even the angels—remonstrated with Him for what He tolerates: "Is this the Torah," they are supposed to have cried, "and this its reward?"

— Indeed the meek, like Job's friends, far from inheriting the earth, sometimes displease heaven. Of course, there are some forms of suffering that we must bear in silence and love, but there are agonies as well to which we must say no even to God Himself.

Does God Encourage Dissent?

"It sounds," someone commented, "as if God encourages dissent."

— God, according to scripture, delights even when nature, not to say man, rises, as it were, in protest. He opened the Bible that lay on the podium.

— It is in Chapter 89 of the Psalms. "Thou dost rule the raging of the sea; when its waves rise, thou praiseth them." Note the word "praiseth," said the teacher. This simple word tells a great story, the story of the creative protest, both of nature and man, and it points up the vital tension between heaven and earth. Man, trying to burst the limitations of his mind, is in the same divinely praised category as the sea trying to obliterate the boundaries of the land. Here is how Rabbi Mendel of Kotzk, the Hasidic sage, explains it.

God and the Raging Waves

— Rabbi Mendel thought that there was an inherent contradiction in that passage from the Psalms. If the Creator, as we are told in the fifth chapter of Jeremiah, had "placed the sand as the bound for the sea, a perpetual barrier that it cannot pass, though the waves toss, they cannot prevail; though they roar, they cannot pass over it," why then do the waves rage on and beat against the shores, trying, as it seems, to break the barriers and flood the land? Why does the sea rebel against God's will and fight on so fiercely, spewing forth foam like a dragon without end? Surely it knows that it cannot destroy God's established order, that it cannot possibly prevail against Him! "Yes," Rabbi Mendel replies, "the sea knows this only too well, but rages on nevertheless, and the Almighty praises its passionate desire to ravage the boundary. The sea knows that it does not have the power to win, yet it rages on as if it had. That is where the glory of the sea lies, as well as the glory of the God who created it. The same is true of God and man."

Friends and the Human Soul

Job's three friends aroused further interest from the class. A student commented that according to the Bible, God permits Satan to deprive the good man of absolutely everything but his soul, his life. And, accordingly, the adversary leaves Job with nothing but his life. But why does Satan not take Job's friends away when he would have been permitted to?

Lithuanian Mussar sages, replied the teacher, supplied a wonderful existential answer to this question. They said that so vital are friends to the very life of man that they belong to the category of the soul. It follows that Satan, who was under orders not to touch Job's soul, could not touch his friends either. The very life of man—his physical, not to speak of his spiritual life—quite often depends on the dialogue his soul conducts with kindred souls. If you take a man's friends away, you take his soul away. They say of a Hasidic master who died young that he would have lived longer if he had only had someone to talk to. The sages of the Talmud put it bluntly: Give me friends or give me death.

Job's Real Sin?

A class member remarked that she had recently come across an interpretation of Job's predicament that said that Job may not have been as guiltless as it appears. For why did the righteous Job raise his voice in protest only when he himself was afflicted? Did he not find cause to raise the question of God's ways with man before his own ordeal? Did he really think, when God's blessings were lavished on him personally, that all was right as well with the world? Did he not know, before he himself was stricken, of all the suffering, sorrow, cruelty, and misery around him? Why did he not rise up then and curse his day? The source of this interpretation was an article written during the last year of World War II by Dr. Judah L. Magnes, chancellor of the Hebrew University.

The teacher remarked that under the impact of the Holocaust, Dr. Magnes had undergone, in the last years of his life, a drastic metamorphosis: The former American reform rabbi had become, so to speak, a penitent. His process of *teshuva*, the Hebrew word for "return" or penitence, began during the war. Magnes had founded the group Seekers of Thy Face and it culminated with his renaming that group *Ha'ol*, "The Yoke." Profoundly shaken by the bestialization of man as demonstrated in the wildly idolatrous Nazi era, Magnes concluded that the only path to follow was to draw closer to God by total submission to what the sages call "The Yoke," the yoke of the kingdom of heaven as embodied in the Law as a deterrent against evil. Magnes was convinced, and he was not alone in this conviction, that the extreme opposite of The Yoke was not just idolatry, but ultimately mental sickness. He thus regarded the world as deranged.

Sin and Mental Sickness

Prefatory to his explaining the connection between sin and sickness as viewed by the Bible, Ariel Halevi said that the word "sin" is widely misunderstood today. — Some apply it only to obvious breaches of the criminal code and therefore exclude it glibly from the personal vocabulary. Others vaguely connect it with sex and thereby completely, and conveniently, miss its all-embracing implications. "An awareness of sin," the teacher went on, quoting Samuel Terrien,

> existed at a very early date among the ancient Hebrews. While their pagan neighbors were chiefly concerned with sin as a cultic offense, they, [the Hebrews] understood, by the same word, not only an error of ritual but also an ethical crime. Biblical sin is basically a manifestation of man's arrogance against his Creator. The

story of the Garden of Eden intends, among others, to show that
man is a sinner whenever he tries to become "like gods." The ancient Hebrews knew the process of psychological disintegration
which proceeds from the act: "Sin lieth in wait at the threshold."
The perpetration of such acts is condemned not because they vio-
lated a tribal custom or the requirements of a local shrine, but
because "they were evil in the eyes of the Lord." When King
David, after he sinned, receives from Nathan the Prophet the en-
lightening blow, "Thou art the man!" he realizes that he has "despised the Lord" and sinned against the Creator Himself, as mentioned in II Samuel, 12:10. Thus even before the great prophets of
the eighth and seventh centuries B.C.E. applied to the recesses of
the human heart their skillful and merciless scalpel, a long tradition of psychological introspection had conferred on Hebrew spirituality its unique ability to see human nature without illusory optimism. Sin, in Biblical terms, means the incomplete life, the stupid, ignorant, arrogant life.

—Now, can you think of an instance in scripture, the teacher
asked, where we read that sin is a form of mental sickness or, to be
more exact, that it produces a sickness of soul? Not waiting for an
answer, he continued, first mentioning the various names the Bible
uses for fools and folly: *shoteh, sahal, tipesh, pety, ba'ar, kssil, evil.*
What kind of fool was *evil* (pronounced like "evil" in English)? Someone replied that since *iveleth* was usually translated as an aggravated
form of folly, *evil*, he assumed, stood for some kind of dangerous fool.
The teacher agreed, though he stressed that the folly denounced in
the Bible was opposed not to cleverness—the biblical fool may very
well have been a real "smartie"—but to wisdom. —But we have already discussed this. At the moment we are interested only in a particular fool called *evil.* Can you recall a chapter in Psalms where it
speaks of *evilim*—fools—who are literally sickened by their sins?

"I am not sure," someone said. "But are you refering to the passage
'fools—*evilim*—on account of their transgressions?'"

—Exactly, the teacher replied. It is part of the formidable one hundred seventh chapter of Psalms. The full quotation is "fools on account of their transgressions, and afflicted because of their
iniquities."

"But it doesn't say '*sick*' on account of their transgressions," someone
parried. "It says 'fools'!"

—The sentence that follows, the teacher replied, makes it clear that we are dealing here with sick people: "Their soul abhoreth all manner of food and they draw near unto the gates of death." If their souls abhor all manner of food, is it not obvious that they must be sick people?

Someone asked the teacher whether the biblical *evil* was ever actually translated as "sick," and the teacher replied in the affirmative. —More than a century ago, he said, Rabbi Samson Rafael Hirsh, a latter-day sage, translated *evilim* to mean men literally sickened *by* their sins. In the same chapter in Psalms, the teacher went on, there are, in fact, some perfectly identifiable descriptions of symptoms of mental sickness. He quoted from the text before him: "Such as those who sit in darkness and in the shadow of death, bound in affliction and iron. . . . Because they have rebelled against the words of God and condemned the counsel of the Most High: therefore *they* brought down their hearts with labor; they fell down and there was none to help." Is it not obvious, the teacher said, that the psalmist speaks here of those who, having overthrown the freeing yoke of the kingdom of heaven, languish in the slavery of their own yoke? The psalmist is speaking unmistakably of the depressions caused by transgressions, depressions that ultimately fetter people like iron, a darkness of soul that is bound to bring down their hearts in labor. The psalmist speaks moreover of a sickness of soul that afflicts bodies, also, for "they abhor all manner of food." Samson Rafael Hirsh was a contemporary of Kierkegaard, though it is unlikely that they knew of each other. But those two great contemporaries were the first modern thinkers to see sin as a form of mental sickness, an idea that now seems to be eclipsing some cherished Freudian theories.

The Denial of Death

To illustrate his point, the teacher mentioned a recent book titled *The Denial of Death*, a Pulitzer Prize winner written by Ernest Becker. —In this book, said the teacher, the author reaches the conclusion—from a purely psychological angle—that mental sickness is a form of sin or, if you wish, that sin is a form of mental sickness. Such an idea would be anathema to orthodox psychoanalysis. Right now, however, Freud's biological image of man is seen by some as reductionist and one-dimensional insofar as it limits man's primary concerns to himself and disengages him from religion, society, and philosophy. It seems to disconnect him from life itself as a human struggle with values and ethical and moral choices—in brief, a wrestling with himself for the sake of self-transcendence. Insofar as Freud seemed to present a view of man as not having any spiritual and transcendental dimensions, he almost fatalistically defined the human being as devoid of any moral imperatives. But the new school of humanistic psychology simply rejects this view. To Abraham Maslow, for example, religious experiences are symptoms of health, not neurosis. Ackerman sees guilt feelings not as highlighting an imbalance, as psychoanalysis claims, but as a genuine emotion of remorse for actual wrongdoing, so vital for inner growth. Mowrer emphasizes that each person has both the knowledge and the option of choosing right or wrong. Rollo May deemphasizes the unconscious—man's biological background, his repressed and hostile anger, his childhood experiences, and so forth. Instead, he stresses the existential primacy of the "here and now." A tendency is developing, the teacher continued, to regard moral questions and life's meaning as interrelated and, hence, as primary in psychotheraphy. Thus Victor Frankel views neurosis as a deficiency of conscience, and Erich Fromm boldly declares that the psychiatrist is a physician of the soul.

The teacher went on to say that Hebrew may be the only language in which mental sickness, *mahalot nefesh*, is frequently referred to as *mahalot ruah*, which literally means "spiritual sickness," thus implying the connection between insufficiency of conscience and neurosis.

—The two Hebrew names for mental sickness, Ariel Halevi continued, which may have their equivalent only in Greek, are particularly significant in view of the three Hebrew words for soul: *nefesh, ruah, neshama. Nefesh* is the lowest form of soul, as it is written, "For the blood is the *nefesh.*" Animals, too, have a *nefesh. Ruah,* however, is the distinctly human soul, while *neshama* is the distinctly divine in us. There can therefore be sicknesses of the *nefesh,* which one may call clinical, and the sicknesses of the *ruah,* which may be described as existential. The *neshama,* however, which is pure and divine, can either be there or not be there, but can never be there as sick!

—This brings me back to Ernest Becker, the teacher went on. Becker was obviously speaking of *mahalot ruah,* that is to say, existential sickness, or existential neurosis, as Frankel calls it. The point Becker makes is that at the very furthest reaches of scientific description, psychology has to give way to theology, that is to say, to a world view that absorbs the individual's conflicts and guilt and offers him the possibility of what Becker calls a "heroic apotheosis." Man, he writes in truth, *cannot endure his own littleness* unless he translates it into meaningfulness on the largest possible scale.

—Here Rank, a former disciple of Freud, and Kierkegaard meet in what Becker rightly describes as an astonishing merger of thought: that sin and neurosis are two ways of talking about the same thing—the complete isolation of the individual, his disharmony with the rest of nature, his hyperindividualism—another word for narcissism. In sin, as in neurosis, man makes a fetish of something near at hand and pretends that the whole meaning and wonder of creation is limited to that. For Rank the neurotic world view is the same as that of the sinner: The neurotic loses every kind of collective spirituality and makes the unheroic gesture of placing himself entirely within the "immortality" of his own ego. The neurotic and the sinner also have in common their low esteem of themselves even in their egocentricity, which is primarily due to their loss of the courage to overcome the terrible power of gravity that drags them down. Just think, the teacher exclaimed, how expressions of the psalmist like "hearts brought down in labor," "sitting in darkness," and "chained in iron" describe the nature and terror of the sickness! The spiritually sick man is chained in his inability for self-transcendence, chained in his failure of heroism, to the iron of a dark gravity that constantly pulls him down.

How Do We Know We Are Right?

"What bothers me is the question of the ultimate validity of our opinions," someone in the group said. "I remember the report of the deliberations of the Rockefeller Foundation council after Kennedy's assassination. It was as remarkable for its frankness as for its helplessness. Regarding the question of what had gone wrong with our society, it said, in effect, that we would have certainly done what was right if we only knew what right was. So how do we really know what is good and what is right, not merely in questions of a religious nature, but when we are confronted with worldly problems?"

The Metaphysical Roots of Ethics

The teacher promised a clear-cut biblical answer to this extremely important question. — But first, he said, I would like to tell you a little story. The Rabbi of Ponivezh, in Lithuania, a latter-day sage, said of the great Hazon Ish: In matters concerning the interpretation of the Law, of the Torah, you might agree with him or you might not. You might say he was right or you might say he was wrong. In *worldly* matters, however, he was always right! Now, how are we to understand such a statement? asked the teacher rhetorically. We must understand it as a statement of faith in the metaphysical roots of ethics. Those roots have to right one's thoughts. The Hazon Ish was a saintly man, a man who perfected his deeds to the point of total commitment to the God of truth. When our deeds — deeds, not merely thoughts — are totally committed to the truth of God, our opinions, in turn, become truthful, right, or, to be more exact, *rightened*. Do you follow me?

A question-filled silence followed. Ariel Halevi continued. — What I am saying is that a person whose deeds are perfect draws on himself a divine illumination that renders him capable of seeing things as they truly are. The perfect person is thus right in his views about the world because his self-perfection makes it possible for him to know what is right.

"Is that what the Bible says?" someone asked.

And Your Thoughts Shall Be Rightened

— Precisely, the teacher replied. In the sixteenth chapter of Proverbs is a passage that contains an entire philosophy of life and an answer to some burning questions. It says, "Commit your deeds to God and your thoughts shall be rightened." This simple passage is saying that in actuality something happens to us in response to our making something happen with us. Something mysterious, a mysterious process of *rightening*, takes place in the person who has reached a state of deedful commitment to his Maker. Such a person is not just enlightened but illuminated and, what's more, the things around him, things one cannot usually see clearly, become illuminated for him. We might call this mystical psychology.

Light Is Sown for the Righteous

—"Light is sown for the righteous and gladness for the upright in heart," says the ninety-seventh psalm. This means, said the teacher, that the righteous person walks on an illuminated path. Because light is "sown" for him on account of his righteousness, he sees things that others do not see. That is why his opinions are right, too. The right deeds lead to the right thoughts. This is what Rabbi Israel Salanter, the sage founder of Lithuanian Mussar, meant in this epigrammatic summary: "How do you know that your thoughts are right? If your *midess* are right, your thoughts are right." Now what is meant by *midess*? *Midess*, or *midoth* in modern Hebrew pronunciation, means literally "measures." In the terminology of Hebrew metaethicism, however, particularly of the metaethicist movement of Lithuanian Mussar, it meant traits, good and bad. To use the same word for traits and measures is in itself an astounding feat of psycho-social insight. For when all is said and done, we are what we measure ourselves against. Sartre's famous line "Hell is other people" implies a state, a dreadful, absurd state in which other people—that is to say, the social gaze—become the measure of man. Nobody explained this awful state better than Kierkegaard. A herdsman, he says, who is a self only in the sight of his cows is a very low self indeed, and so also is a ruler who is a self in the sight of his slaves, for in both cases the scale or measure is lacking. The child who has had only his parents to measure himself by becomes a self when he matures by getting the state as a measure. But what an infinite spell falls on the self by getting God as a measure! With God as a measure, one's measures—*midess*—are right, and when one's *midess* are right so are one's opinions.

—The right thoughts, moreover, the results of an illuminated path, illuminate even the person's face, as it is written in Proverbs, "Man's wisdom illuminates his face."

Man's Wisdom Illuminates His Face

The teacher paused to locate a particular note. —I want to read to you, he said, a few lines by Eugene Ionesco, the great French playwright, concerning illuminated faces.

The luminous images of the mystics reveal a full and luminous extra consciousness on which shadows or nothingness have no hold.
This is why the feeling, the consciousness of "being" is expressed in
images of light, and it is also why light, presence, plenitude are
synonymous with "spirituality." Initiation means illumination, the
dispersion of shadows, nothingness held off.

Ariel Halevi put the note aside and went on. — An astonishing line
in the Talmud says, "A *talmid haham*, a learned man, unless his face
is like that of an angel of the Lord, . . . cannot be a teacher of Torah."
How are we to understand this? The answer is that if the study of the
Torah has not left an imprint of luminous refinement on the person's
face, it is highly doubtful whether it has gone deep enough to refine
his soul. We do not know how an angel of the Lord looks, but we do
know that the luminosity of the great-souled men was reflected in
their faces. Those men were truly made in the image of God. Thomas
Carlyle also said that man's face is sooner or later bound to become a
clear mirror of his thoughts.

More On Rightening One's Thoughts

"How can we explain," asked someone, "that saintly men of different religions whose deeds rendered them eligible to be 'rightened' in
their opinions did not necessarily see God the same way?"
— If "rightening" meant a universal and uniform knowledge of the
nature of God, said the teacher, there would have been no real
freedom of choice. In matters concerning the relationship between
man and man all illuminated souls down the ages have spoken a similar language. But that does not mean they could possibly speak a similar language concerning the relationship between God and man, concerning God's ways with man. These are supposed to remain hidden
till the end of the days and be understood only in retrospect.
"Is that what the Bible says?" someone asked.
— Yes, the teacher replied.

Show Me, I Beseech Thee, Thy Honor

The teacher quoted from Exodus 33:18. Moses asks the Lord to
show him the secret of His glory, His honor, that is to say, to show him

how he could reconcile His glory and honor with some of the dreadful things that are going on here below: "Show me, I beseech Thee, Thy honor," Moses pleads. The request is denied. "You can see only My back; but My front cannot be seen," is the divine answer. Rabbi Samson Rafael Hirsh's interpretation of this enigmatic answer is this: God tells Moses that His ways will be fully understood as adding up to His honor only when looked upon backward with hindsight. In other words, everything will fall into place and make ultimate sense only at the summation and end of history, not as history is still in the process of unfolding.

7

Does God Change Man?

Two Kings

A young man raised the question of King Saul. He had always felt, he said at the outset of our next class, that a great injustice had been done to Israel's first and most tragic king, and that the prophet Samuel had treated him, to say the least, unfairly. "One cannot escape the impression," he went on, "shared by many historians and secular critics of the Bible, that Samuel, though he may have anointed Saul by divine order, was nevertheless jealous of his power. The Bible makes it abundantly clear that Saul transgressed. But so did King David, his successor. Why then has David remained forever a favorite of the Lord and his people while Saul died disgraced?"

The teacher shook his head. — Not disgraced, he said. Abandoned. Yet in the whole of ancient literature, religious or not, there is no more shattering lamentation or more moving poetry than David's eulogy on Saul and Jonathan: "The beauty of Israel is slain upon thy high places.... How are the mighty fallen!"

"But Saul died 'abandoned,' as you put it," the young man persisted.

— Abandoned, yes.

"Because he transgressed? Is that it?" the young man inquired.

— No, the teacher replied. Because of the nature of his transgression.

"Meaning what?"

— You mentioned, the teacher replied, that David, too, had sinned. And he surely did. But the sins of Saul and David were of a different nature and they affected two different realms of life: the political and the emotional realms, or, if you wish, the national and the personal.

70

But before I go any further, let me ask you this: Does the Bible tell us anything about Saul's private life?

There was no answer.

— But it tells us something about David's private life, does it not? Ariel Halevi prodded.

"It does," someone replied.

— What exactly does the Bible tell us about David's private life? the teacher asked.

"From what it tells us," was the answer, "it is quite clear that King David was a very passionate, very 'romantic' man, and very compulsive in matters of love. He falls in love with Bathsheba at first sight; sends her husband, a general, to die on the perennial battlefield with the Philistines, and marries her."

— What else does the Bible tell us about it? the teacher asked. Because there was no immediate answer, he went on. — It tells us a good deal about the intensity of David's repentance as well as about the lofty status of the prophet in those days. Nathan, the prophet, comes to the king as to an underling, and the king breaks down before him as before a superior whose authority was unquestionable. Only scripture knows of prophets who could force kings to their knees. Now let us see what was the nature of Saul's transgression. His first transgression consisted of insubordination to the divine order, transmitted through Samuel, not to touch the spoils of the defeated Amalekites and not to spare their lives. Now, can you recall what the king told the prophet when the latter accused him of insubordination?

"He told him a lie," someone replied.

— Did David tell the prophet a lie? the teacher asked.

"No, he didn't," was the answer. "He confessed right away."

— But Saul confessed, too, did he not? the teacher asked.

"He did," was the answer. "He said he was afraid to antagonize the people who clamored, as he put it, for the booty—the oxen, the lambs, the fatlings, and so forth."

— In other words, the teacher proposed, Saul admitted to Samuel that in this instance, his first real test as a king, there was a clear failure of leadership?

"Obviously."

— Then, the teacher went on, when Saul begins to suspect David of conspiracies—David who, to the very end, referred to Saul as the

"God-anointed" — and tries to kill him, and the latter, running for his life, seeks refuge from the king's wrath in Nob, the city of the priests, Saul destroys Nob, lock, stock, and barrel, as they say. Isn't that what the Bible says?

"It certainly is."

— And is it not true, the teacher went on, that by destroying the priesthood Saul had undermined the whole system of government as practiced in those days?

"No doubt about that."

— Would you then define King David's sin, in view of the above mentioned, as political?

"Moral," was the reply.

— And Saul's sin?

"Political — to use a modern term."

— Right, the teacher agreed. Now let me tell you what Don Isaac Abarbanel, the great sage of Spanish Jewry, says about the difference between the two kinds of sin: Saul's sins affected the nature of his *kingship* while David's sin was related to the nature of his *manhood*. Thus the sin of Saul was that of *subversion* while David's sin was a sin of *passion*.

— In the "Letters from Prison" of martyr-priest Dietrich Bonhoeffer, hanged by the Nazis in 1945, there appear remarkable observations on the God-man confrontation as depicted in scripture. "The Bible," Bonhoeffer writes, "would forgive sins of weakness, but not sins of strength . . . . The Bible doesn't think it necessary to spy out things." Do you understand now? the teacher asked. Saul's sin, the misuse of power, was one of *strength*, while David's sin was one of *weakness*, human weakness.

One King

"While we are on the subject of Israel's early kings," someone interjected, "what about the passage in scripture that says that Solomon was wiser than all other men? I know the sages say 'even wiser than the fools,' but what meaning can there be in a statement suggesting that it takes much to be wiser than a fool?"

The teacher replied. — There is great and relevant meaning in this statement about Solomon. We should mention again that the biblical fool—except, perhaps, for the sort of whom the Bible says, "God protects the *pety*'s" —is not a fool in the sense of being devoid of cleverness but, to the contrary, may be very "clever," very "smart," very "successful." But precisely on account of his cleverness, smartness, and success, he grows so arrogant in his satisfied ignorance that he regards wisdom as a silly, meaningless pursuit or, worse, regards himself as "wise." We meet such people everywhere, the teacher went on. So sure of themselves, so opinionated, so self-sufficient in their narrowness that nobody in the world would be able to convince them of their folly. If "the wisdom of the unfortunates is mocked," as Solomon says in Ecclesiastes, it follows that the folly of the powerful is applauded. Rabbi Levi Yitzhak of Berditshev, the Hasidic sage, explained the Talmudic comment on this question as follows: It is not too difficult to convince an open-minded, educated, non-self-satisfied man that he acts or thinks foolishly. The wiser the man, the more he is inclined to listen to those wiser than he and the more likely that he will not consider himself wise. It will take a Solomon, however, to convince a "smart," self-satisfied, successful fool of his folly.

For Zion's Sake

"Speaking of Solomon," someone said, "I really think, as we all do, I am sure, that it will take the wisdom of Solomon to come up with what they call a comprehensive solution to our conflict with the Arabs. But the question that keeps bothering me is, don't the Arabs too, have a case, in their dispute with Israel? My question is not political, but moral. If the whole question were political, that is to say, if our history in this land began with political Zionism and not with Abraham, Isaac, and Jacob, our case would not be stronger than that of the Arabs. But since I do believe that our basic rights to this land emanate from the Bible, even if I don't really believe—not yet, at least —in the divinity of the Covenant with the patriarchs, I simply wonder how we can explain the lack of reference in the prophets to a conflict of world-shaking proportions, such as that between us and the Arabs, in which both sides, claiming the same land, will be equally convinced of the justice of their cause. The prophets speak, of course, of the 'ingathering of the exiles,' of the 'blossoming of the desert,' of 'God's word coming forth from Zion.' But how are we to understand, we who want to believe that God spoke through His prophets, that there is no word in the Bible about the critical moral issue as well as the lasting nature of the violent Israeli-Arab dispute?"

— That the conflict over rights to the promised land, replied the teacher, will be a lasting one is implicit in the Bible but is made explicit only in the words of the greatest post-Talmudic interpreter of the Bible, Rashi, who lived in France almost a millennium ago. He states at the beginning of Genesis in the name of Rabbi Yitzhak that the nations will keep on telling the Jews, "*listim atem*": "You are robbers for you have stolen a land that belongs to others." The critical and lasting moral nature of the dispute is underscored in the Bible by the fact that it depicted it as insoluble by natural means.

"Insoluble by natural means?" someone asked.

— That is right.

"Where in the Bible?"

— In Isaiah, the teacher replied. Look, he went on animatedly. Let me ask you something: If I felt constrained to make a statement to the effect that I would not rest until I proved the justness of my cause, would that not imply that I was on trial?

"It certainly would," was the answer.

— And would it not further imply that I had not as yet succeeded, in the course of my trial, in convincing people that justice was on my side?

"It would."

— Well, then, the teacher said, all we have to do is see what is written in Chapter 62 of Isaiah, which most of us know by heart, I am sure: "For Zion's sake I shall not remain silent and for Jerusalem's sake I shall not rest until their righteousness go forth as brightness and their salvation as a lamp that burneth." Has it occurred to you, the teacher asked, that this famous passage clearly implies how difficult it will be to prove our righteousness, how it will take nothing short of messianic salvation to prove it?

"I thought," ventured a student, "that the righteousness mentioned in this passage referred to the dispute between Israel and its God, not with other nations."

— The next passage, the teacher answered, clearly states the exact nature of the confrontation in question: "And the gentiles will see thy righteousness, and Kings thy glory, and thou shall be called by a new name which the mouth of the Lord shall name . . . . Thou shall also be a crown of glory in the hand of the Lord and a royal diadem in the hand of thy God." Surely this is a righteousness that other nations will recognize, but by supernatural processes. The righteousness of our cause will be willingly, almost gladly recognized by the others. The others will not be humiliated and defeated by it, but redeemed and illuminated.

— From what all the prophets had to say about the end of days, it is clear that, no matter how the messianic transformation of mankind manifests itself, all the peoples of the world, not only the Jews, will ultimately bask in the light of God's revealed glory.

Someone asked the teacher what exactly he meant by "messianic transformation."

He replied: — By now it is quite clear that the solution to the problems of humanity is not a matter of a change in political attitudes but of a change in human nature. Nothing less will do. The prophets knew this all along.

"They knew what?" asked a listener.

— That there can be no redemption without a change in human nature.

"The prophets say this?" rejoined the student.

— Exactly, the teacher replied with emphasis. And the fact that it comes as a surprise to you proves the extent to which, in the Bible, we fail to see the trees for the forest.

And a Wolf Will Dwell With a Lamb

The teacher read from Isaiah XI:

> And a wolf shall dwell with the lamb; and a leopard shall lie down with the kid; and the calf and the young lion and the fatling together; and a little child shall lead them . . . . And the cow and the bear shall feed; their young ones shall lie down together; and a little child shall lead them . . . . And the suckling child shall play on the hole of the asp, and the weaned child shall put his hand on the cockatrice' den . . . . And they shall not hurt nor destroy in all My holy mountain, for the earth shall be full of the wisdom of the Lord as the waters cover the sea.

—Now, the teacher went on, if the wolf dwells with a lamb without any urge to harm it, will it not require a change in his nature? And will it not require a change in the nature of an asp if he is to lose his need to sting and poison? "And they shall not hurt nor destroy in all My holy mountain"—this refers then to an ultimate change in human nature, which has hitherto been like that of the wolf or the asps.

"In other words," someone proposed, "in the grand discussion of whether aggression is innate in man, the prophetic answer is yes."

—Correct, the teacher replied. Nobody can completely overcome it, but the select few, through their deeds, can draw from this aggressive urge, which the sages call the *yetzer hara*, an added energy they use for the intensification of the good. In the messianic era this energy will be drawn from the wisdom that will "fill the earth like waters that cover the sea."

Does God Change Man?

"In view of what you have just said about innate aggression," someone queried, "does it not follow that man can hardly count on God's help in trying to change himself?"

—The sages say, replied the teacher, that "whoever comes to purify himself is helped from above." This does not mean, however, that God changes man if man does not first make a supreme effort to change himself, indeed, to create himself. The self-change, and the self-change alone, makes him eligible for the illumination that comes with knowing the truth, or at least with knowing what is an untruth.

—Let me tell you again how a Hasidic sage interpreted the passage in Micah "And Thou giveth truth to Jacob." Why "giveth" truth to Jacob or to anyone of high merit? "Truth," said the Rabbi of Kobrin, "is not something that can be attained." But what happens is this: God looks at a man who has devoted his entire life to attaining the truth and suddenly gives him a free gift of it. That is the meaning of the passage in scripture, "And Thou giveth truth to Jacob." It is told that the rabbi, as he was making this comment, took a pinch of snuff between two fingers and scattered it on the floor. "Look," he said, "Even less than this!" Again he took some snuff—a few shreds of tobacco—and added, "And it can be even less, if only it is the truth!"

The Mantle of Elijah

— Let me tell you, continued the teacher, how another sage of Has-
idsim saw the possibility of change in man through the right dialogical
contact with another person. A disciple of the great Rabbi Bunam of
Pshisha was asked what was so wonderful about his teacher that such a
great to-do was made over him. He replied,

> Elijah found Elisha when the latter was ploughing the field with his
> oxen . . . . Now you must not think of Elisha as a prophet, but as a
> real farmer who calls to him team: "Giddap! . . . Giddap!" Then
> Elijah came and cast his mantle over him and instantly Elisha's
> soul burned bright as a flame. He slaughtered his beasts, he broke
> his plough.
> 'What have I done to you?' asked Elijah.
> 'Oh,' Elisha cried, 'What you have done to me!'
> Elisha left his father and mother and ran after the master, and
> no one could tear him away from him. That is how it is, said the
> disciple, when Rabbi Bunam takes one of his disciples by the hand.
> No matter how simple a man he is, life begins to stir within him so
> strongly that he yearns to offer himself up on the altar of the Lord.

— Indeed the question "What have I done to you?" contains an entire philosophy of life as a confrontation with something, or someone,
larger than life. Every Elisha seeks his Elijah, and the other way
round. The need of one for the other goes much further than the Buberian dialogue. We all have voices but only an Elijah can make us
sing.

With Thee

— The entire social part of the Law, continued the teacher, which is
in actuality the basis of the whole Law of Moses and Israel, is ground-
ed in the idea that one must always have someone at his side who will
help him "sing" and the other way round. Since everyone's lonely
voice is bound to go through a process or a period of faltering in life,
everyone must see to it that there is someone at his side whose ears are
attuned to his "music," and the other way round. To say, or to be
told, "I am with thee" is the heart of the matter.

The teacher repeated the Hebrew word for "with thee" — *imha* —
several times as if he were waiting for his audience to pick it up. Some-

one caught it. "Are you referring," she asked, "to that recurrent word in the third book of Moses dealing with the law of sustaining a neighbor in distress? 'And if thy neighbor has waxen poor *with thee*' — 'And thy neighbor should live *with thee*' — 'And if his hands should droop *with thee*'? I admit," she went on, "that I never quite understood the 'with thee.' It couldn't possibly mean '*along* with thee' — that is to say, that both you and your neighbor wax poor together! The admonition clearly refers to a state in which one has lost all one's material goods, or faith, or courage to go on, as suggested by the 'drooped hands,' while his neighbor, his friend, was in a position to do something about it. But if that's what the admonition is all about, why not say 'If thy neighbor has waxen poor, thou shall help him'? Why 'waxen poor *with thee*?'"

Elaborating on *imha*, the teacher remarked that in most cases it is translated "in your midst." — But *imha*, he exclaimed, is not "in your midst"; *imha* is "with thee." That is the whole point! People nowadays are no longer "with thee." People do not talk *to* each other, but *at* each other; they do not want to know what is bothering you, for they are not *with you*. People do not want you to tell them how you feel, for if you tell them you may lose them. People do not want to be bothered, to get involved, to stick their necks out. There is no dialogue but rather, in Buber's apt words, "a monologue masquerading as a dialogue." Rollo May, the existential psychotherapist, says something in a book of his that impressed me very much. He spoke of a girl patient who told him that a certain man in her village would not have committed suicide "if *one* person had really known him." That is what happens, or can happen, to a man who has no *imha*, no "with thee." If there is not such a one who truly knows you and sticks with you *on account* of his knowing you, your "Thou" is not only unhappy, but muted. You are unable to "sing." Of course, one can also sing in unhappiness, but only as long as it is a matter of genuine pain, not dull despair. An existence without an *imha*, without a "with thee," is a muted existence. Rabbi Pinhas of Koretz, the Hasidic sage, said, "When a man is singing and cannot lift his voice, and another comes along who *can* lift his voice, then the first will be able to lift his voice, too. That is the secret of bond between spirit and spirit." That, my friends, is also the meaning of *imha*.

Love

Finally, the teacher was asked a question about love. "We are told in the Bible," a young girl said, "that Jacob worked for Rachel fourteen years, and they were like one day to him, so great was his love for her. How are we to understand it? If Jacob's love for Rachel was so great, fourteen years should have been like an eternity to him, shouldn't it?"

The teacher smiled. — That is a good question, he said, to which a sage of Lithuanian Mussar provided a good answer. Rabbi Eliyahu Lupian of blessed memory explained this enigmatic passage this way: A man *loves* fish, for example — he's *crazy* about fish — so what does he do? He buys it, cuts it to pieces, fries it, boils it or broils it, and devours it in no time. That is one kind of love. Jacob's love for Rachel was apparently of a different order.

8

"I Gave Him Everything, Your Honor"

Where Art Thou?

Someone asked, "How is one to understand the meaning of the question 'Where art thou?' which God hurled at Adam, the first man, when he was hiding from his Maker after committing the first sin? The question sounds too human, too simple. Didn't He, the all-knowing God, know where Adam was?"

The teacher, in reply, told the story of the Hasidic sage Rabbi Shneur Zalman of Liadi and the chief of gendarmes at the prison in St. Petersburg. — Denounced by his opponents, the rabbi was imprisoned by the Tzar. The great man was calmly awaiting trial when the chief of gendarmes entered his cell. The majestic, radiant face of the old master suggested to the chief, who was a thoughtful man with a discriminating taste, what manner of man he was keeping as a prisoner. He began to converse with the sage on spiritual matters and finally brought up the question of the biblical "Where art thou?" He asked the master how we are to understand that the omniscient God had to ask Adam where he was.

— "Do you believe," the master replied, "that the scriptures are eternal and that every generation, every era — nay, every man is included in them?"

— "I believe, Rabbi," said the chief.

— "Well, then," the master said, "What this question means is this: In every era God calls to every man at a certain stage of his life and puts the question to him: 'Where are you? Where do you *stand* now? So many years and days of those alotted to you have passed,and how far have you gotten in your world?' God says something like this: 'You have lived forty-six years, how *far along are you?*'"

— The story is told that when the chief heard his age mentioned, he pulled himself together, jumped to attention, said "Bravo!" and left.

"I Gave Him Everything, Your Honor"

"While we are on the subject of Adam and Eve," an elderly gentleman interjected, "I may as well mention the serpent. I was always bothered by the serpent's punishment for having seduced Eve. The Bible tells us that God cursed the serpent and told him, 'On thy belly thou shall crawl and dust thou shall eat all the days of thy life.' But there doesn't seem to be much of a curse here. If the serpent, of all God's creatures, can subsist on dust, which is to say that he can find his food everywhere, anywhere, with no need whatsoever to struggle for it, it is a blessing, not a curse!"

The teacher nodded knowingly. — The sages of the Talmud, he said, have already raised this question, and you know what they say? They say that is precisely where the curse lies! When a living creature — any creature, whether man, animal, or reptile — does not have to struggle for its livelihood, getting all it needs without labor or effort, it knows no enjoyment either. It is a curse, not a blessing, not to have to labor for one's livelihood. The creature that knows not the satisfaction that comes with this labor — like the serpent — thus knows only the satisfaction that comes with using its venom.

Another member of the class spoke excitedly. "I—I must tell you something," he said. "I know of a case in California, the son of a well-to-do family — his father was a successful physician — who was caught burglarizing the neighbors' house. His mother, appearing before the court, pleaded with the judge for mercy. 'We gave him everything, your honor,' she wept. Perhaps this is why her son became a criminal."

Why Was the Serpent Cursed?

"But why was the serpent cursed?" asked the elderly gentleman again.

"Actually, the serpent spoke the truth, didn't he?" said another student.

— He did, the teacher replied. The truth that the primeval serpent spoke was a *lying* truth. About a century ago, Swinburne summarized the serpent's words, without at all realizing it, in his famous "Hymn to Man": "Glory to man in the highest, / The maker and master of things."

— Is it not strange that the serpent had actually sung the first known hymn to man in almost identical words? For what had the serpent told man according to the Bible? He told him, in essence, that if he only proclaimed his rational self-sufficiency and, hence, his independence from God, he could be like Him, the Maker and Master of things. God Himself later confirmed that the serpent had not lied. Why then was the serpent cursed? Because he uttered a lying truth. Human reason, which gained a measure of dangerous independence with the advent of the primeval serpent, began slowly to infringe on the domain of the Absolute by claiming that man could work out his salvation without God and even against Him. But this process of increasing rationalism pushed man into darkest irrationality.

Who Created the Serpent?

"But who created the serpent?" someone asked. "Didn't God Himself create him?"

— That is right, the teacher nodded. Buber summarizes the preceding argument as follows: The evil that God created is the power to do that which He desires not to come to pass.

"Then why has He created it in the first place?" asked the same person.

— Had He not created it, the teacher replied, no one could commit a sin against Him, but the whole point is that He desired His creatures to be able to oppose Him, to wrestle with Him. That is what freedom of choice is all about. He has given them the power to act as though omnipotence did not exist. They are not deluded in thinking that they can act contrary to God's will; they really can. They have the power. But the problem is that they have misused it.

— We raised the question some time ago why the second and sixth days of creation are not summarized with the words "and God saw it was good." The Kabbalah, specifically the Zohar, has something to say on the subject, but I must warn you that any explanation of a subject so profound and delicate will of needs be very sketchy. The Bible tells us, as we all know, that on the second day the Lord separated the waters that were above the firmament from those that were below it. As I mentioned on another occasion, the very notion of waters above the firmament clearly implies an open system or a process of creation that is ongoing and endless, as it is written, "He Who renews every day the works of creation" — that is, as far as the physical universe is concerned.

— But since everything physical in the universe has its equivalent in the spiritual domain, and vice versa, as it is written in Ecclesiastes, "One as against the other He created them," the division between the waters of above and below has a mystical meaning. The meaning of waters of above is implicit in the very notion of "above," which is utter mercy. The waters of below thus imply another aspect of divine emanation — the Kabbalah, as you know, explains creation in terms of ten *Sefiroth* — "emanations" of God — the aspect of rigid judgment, as opposed to mercy. The Zohar maintains that the quality of mercy became separated from the quality of judgment, and that judgment by itself, rigid judgment, untouched by mercy, is what evil often uses to strengthen its power. This process is needed, it seems, for the sake of a complementarity so subtle that it pits not only good against bad, but judgment against mercy. Some medieval Kabbalists even maintain that there is no purity except through impurity, a mystery contained in the fourteenth chapter of Job where he speaks of "a clean thing out of an unclean." Indeed, as Abraham Joshua Heschel remarks, the most horrible manifestations of evil occur when it acts in the guise of good. We are all too familiar with this phenomenon today.

And Evil Will Kill the Evildoer

— The idea that we are punished *by* our sins rather than *for* our sins is biblical, but it is passed over almost unnoticed. One example can be found in Isaiah, another in Psalms. In both cases evil is depicted not as something that man does, but as something done to man by virtue of a dark, self-sufficient strength. The first passage, in the fifty-seventh chapter of Isaiah, is universally mistranslated and hence misunderstood: "The righteous perisheth and no man takes it to heart; and merciful men are taken away, none considering that the righteous are taken away from the evil to come." But the actual Hebrew text says something entirely different: The righteous are taken away *from* the evil *to come*, that is, from—or prior to—*future* evils, but "nobody understands that the righteous are taken away *on account of evil.*" The prophet tried to prevent a possible misunderstanding by saying "Nobody understands," which is to say it takes a special kind of understanding to realize that the righteous man dies not because he has sinned but because of an onslaught of evil in the whole environment, an evil that kills not only the good, but the bad, too. The reference to evil as a killer even of the bad appears in the thirty-fourth chapter of Psalms, where it says, "Evil shall kill the evildoers." Indeed, evil in the world is a terrible reality, so real and so potent that it acts as if it were a semi-autonomous force.

"How frightening!" someone exclaimed.

—Yes, the teacher said. But no more frightening than the passage in the forty-fifth chapter of Isaiah in which the Lord God is depicted not only as the Maker of peace, but also as the Creator of evil. In the seventh passage it says, "I form the light and create darkness; *I make peace and create evil*: I, the Lord, do all these things."

"There is something strange about the lack of symmetry in this portentous passage," said a listener. "At the beginning of that passage it says 'I form the light and create the darkness.' So should it not then have said, 'I make *good* and create evil'? Why 'I make *peace*'"?

Peace and the Redeemability of Evil

—A good question, smiled the teacher, and to answer it, I cite Sartre again. Evil, Sartre says, is not just an appearance; it is not opposed to good as a confused idea is to a clear one; it is not the effect of passions that might be cruel, of a fear that might be overcome, of an ignorance that might be enlightened. We, who heard whole blocks screaming (under Nazi occupation), Sartre says, understood that evil, like good, is absolute. In spite of ourselves, Sartre stresses, we came to this conclusion, which will seem shocking to lofty souls: "Evil cannot be redeemed!" Only in their conclusion do Sartre's fearful words run contrary to biblical faith. Evil, as a semi-autonomous force, so to speak, may appear, at times, as absolute, yes, but the whole point is that it *is* redeemable! That is what the above-quoted passage in Isaiah is, in fact, all about: "I am the Lord Who makes peace and creates evil." What does it mean? It means that even prior to the creation of evil — which antedates original sin — there was a divine commitment to the ultimate redemption of evil. But even more important, it means that the ultimate redemption of evil is predicated on a state of universal peace, which in turn is unthinkable without a messianic change in human nature. Only peace, ultimate peace, which is impossible in the biblical view without a revelation of the Divine, can redeem evil.

The Two Waters

Someone in the audience reminded the teacher that he had begun to say something earlier that evening about the separation that took place on the second day of creation between the waters of above and those of below. "I am confused," he said, "and I admit it. I assume that nothing short of Kabbalah will do to unconfuse me, so to speak, if it will not confuse me even more. But so as not to be carried away by a stream of many questions that come to my mind, let me ask you just one: Judging by what you have said tonight, I am assuming that the waters of 'below' mentioned on the second day of creation are the negative waters, so to speak, the abyss. Isn't that what you are implying?"

— That is right, the teacher said.

"Then how are we to understand that passage in Psalms — I don't recall the chapter — that says, 'Thy righteousness is like the mighty mountains; Thy judgment like *the deep abyss*.' How are we to understand it?"

— It is in the thirty-sixth chapter of Psalms, the teacher said, and I am glad you brought it up. Aside from what I said before about rigid judgments being on a collision course with pure mercy, and about Satan's doing his best to see that rigid judgment, untouched by mercy, prevails, the abyss below stands not only for rigid judgment, but for creative energy — it stands, in fact, for *creativity*.

Creativity

— The juxtaposition of the abyss below as judgment with the heights above as mercy touches on the dialectical meaning of creativity, said the teacher. Do you remember Jacob's blessing for Joseph?

He digressed for a moment on the meaning of the Patriarch's blessing for Dan, which starts by saying "Dan shall judge his people" and ends with the odd words, "I have waited for Thy salvation, O Lord! — This prophecy means that without divine salvation, which is mercy, judgment alone, Dan's vocation, can be frightful. Now the blessing to Joseph is

> Joseph is a fruitful bough, even a fruitful bough by a well whose branches run over the wall.... The archers have sorely grieved him, and shot at him, and despised him.... But his bough abode in strength, and the arms of his hands were made strong by the hands of the Mighty God of Jacob; from thence is the shepherd, the stone of Israel.... Even by the God of thy father Who shall help thee; and by the Almighty Who shall bless thee with the blessings of heaven above, *blessings of the abyss that lieth under*, blessings of the breasts and of the womb.

— No translation can do justice to these words, which flow like a river into the sea of eternity, but Thomas Mann has somehow captured its meaning in an essay:

> When I was young, I was infatuated with that pessimistic and romantic conception of the universe which set off against each other life and spirit, sensuality and redemption, and from which are derived some most compelling effects — compelling and yet, humanly speaking, not quite legitimate, not quite genuine. In short, I was a Wagnerite. But it is very likely in consequence of riper years that my love and my attention have more and more fixed upon a far happier and saner model — the figure of Goethe, with that marvelous combination of the daemonic and the urbane which made him the darling of mankind. It was not lightly that I chose for the hero of that epic [Joseph and his brothers] which is becoming my life's work a man "Blest with blessings from the heavens above and from the abyss below." ... Jacob, the father, pronounced the blessing upon Joseph's head. It was not a wish that he might be blessed, but a statement that he was so, and a wish for his happiness. And for me it is the most compendious possible formulation of my ideal humanity. Wherever in the realm of mind

and personality I find that ideal manifested as the union of darkness and light, feeling and mind, the primitive and the civilized, wisdom and the happy heart—in short, as the humanized mystery we call man—there lies my profoundest allegiance, therein my heart finds its home. Let me be clear: what I mean is not subtilization of the romantic, nor refinement of barbarism. It is nature clarified; it is culture; it is the human being as artist, and art as man's guide on the difficult path toward knowledge of himself.

The Abyss

—The demonic aspect of creativity, the teacher went on, was suggested by Nicholas Berdyaev, whom I shall cite:

The asceticism required by creativity is different from that which is concerned with personal perfection and salvation. No amount of ascetic practice will give one talent or ability, to say nothing of genius. Genius cannot be earned, it is given from above, like grace. What is required of the artist is intensity of the creative effort and not an artistic struggle for self-improvement. If Pushkin had practiced asceticism and sought the salvation of his soul he would probably have ceased to be a great poet. Creativeness is bound up with imperfection, and perfection may be unfavourable to it. This is the moral paradox with regard to creativeness.... If a man feels nothing but humility and a perpetual sense of sin, he can do no creative work. Creativeness means that one's mind passes on to another place of being. The soul may live simultaneously on different planes, *in the heights and in the lowest depths*; it may boldly create and be humbly penitent. But creativeness in all its aspects, including the moral—for there is such a thing as moral creativeness—testifies to the presence in man of a certain principle which may be the source of a system of morality different from the ethics of law and the ethics of redemption. Creativeness, more than anything else, is reminiscent of man's vocation before the Fall, and is, in a sense, beyond good and evil. But since human nature is sinful, creativeness is distorted and perverted by sin, and may be evil.

—The Bible treats the abyss, which sometimes stands for the unfathomable and sometimes for the demonic, reverentially. And the sages of the Talmud, continued the teacher, make the startling statement that a man should seek to serve God with *both* his urges, the good and the bad. In my view, this is possible only as a striving of the great soul to endow the good it generates with an energy equivalent to that generated by evil. For that the energy of evil is inexhaustible we learn from another saying of the sages: "The greater the man, the stronger his sinful urge." The sages never said, "Destroy the sinful urge in you!" All they said was, "Let the good in you acquire some of its energy!" The heights, in other words, need the depths, and the other way round. Rainer Maria Rilke said, "If my devils are to leave me, I am afraid that my angels will take flight as well."

— Let me conclude with a brief Hasidic story:

Cain's Good Traits

— Rabbi Uri of Strelisk, who was called "The Seraph," made the following comment: "My teacher, Rabbi Shlomo of Karlin, of blessed memory, had the soul of Abel. Now there are people within whom the good traits of Cain's soul have their habitation, and these are very great!"

9

What is Mussar?

And God Made Them Clothes

At the end of the class, late at night, a question was raised about a biblical passage whose meaning did not seem, at first, to present a problem. Adam and Eve, after they ate of the fruit of the tree of knowledge, realized that they were naked and were greatly embarrassed. Subsequently, after the severe divine reprimand—if not verdict—that was to change the mind and destiny of man forever, God, so scripture tells us, made clothes for Adam and Eve. "What I don't understand is this," said the questioner. "Did the Maker of heaven and earth really have to make clothes for His two sinful creatures Himself, and dress them? I thought the term 'and God made' was reserved for major acts of creation. But since the making of clothes for the first disobedient human beings can hardly be placed in this category, wouldn't it have been enough for God the Creator just to tell Adam and Eve how and with what to cover their bodies? What special significance, if any, is there in the simplistic biblical account about God—excuse the expression—the tailor?"

The teacher replied that this was a most important question, which was dealt with by Dietrich Bonhoeffer. A letter he wrote from a Berlin prison cell sheds light on it. —A couple of weeks earlier Bonhoeffer had written a letter to his friend Eberhard about fear under the bombardment of Berlin by the allies. The prison sustained—or almost sustained— a direct hit, and Bonhoeffer was witness to the double terror of the prisoners: the terror of the air raid and of the ground-trap they were in. He said in his letter that the shouting and the screaming of the prisoners in their separate cells was nothing short of horrifying. (They had no dead, only injured.) Afterwards, Bonhoeffer said, people talked quite openly about how frightened they had been while he, Bonhoeffer, did not quite know what to make of it, for, as he put it, "fright is surely something to be ashamed of." He had the feeling, he said, that fright should not be talked about except, perhaps, "in the confessional." On the other hand, Bonhoeffer argued, naive frankness could be quite disarming, but a cynical, ungodly frankness was disgusting. He was speaking, he said, of the kind of frankness that breaks out in heavy drinking and fornication and gives the impression of chaos. Bonhoeffer wondered whether fright was not one of those shameful things that ought to be concealed. In a subsequent letter, written a few weeks later — he was not permitted to write very often — Bonhoeffer quoted the Bible to prove a vital point.

God Himself Made Clothes for Men

Again speaking of fear, the teacher went on, Bonhoeffer observed that under the guise of honesty, something was being passed off as "natural" that was, at bottom, a symptom of sin. It was quite analogous, he said, to talking openly, obscenely, about sexual matters. "Truthfulness, after all, does not mean uncovering everything that exists." And here, the teacher commented, Bonhoeffer made an observation that gives a lasting, relevant, almost contemporary explanation for the biblical assurance that God Himself made clothes for man. If God Himself made clothes for man, Bonhoeffer said, it can mean only that in *statu corruptionis* (a state of corruption) many things in human life ought to remain covered, and that evil, even if it cannot be eradicated, ought at least to be concealed. Exposure is cynical, and although the cynic prides himself on his exceptional honesty, or claims to want truth at all costs, he misses the crucial fact, so vital for our spiritual survival, that since the fall there must be reticence and secrecy. God the tailor, it seems, performs with His "tailoring" an act of creation that had to serve as a warning to men till the end of the days that reticence and secrecy are not the concealment of truth, but truth itself.

What is Truth?

"But how would you define truth?" someone asked. "The Patriarch Jacob, always close to my heart, lies to his blind father about his true identity and thus deprives his older brother, Esau, of his right as the firstborn. Yet the prophet declares 'Thou giveth truth to Jacob.' How are we to understand truth?"

— We must remember to distinguish between truth and fact, the teacher replied. A truth is *not* a fact and a fact is *not* a truth. It is a fact, for example, that a wolf devours a lamb, but it is not a truth. It is a truth that you are your brother's keeper, but it is not a fact. Truth must have a dimension beyond the visual and the factual.

"What about scientific truth?" someone asked.

— Science, the teacher replied, is interested in *verifications*, not in truths. How can science be interested in truths when it is, according to its own admissions, morally neutral?

"Then truth must have a moral dimension?"

— Precisely, the teacher replied.

"Does speaking the truth always have a moral dimension?" someone asked.

— It does not, the teacher replied. That is why to tell the truth about a fact can sometimes be immoral.

"Can you be more specific?" a student requested.

— There is an ancient admonition by the sages of old that says, "Teach your tongue to say: I don't know." Does it not clearly imply that you should teach your tongue to say "I don't know" even if you *do* know?

"That's what it implies."

— But that would be a lie, wouldn't it? pressed the teacher.

There was no answer.

— What I am saying is this: When a fact, a naked fact, which is not, as we said, in itself a truth is expressed by a man who is himself a lie, then *infidelity* to that fact by a man of truth is fidelity to truth. Thus when a famous writer, a master at describing base instincts, his own to start with, declares that it is the vocation of a writer to make his private life public, he is not a liar, he is a lie. Conversely, if a person in search of a higher truth is unfaithful to the lower one — to a fact about himself or about another self who is a lie — he may very well be on the way to becoming a man of truth.

—Charles Peguy's thoughts come to mind. "The honest man," he read,

> must be a perpetual renegade; the life of an honest man must be a perpetual infidelity; because the man who wishes to remain faithful to truth must make himself continuously, relentlessly unfaithful to all the successive, indefatigable renascent errors. Thus the man who wishes to remain faithful to justice must make himself unfaithful to the triumphant injustices.

—Thus Jacob, the teacher concluded, faithful to truth, had to make himself unfaithful to a lie.

"Where does the Bible say that Esau was a liar?" someone asked.

—It does not say he was a liar, but it clearly implies that he was a *lie*, responded the teacher.

"I don't understand," exclaimed the questioner.

—Well, let us see how scripture depicts the main characteristics of Jacob and Esau. Jacob, the Bible says, was an *ish-tam*, a "whole man," "dwelling in the tents," that is to say, studious; while Esau a hunter, was roaming the fields. One day, Esau comes home tired and hungry. He sees the pot of red lentil soup in the kitchen and tells his brother he wants some. Do you remember the words?

"'Pour that red stuff down my gullet,'" someone quoted.

—Exactly, the teacher said. That is what he said, but that is not at all what comes out in any translation of the Bible. Now let me ask you this: What kind of man, what kind of character, would use this kind of language?

"Coarse," someone said.

"Vulgar," said another student.

—The sages indeed say, the teacher agreed, that the line indicates Esau's baseness of character.

"Then why did Isaac love him?" someone asked.

—Because "there was hunting in his mouth." There was no need to say, as the Bible does, "there was hunting in his mouth" if the intention was just to tell us that Esau was a hunter. The phrase "hunting in his *mouth*," in my view, stands not only for his profession, but for his

deception. Don't you have somehow to deceive the animal you are trying to catch? Esau deceived his old, blind father with his sweet and
misleading talk. True, the Bible nowhere says that Esau lied, but it es-
tablishes a much more important fact, namely, that he was a lie, a
thing of falsehood.

"How is that established?" someone queried.

A Thing of Falsehood

Instead of answering the question directly, the teacher put another:
—Have you ever asked yourself the question why there is no
commandment saying "Thou shall not lie"?

"What about the commandment 'And thou shall not bear false witness against thy neighbor'?" someone asked.

—The commandment against bearing false witness is clearly social,
while one that would prohibit lying, even if nobody was hurt by it,
would be of a distinctly moral nature. But you remember, I am sure,
the teacher went on, that passage in the Bible, quite close to the Ten
Commandments, which warns against any *proximity* to falsehood?

"'Keep away from a thing of falsehood,'" someone quoted.

—Yes. "Keep away from a thing of falsehood," the teacher said
with great emphasis, is a commandment for today. It could not have
followed the other "Thou shall not's," for its meaning is not as obvious. It is, in fact, a category in itself, containing a warning for our
time, for all times. But first let us return to Jacob and Esau. Esau,
ladies and gentlemen, was "honest": He was hungry, terribly hungry
one evening and on seeing the red lentil soup in the kitchen, told
Jacob to "pour that red stuff down my gullet." That is honest, isn't it?
He said what he felt. He did not conceal, did not hide, did not
hesitate, did not look for a nicer way to express himself. Yet the sages
say it was that "honest" line of his which disqualified him as a firstborn. Why? Because it was a coarse, crude, vulgar honesty, and a vulgar honesty is a thing of falsehood.

—Two nineteenth-century giants, Kierkegaard and Nietzsche, desperately seeking the truth in two different directions, came to the
same conclusion concerning truth. They thought, namely, that it was
impossible to grasp or teach the truth when the mode of thinking was
base. This profound observation implies that you do not have to lie in

order to lie; if one is base, vulgar, coarse, one *is a lie* even if, strictly speaking, one does not lie at all! One is, in other words, a thing of falsehood even if one is "honest."

At Least I Am Honest

"A statement comes to my mind," someone commented, "which I heard on an American television program about prostitution. A prostitute appearing on it declared 'At least I am honest!'"

— Did you see anything wrong in that statement? the teacher asked.

"Frankly, I didn't," the man admitted.

— You see, the teacher said, there is a sick idea now being expounded everywhere — in art, literature, the media — that honesty and nature — human nature — are the same. You know what I am talking about? the teacher asked.

"N-not exactly," the man replied.

— To be true to one's nature is generally regarded as honest, isn't that so?

"It is," the man said, "But—"

— What is wrong with it? Is that what you want to ask?

The student hesitated. "Well—"

— We have established, said the teacher, that the Bible does not regard man's nature as good but, at best, as imperfect and, at worst, as naturally inclined toward evil, as it is written "For the imagination of man's heart is evil from its inception!" Hence man is there to fight his nature. Man is there to transcend it. Of course I pride myself on my freedom to do as I please, but I derive my quality as a true human being from my acquired ability *not* to do as I please! That is why sin is so vital for the very exercise of my freedom: I can sin if I want to, but it requires more strength to abstain from sinning when my whole nature inclines me to it. To be one with one's nature is to be animalistic, not honest.

A student interrupted. "I am not quite sure I follow you. Isn't it true that to act naturally, for example, is something praiseworthy?"

— There are two kinds of acting naturally: to act naturally as opposed to being pretentious and to act naturally as opposed to being restrained. The first is a truth; the second, a lie.

The teacher paused, to catch a thought. Then he said: — A strange thought has just occurred to me. It is very possible that the "missing" commandment "Thou shall not lie!" is not only contained in but, as it were, reinforced by the commandment "Thou shall not steal!"

The Mind-Thieves

— There is an expression in Hebrew, the teacher went on, whose equivalent, as far as I know, does not exist in any other language, *Gonev da'ath haberioth*, "He who steals the minds of his fellowmen." The sages in Tosefta Baba-Kama speak of seven kinds, or types, of thieves, the worst of them being "he who steals the minds of his fellowmen." Whom would you classify as such a thief?

"As I see it," someone said, "to steal the minds of people is to brainwash them in a way, to seduce them into believing something that you, yourself, may not believe in but that is convenient to you to have others believe."

"To steal the minds of people," another opined, "is to pretend."

"Hypocrisy," said a young man, "is what stealing the minds of people is all about."

"If you ask me," was another answer, "politicians are actually in the business of stealing the minds of people."

"Don't forget Madison Avenue!" someone added.

"Image making, to be more specific!"

"Propaganda! Propaganda is the art of stealing the minds of people without their noticing it."

The teacher nodded. — All this is very true, of course, but let me add one major kind of stealing that has not been mentioned here: the stealing of the *image*.

"Of what?" clamored several voices.

— Of the image, the teacher replied. The term belongs, if my memory serves me well, to Jacques Maritain, and what he said, in essence, was this: A revolution has been going on for more than half a century against whatever in man and in the human world bears the likeness of God. In Marxism, there is "alienation," which, substituted for the likeness of God, demands the giving up of personality and the organization of collective man into one single, faceless body whose supreme destiny is to gain, at any price, dominion over matter and human history as determined by matter. In capitalism there still is a thirst for communion, but it is sought in economic activity, in pure productivity, in marketability. Capitalism is engulfed in the demiurgic task of fabrication and domination over things. When the human person is sacrificed to industrial titanism, his image is a stolen one, for it is no longer derived from God, but from "society." A human image derived from society is not just a lie, but a theft: The image was stolen, and it was stolen from God. No wonder that the thief, the stealer of the image — narcissist, for example, madly in love with himself, yet constantly seeing his image in other people's gaze — is so totally incapable of self-condemnation. On another level of society, a less complacent one, there roams another kind of image stealer, the radical one, whose self-image is a derivative of a party line or a group discipline, and who condemns the whole world but himself. The more capable we are of self-determination, the less stolen our image.

What is Mussar?

— I want you to remember this, said the teacher, for it may answer many questions about people who are out "to save the world," so to speak: Rabbi Israel Salanter, the founder of the Lithuanian Mussar movement, said of himself, "At the beginning, before I took to Mussar, I would condemn only the others for all the wrongs of the world. Later, when I got involved in the study of Mussar, I condemned the others along with myself. Now I condemn *only* myself."

"But what *is* Mussar?" someone asked.

— Another time, the teacher replied.

Shem, Ham, and Yaphet

The teacher opened the next class with the question, What is the first biblical prophecy? He prefaced his answer as follows: — The prophecy in question prefigures and symbolizes the major currents in the cultural and spiritual development of mankind to this very day. It is the one that summarizes the relationship between Noah and his three sons, Shem, Ham, and Yaphet.

— We read in the ninth chapter of Genesis, the teacher went on, that Noah got drunk and fell asleep naked. Ham saw the nakedness of his father, and instead of covering it, he — perversely amused, as it seems — told his brothers about it. "And Shem and Yaphet," says the

Bible, "took a garment and laid it upon their shoulders and walked backwards, and covered the nakedness of their father. . . . And they saw not their father's nakedness." Then Noah awoke and, realizing what happened—the Bible does not tell us how—he pronounced a prophecy:

—"Blessed be the Lord of Shem, and Cana'an shall be his servant."

—"God shall enlarge Yaphet, and he shall dwell in the tents of Shem; and Canaan shall be their servant."

—Canaan, the teacher went on, as we find out a little later, is "Ham's issue," as the Bible puts it. We also find out that Yavan, the Hebrew name of Greece to this day, is "the issue of Yaphet." And we are also told that *Ever*—Hebrews—are "the issue of Shem." We must bear this in mind, for what is so remarkable about the story is that it deals with refinement of spirit not only as an ontological but as an anthropological category. I used the word "refinement," but "fineness" may be a better word. Nietzsche, in fact, whom I am going to quote on the subject, uses the word "finesse." You have heard me quote Kierkegaard and Nietzsche to the effect that the truth can neither be taught nor grasped when the mode of thinking is base. "Fineness," the opposite of baseness, is thus the mode of thinking conducive to the grasping of truth. It is not a moral but an ontological conclusion. Meaning itself, or the search for it, is a category of fineness. I would like to say something else before we come to the heart of the matter: This age of ours *is the least refined* in the history of civilization. Never in the history of the emerging human spirit has the mode of thinking been so base. The "Garden of Eden," literally translated, means "garden of refinement," which is to say that the soul, when it attains to ultimate truth, attains it through ultimate refinement.

—The sages of the Talmud tell us that the purpose of the Law is to refine man. Someone asked me at our previous class, "What is Mussar?" and though my answer may seem a bit farfetched, I will stand by it. If messianic redemption means a universal change in human nature in general through an act of divine interference, Lithuanian Mussar tried to achieve a change in the nature of the few through an act of the will. Lithuanian Mussar taught that men of moral depth—not to be confused with "morality"—warmth, and delicacy may be more important for the improvement of mankind than the newest and truest ideas of science and morals. It was Gedalyahu Alon, himself a former Mussarist, who uses these three characteristics to define Mussar: depth, warmth, and delicacy. Two stories come to mind: one about the Hafetz Hayim, of blessed memory, and the other about another man of blessed memory, Rabbi Israel Salanter.

The Hafetz Hayim Becomes a Grocer

—The Hafetz Hayim the teacher said, so-called after his unique thesis about the evils of bad tongue, was unwilling to enter the rabbinate. So what did he do? He decided to open a grocery shop. The arrangement was that his willing wife, whose idea it was in the first place, would attend to the store while he attended to his studies. Soon word spread in the village of Radin that the saintly man had become a grocer. That was enough for the inhabitants, Jew and Gentile alike, to flock to his store. When the Hafetz Hayim saw the lines forming outside, he told the people that unless they kept patronizing other groceries, too, his would constitute unfair competition. When the appeal proved futile, the Hafetz Hayim closed the store in the afternoons, only to find that the lines in the mornings had doubled. He resorted to one last attempt to cut his clientele to the desired size: He kept his store open only two days a week. Realizing, however, that the customers were still numerous enough to pose a threat to the other grocers, he gave up and closed his store altogether.

The Worry of a Dying Man

The teacher went on with the other story:
—Rabbi Israel Salanter, he said, died in Koenigsberg, East Prussia, where he had come to seek medical help. The Jewish community hired an elderly man to stay with Rabbi Israel at night, and the man watched over the sick rabbi, night after night, with a great and loving consideration. On the night Rabbi Israel passed away, he called in his attendant, a highly sensitive man, and asked him not to be afraid to remain with a dead body at night. He explained to him that a body, once the soul that inhabited it is gone, must not be looked on as anything frightening. "You must promise me," he pleaded with

the tearful old man, "that you will not be scared." That was Rabbi Israel, the teacher concluded, and that is Mussarist consideration at its loftiest. Fineness, as understood by Mussar, is not only voluntary consideration, but consideration as the *duty* to gladden one's heart, or, at least, to avoid saddening it.

— One more story, taken from the Talmud, will further illustrate this point.

The Jesters

— Rabbi Beroka used to visit the marketplace, where the Prophet Elijah often appeared to him. It was believed, as you know, that Elijah appeared to some saintly men to offer them spiritual guidance.

— Once Rabbi Beroka asked the prophet, "Is there anyone here who has a share in the world to come?"

— "No," the prophet replied.

— While they were talking, two men passed them by. On seeing them, the prophet remarked, "These two men have a share in the world to come."

— Rabbi Beroka then approached and asked them, "Can you tell me what is your occupation?"

— "We are jesters," they replied. "When we see men depressed, we cheer them up."

Rigor and Mercy

Someone in the audience confessed to a sense of frustration at the antinomies of the Bible. "You have given us some moving examples of divinely inspired kindness, which you rightly regard as indistinguishable from finesse; but how are we to understand the pronunciations and manifestations of divine rigor, if not rigidity, in the Bible?"

— Only in adversity, I think, can one realize that those manifestations of divine "rigidity" are also, dialectically speaking, aspects of mercy. Bonhoeffer was more and more drawn to the Old Testament, as it is called *precisely* on account of that rigidity, for it is the rigidity along with the mercy that makes it possible for the Absolute Spirit to address Himself to all human, and inhuman, situations till the end of the days. In the Old Testament, that Absolute Spirit had jotted down, in Heine's words, the events of the days — of all days — with the accuracy of one listing his laundry. The "laundry," so to speak, is sometimes dirty, sometimes bloody. But a Jew in Auschwitz, I say, could definitely console himself with the thought that "a God of vengeance is the Lord."

— "But what we are to do with the passage that speaks of the sins of the fathers being visited upon their children?"

Visiting the Iniquity of the Fathers Upon Their Children

— This puzzling and disturbing warning, the teacher said, which is part of the Ten Commandments, promises to have the iniquites of the fathers visited upon their children "to the third and fourth generation of those who hate me." How are we to understand it?

— In my view, a view for which I find support in Rashi's comments on the Torah, it is Noah's prophetic curse that provides, as it were, an a priori answer to that enigmatic passage. Noah's prophecy teaches us the great lesson that when the human psyche began to be formed, the Almighty, who created man with an opportunity for self-perfection, also left it to him to create his own *imperfections*. The Almighty, in other words, made it possible for man, after He created him in His image, to mold his own character and, by doing so, to determine, for better or worse, the character of his issue for generations to come. Thus Ham's lewdness was bound to manifest itself in his son as a deformity of character.

"But why should a deformity of character, if that is the word for it," someone asked, "be punishable by slavery?"

— That is the whole point, the teacher replied. Slavery here is not just the punishment, but *the diagnosis as well as manifestation of sin as a deformity of character*; it is sin *as* punishment. We have discussed that before in another context, haven't we? Maybe this first Noahite prophecy will make it clearer. What essentially did Ham do? He could not resist an obscene urge to see his father's nakedness and then make fun of it in front of his brothers. He succumbed, in other words, to a base impulse that involved not only a vulgar curiosity, but a flagrant disrespect for the seniority, indeed superiority of fatherhood. Ham, at that moment, was a slave to ugly impulses that he was either powerless or unwilling to resist.

— You can see now what I am driving at: The powerlessness to resist slavery to his own ugly impulses degenerated into a powerlessness to resist slavery to the ugly dominance of others. Sin thus became a punishing character trait to be visited upon Ham's children, for it involved not only yielding to a base slavery from within, but *not* granting the respect due an honorable authority from without, as represented by the father. To the degree that Ham's transgression became Canaan's trait, can we not say that the father's sin was visited upon his issue?

"It will be a while before I fully comprehend it," someone remarked, "though it seems clear that the Bible here was going out of its way, so to speak, to stress the thought that an inconsideration to man — not to say a mean, coarse inconsideration — is a sin against God."

— That is Mussar! the teacher exclaimed. The Bible here is also going out of its way to stress the corresponding thought that *fineness*, pure consideration, is not only something that endears man to man, but that which draws him closer to God. That, too, is Mussar. Look at the cryptic yet explicit way the Bible describes the finesse and discretion of Shem and Yaphet when they went to cover up their father's nakedness!

Some people in the audience still seemed troubled by the story. "I am profoundly impressed," said one, "by the thought that the first biblical prophecy was, in fact, based on a denunciation of vulgarity, but I am very bothered by the idea that the manifestation of Ham's slavish and coarse character trait merited a curse on his issue."

— A *forecast* about his issue would be more exact.

"Meaning what?" someone asked.

— It was a forecast about a curse on his issue, the teacher explained, not a wish that such a curse be their lot. Commenting on the terrifying list of curses in Deuteronomy, curses that will befall the Jewish people if they do not obey God's will, Don Isaac Abarbanel says, "We should know that the curses in this chapter are not invoked as a warning and threat, but were meant as a revelation of the Holy One concerning what lies ahead; and all these [prophecies] were fulfilled in the generations of the sinners in their soul." Nachmanides sees these curses the same way. The prophecy about a curse to come was even more plausible in Noah's case, for he was made to see prophetically a character deformity as a destiny. This is very much in the biblical line of seeing a sin — and a character deformity *is* sin — as its own punishment, as it is written, "Thine own wickedness shall punish thee."

And He Does Not Cleanse

— There is a mighty passage in Exodus 34, said the teacher: "And the Lord descended in the cloud, and stood with him there, and proclaimed the name of the Lord.... And the Lord passed by before him, and proclaimed: the Lord, the Lord, mighty, merciful and gracious, long-suffering, and abundant in goodness and truth.... Keeping mercy for thousands, forgiving iniquity and transgressions and sin, but Who does not *cleanse the guilty*; visiting the iniquity of the fathers upon the children's children, unto the third and fourth generation." Now the Hebrew words *yenakeh lo yenakeh*, usually translated "and He doesn't cleanse the guilty," have been discussed down through the ages of biblical commentary. It seems to me, however, that the simplest and most literary translation of those three words is also their most likely interpretation: God forgives and loves, is abundant in goodness and truth. He forgives iniquity and transgressions and sin, *but He does not do the cleansing of man; He does not change man. Man must change himself.*

Haliteini na and *Hagmieini na*

— In Genesis 24, continued the teacher, we read a marvelous account of human finesse that tells us how Eliezer, Abraham's servant and "master of his household," came to Abraham's distant relatives to look for a wife for Isaac. Abraham, repelled by the abominations of the Canaanites among whom he dwelled, makes it clear to Eliezer that Isaac's wife cannot be one of them. So Eliezer goes far away, to Abraham's family. The way he tells them of his mission is so utterly beautiful that it led the sages of the Talmud to exclaim, "The conversation of the servants of the Patriarchs is greater than the teachings of the children." Before this conversation is the story of Eliezer's first encounter with Rebecca at the well. One passage in it cries out to be juxtaposed with another that deals with a similar situation and, strangely enough, has the same rhythm: Esau, as we all remember, asks Jacob for food as Eliezer asks Rebecca for water. But there is a difference. Esau starts his request with the words *Haliteini na*, "fill me up with" or "pour that stuff down my gullet." When Eliezer asks for water, however, he says *Hagmieini na*, which does not even mean "Make me drink, I beseech thee" as it is usually translated. It is so tender an expression that it simply defies translation. Eliezer, Abraham's servant, was the master of his household because he was, as is clear from the biblical narrative, a masterfully refined man. Finesse, in other words, made a master out of a slave.

— Now I want to return to the question of inherited mean traits eventually shaping a mean — not to be confused with a tragic — destiny, said the teacher. This is my own interpretation of the biblical warning about the sins of the fathers being visited upon their children. However, it was implied by the sages of the Talmud in Tractate Sanhedrin, where it is said that the "visiting" of the iniquities of the fathers upon their offspring applies only to offspring "who hold on to the iniquitous deeds of their parents." This is the same as saying that those "deeds" that have become character deformities cling to them unless or until they resort to radical means.

— Now, the teacher went on, let us look at the prophecy from the angle of culture and civilization as it developed down the ages: Both Shem and Yaphet were called on, after the flood, to cover, symbolically speaking, the animal nakedness of mankind, that is to say, to elevate man to ethical and aesthetic levels and thus render him more human. Ham, however, who was the personification of hot-blooded coarseness and delighted in brutish nakedness, was delivered through his own moral insensitivity into the hands of the two brothers to tame and teach him.

Sounds Like Colonialism

"Sounds like colonialism!" someone remarked, not without bitterness.

— It does, the teacher replied. Since nothing happens in a vacuum, colonialism has evidently happened in the context of a curse of which Ham was the creator. But at the risk of rubbing some of you the wrong way, which I would not like to do, I will say this: A look at a good part of Africa today is enough to make us wonder whether the curse has run its course.

"Meaning what?" someone demanded.

— Meaning, the teacher replied, that one can free oneself from political slavery from without and remain a slave to coarse and brutish impulses from within. It is the shame of Yaphet that for centuries it compounded the curse, but it is the shame of Shem, Ham, and Yaphet that they cover up, as they do even today, the atrocities that are being perpetrated in Africa by the issue of Ham against the issue of Ham!

After a long, heavy silence the teacher went on. — Returning to the all-embracing vision of the first prophecy, he remarked, we are immediately struck by the fact that it has divided the world for all time into Hebraic and Hellenic divisions. These two major currents account for the spiritual, cultural, and intellectual life of the world. They have shaped, directly or indirectly, the opinions, customs, institutions, ideals, and actions of people all over the world and are, in essence, representative even of trends that, historically speaking, knew little or nothing of them, like Buddhism and other spiritual trends of the East. According to Heinrich Heine and, later, George Brandes, both following many others, mankind's cultural river is divided into two tributaries: the Hellenic and the Hebraic, Hellenism dealing with the spirit of beauty and Hebraism dealing with the beauty of the spirit. Christianity and Islam, of course, must thus be regarded as Hebraic.

"Forgive the interruption," a young man said, "but would you also regard as 'Hebraic' the not very complimentary description of Ishmael's traits in scripture? The Arabs, after all, regard themselves, and rightly so, we think, as the issues of Ishmael."

— We were just speaking of *trends*, not of *traits*, the teacher explained. Included in one or the other trend can be any part or any people of the world. But since you mentioned Ishmael, I may as well remind you of the prophecy about him, which, if properly understood, reads like today's headlines. Our next lesson will begin with it.

10

And Thou Shall Not
Put a Stumbling Block
Before the Blind

Everybody Will Need Him

The teacher read the twelfth verse of the sixteenth chapter of Genesis: —"And he [Ishmael, says the Lord] will be a savage. . . . His hand will be against every man and every man's hand will be against him. . . . And he shall dwell in the presence of all his brethren." Onkelos, he said, the inspired translator of the Bible into Aramaic, interpreted that verse two millenia ago. This ancient sage, a member of the royal family of Rome who embraced Judaism, gave the following interpretation: "He will need everybody and all people will need him." What better describes the almost universal dependence on Arab oil, for example?

God Will Enlarge Yaphet

—What do the sight and sound of the word *Yaphet* in Hebrew remind you of? asked the teacher.

"*Yafeh*" was the answer from all sides. "Beautiful."

—Correct, the teacher replied. Now, Noah's blessing to Yaphet was, as we all know, *Yaphet Hashem Leyaphet*, which means "God will *enlarge* Yaphet." Now, after we have established that *Yaphet* stands for the spirit of beauty, we must draw a second conclusion from the biblical text, namely, that "enlarge" means exactly what it says' expansion, dominion, and what the French call *grandeur*. Now combine the spirit of beauty and the sense of visual grandeur and you have defined the essential components of Hellenism.

— Moving on to Shem, the teacher continued, if the combination of the beautiful with the grand has given us the Parthenon, the Acropolis, the Coliseum, the Arc de Triomphe, in short, the symbols of the grand and the palatial, where would you expect the beauty of the spirit — as opposed to the spirit of beauty — to dwell?

Silence.

— What dwelling place, then, what habitation, in biblical terms, would be the very opposite of the palatial?

"The tent?"

— Exactly! the teacher exclaimed. The tent. Now tell me this: What does the tent stand for in the Bible?

"As you mentioned on another occasion," someone responded, "the passage about Jacob, 'A whole man, dwelling in tents' was interpreted by the sages to mean that he was the learned type."

— The tent, in other words, the teacher said, stands for study?

"For even more than that," offered someone else. "'The Tent of the Tabernacle' is understood in the Bible to mean the place where the divine glory made itself manifest."

— In other words, the teacher went on, the tent, in biblical terms, stands for pure spirit, pure inwardness. Where else is this thought implied?

"In the grand vision of Balaam," someone answered, "who came to curse Israel, but blessed it instead. 'How goodly are thy tents, O Jacob,' he cries."

— Excellent, the teacher exclaimed. Where else?

"'And Isaac brought Rebecca into the tent of Sarah, his mother,'" someone quoted Genesis. "Rashi interprets it to mean, since Sarah was already dead at that time, that he introduced her to the *spirit* of his mother and that she was like her."

— Very good, the teacher said. The "tent," then, stands for the spiritual or, more directly, for the beauty of the spirit. Contrary to the spirit of beauty, which depends to a large degree on appearance, the beauty of the spirit chooses a humble abode, a tent, for its dwelling place. In view of this, the teacher asked, how would *you* interpret the biblical prophecy, the first prophecy, which stresses that while Yaphet will have beauty and grandeur, he will nevertheless *dwell* in the tents of Shem?

"Monotheism?" someone ventured.

— Yes! the teacher exclaimed. It is, after all, the Hebraic concept of one God — the major *tent of Shem*, so to speak — where both Christianity and Islam dwell! Thus Yaphet, though it may, as it does, glory in the palaces of Hellenism, draws its spiritual strength from the tent of Shem.

Yaphet and the Tents of Shem

To the next class the teacher brought a work by Rabbi Samson Raphael Hirsh, a nineteenth-century Hebrew sage and scholar who lived in Germany. — We must realize, said the teacher, that Rabbi Hirsh lived in an era when the exteriorized spirit of Hellenism had little use for the inwardness represented by the tents of Shem. Many Jews, even when they spoke of "the beauty of Yaphet in the tents of Shem," actually longed to be in the palaces of Yaphet. It was an age of reason, the pride and the glory of the Hellenic spirit, which did not have much patience with the faith that dwelled in and emanated from the tents of Shem. Little did Hirsh's contemporaries know of the depths of dark irrationality into which Yaphetic reason, unaided by the spirit of Shem, would one day degenerate. But Samson Raphael Hirsh, interpreting the first great biblical prophecy, sounded, as it were, a warning that unless Yaphet again looked for its spiritual roots in the tents of Shem, it might be in trouble.

— But first, the teacher went on, let us see what Hirsh had to say about the historic encounter between Shem and Yaphet. Prior to that encounter, the pre-Hellenic, Gentile, or heathen world taught man to look primarily outward; expounded to him the phenomena of the world as the manifestation of supernatural powers whose strength was represented to man by idols oveloaded with symbols before whom man had to kneel in fear and trembling and make sacrifices, even human sacrifices, to soothe their wrath and court their favor. Before those supernatural powers, man's personality was reduced to complete insignificance. Only the chosen ones, priests and kings, could stand forth to call on the masses of spiritual slaves to kneel before them

and do as they said. Then there emerged the Hellenic spirit. It
directed man's gaze toward himself and showed him within himself an
ideal of divine perfection and beauty that all could achieve. It set up
the ideal of perfect man in such an all-embracing manner that even
the gods became embodiments of the ideals of human qualities. The
Hellenic spirit stimulated the mind to develop, either through joy in
knowledge or through contemplation of tragedy, a symmetry of harmony and beauty as a means to overcome brutish outbursts of blind
passions. It taught man the virtues of civility and reason and showed
him how to apply reason for the purpose of subduing the evil and
vulgar things in life, which distort the harmony and symmetry of
beauty. Thus Samson Raphael Hirsh, following in the footsteps of
much earlier commentators, interprets the word *Yaphet*, "enlarge,"
to mean "God will open to Yaphet the gates of the mind."

— And indeed He has! the teacher exclaimed. By measuring perfection in terms of sensuous beauty, Hellenism has aroused disgust for all
that is brutish, vulgar, and insensitive in life. By the elevation of tragedy to the rank of a destiny, on the one hand, and, later, by the glori-
fication of reason as the power in us that can make destiny intelligible,
Hellenism has enlarged the mind by constantly stimulating it. If
Alfred North Whitehead was right when he said that all philosophy,
down to our day, is nothing but a footnote to Plato, we shall not be
wrong if we say that all culture that seeks justification for, and beauty
in, man's earthly existence is bound to derive from Hellenism.

Yet the grave crisis in Western civilization, caused to a very large
degree by the degeneration of reason into rationalism and materiality, proves that Hellenic culture, or any derivative of it, if it tries to dis-
regard the tents of Shem and make for itself a fetish of its own corner,
no matter how vast, of civilization, is undermining its own existence.
Hellenic culture, as long as it prides itself on being sublime, self-
sufficient, and exclusive, is bound to fall into error and illusion, degeneration and exteriorization. Hellenic philosophy stimulated the
intellect, created the thirst for knowledge, the need for truth, but was
not capable, in itself, of assuring the spirituality of culture. As long as
Hellenic or, more specifically, scientific culture assumes that the human mind, alone and unaided, that is, autonomous reason, is capable
of grasping the truth, Hellenic reason dissolves into a moral aberra-
tion. The polished exterior of an aesthetically refined culture gives

way to hedonistic pleasure-seeking and brutish animal sensualities. Yaphet contains, in the words of Samson Raphael Hirsh, "only a fraction of that truth which, as we believe, will one day bring salvation to all mankind." For when that fraction moves away from the tent of Shem, even reason, in which it took so much pride, will degenerate into irrationality. The beauty that was Greece needs the wisdom that was Jerusalem.

"What about 'the glory that was Rome?'" someone asked. "Where does it fit into the juxtaposition of Athens with Jerusalem?"

—According to Hirsh, the teacher replied, Rome's essential character, in contrast to Hellas's idealistic outlook, bears the stamp of blatant materialism. Its sole aim was the aggrandizement of material possessions, so that glory and might themselves were only a means toward it. Usefulness—very much like our own all-too-familiar utilitarianism—measured the worth of all things. Rome had neither the time nor the inclination for anything that might elevate the mind and render man more human. The brute force of Rome overpowered Jerusalem, but Jerusalem, as *Shem*, survived Rome. Honor can dwell in tents while glory needs palaces. The honor that rests in tents is hardly known, but the glory that dwells in palaces is famous. Maybe that is why Hebraism, the tents of Shem, is the least known religion in the world, while the glory of Rome, even without "Rome," lives on in a materialism that is now both conquering and destroying the world.

Glory and Honor

—The glory that was Rome! the teacher repeated. Has it ever occurred to you, I wonder, that in the Bible the same word is used for "glory" and "honor," namely *Kavod*? In that famous and marvelous twenty-fourth chapter of Psalms, which begins with the words "The earth is the Lord's and the fullness thereof," God is referred to, time and again, as *Melech Hakavod*, usually translated as "The King of Glory": "Open up, ye eternal gates . . . and let the King of Glory come in." A little earlier in the same chapter, however, there is a description of the excellent man who is worthy of ascending the mountain of the Lord: "Who shall ascend the mountain of the Lord and who shall stand in the place of His Sanctuary? He that is clean of hands and pure of heart, who has not carried his soul in vain and has not sworn deceitfully." Is it not obvious that the kind of man described in here is not a man of glory but of honor? Glory, which is often another word for celebrity, does not always tell us much about the one who achieved it and may even hide from us the real truth about him. Honor, however, tells us a great deal about the man himself, even if there is very little "glory" about him. Napoleon, for example, is associated in our minds with glory, hardly with honor—he may have been, in fact, as a man, quite dishonorable, if not despicable, as Madame de Staël claims. The saint, however, or the sage, can be described, and understood, only in terms of honor, not of glory. It is, in fact, part of their greatness that they escape the glory of celebrity—celebrity is all glory but not necessarily any honor. Now, since in biblical Hebrew glory and honor are the same word, *Melech Hakavod* means "King of Honor." Though the world today may still have moments of glory, there is hardly any honor left. We see and hear what is said and done in the name of religion, of justice, of humanity, of love—and we shudder at the dishonor to each of them. When we perceive the accumulation of dishonor in the world, we sometimes feel like praying to Him on High to save us, to save the world, from its dishonor even more than from its distress. We pray for a rediscovery of honor. "Raise your heads, ye eternal gates, and let the King of Honor come in!"

Our Hands Did Not Shed This Blood

When Ariel Halevi spoke the next time it was in the wake of a murder committed on the seashore between Haifa and Tel Aviv: A girl was found dead, strangled with a fine nylon cord. The reasons for the crime were not yet known, but the crime, as such, was the shock and the talk of the day. The teacher seemed particularly upset by it and seemed to feel constrained to discuss it before anything else.

—At the end of the twenty-first chapter of Deuteronomy, he began without preliminaries, we find an elaborate exposition of a Mosaic Law that is difficult to understand. If an unidentified man is found dead in the vicinity of a city, the city elders, standing over the body of the slain man, shall make in the presence of the priests of the Lord the following solemn declaration: "Our hands have not shed this blood, neither have our eyes seen it. . . . Be merciful, O Lord, unto Thy people, Israel, whom Thou hast redeemed, and lay not innocent blood unto Thy people, Israel," and the blood shall be forgiven them. But forgiven whom? The elders? Has anybody suspected that the elders have shed that blood? The sages posed this question long ago and the answer they gave has momentous implications. They say, in essence, that the declaration the city elders must make over the dead body of the unidentified man has nothing to do with the actual execution of the murder, but with the *atmosphere* conducive to it. Suppose, the sages say, the victim was a poor man who passed through the city and was not fed, a stranger who was not housed, a wanderer who was not helped and thus had to wander somewhere else for aid; in such a case, the city elders have his blood on their hands. According to this Law, then, the mere toleration of an atmosphere conducive to crime *is* a crime. No crime is committed in a vacuum, but rather in a certain social atmosphere, a certain psychological ambience that makes it as possible for the murderer to kill as for the victim to perish. Those responsible for these social and psychological conditions are the leaders, the city elders. They must be regarded as accomplices to the crime unless it is established not only that they have done nothing to create that atmosphere, but that they have done everything to eliminate it. In order to raise their hands before God and men and swear "Our hands have not shed this blood!" the elders must be conscious of a responsibility for the entire social realm. Now, the teacher went on with bitter emphasis, I claim that we cannot say, after that nylon-cord murder, that our hands have not shed that blood.

In the stunned silence that followed, the teacher said he had just learned about a motion picture, televised some weeks ago, that featured in great detail murder by nylon-cord strangulation. He reminded the group that television had introduced Israel to crimes it had never known before. —Now I ask you this, the teacher said, do you think that those responsible for the dissemination of murder and horror stories, if summoned before a court of biblical justice, could say "Our hands have not shed this blood"?

And Thou Shall Not Put a Stumbling Block Before the Blind

One of the Americans in the audience was the first to speak up. As an American, he said, he was both conscious of and disturbed by the undeniable connection between the media and the crime rate. "But," he asked, "wouldn't you say that any attempt to interfere with it would amount to censorship?"

The teacher's dismayed reaction was atypical. — Is restraint censorship? he asked.

"Self-restraint is one thing," the American began, but the teacher interrupted. — And when there is no self-restraint? When what you see or hear actually leads to the *undermining* of self-restraint, what then? Can every man be trusted to restrain himself?

"Once you begin to interfere with certain freedoms," responded the American, "where do you draw the line?"

— The answer is, when you regard the whole area where the mind appears as a dark spot.

"I don't quite follow you," said the student.

— Well, the teacher said, does the mind, in your view, represent a greater enigma than the body?

"If by 'a greater enigma,'" was the reply, "you mean to say that physical problems have proven more amenable to treatment — to surgery, for example — than mental problems, then the answer is yes, it does present a greater enigma than the body."

— And am I right, the teacher went on, that there is now a growing realization, particularly in the United States, where psychoanalysis, as I understand, is on the way out and psychiatry is a failure, that except for chemical tranquilizers, which may prove of temporary help, the mind simply refuses to fit into any preconceived scientific mold? Is that so or not?

"No doubt about that," the American said. "The number of mental cases is on the increase everywhere."

— The mind, in other words, the teacher pressed on, is not only a dark spot for itself, but we are all in the dark when it comes to comprehending its complexities.

"That's right."

— Now let me ask you this, the teacher continued his query. Would you not say that the mind, being less "visible," less clear, less understandable than the body, requires and, indeed, deserves to be treated more delicately, more considerately than the body?

"It certainly does," was the answer.

— And do you think that people actually treat their minds more considerately than their bodies?

No answer.

— Let me be more specific, the teacher went on. In the United States, for example, everybody welcomes the existence of a consumer protection agency set up for the sole purpose of protecting the body and pocket of the consumer against deficient products and reckless profiteers. Then why would the idea of setting up, say a mental consumer protection agency be immediately branded as "censorship," or wouldn't it?

"I suppose it would," was the answer.

— But why is "physical" censorship, so to speak, welcome? Would you not say that the consumer protection agency is there to "censor" the spread of certain harmful mental products and harmful prices before they reach the public?

"Certainly," the American said, "but — "

— And would you not say, the teacher interrupted him, that the public, any public, is likely to know much more about products and prices than about mental reactions and the inner workings of the psyche?

"Obviously."

— Yet you are opposed to restricting the availability of certain harmful products because this is censorship?

"It's a problem," the American replied, "a bitter problem."

— It is a major tragedy, the teacher said emphatically. While we agree that the human mind as a very delicate thing cannot possibly ingest everything that is thrown at it without harm to itself, yet we self-righteously invoke the word "freedom" to justify our treating the mind like a sewer. With the mind we are still groping in the dark; we do not know the nature of the harm that may be caused by the indiscriminate ingestion of whatever visual foods it happens to be served. There is a biblical law about this: "And thou shall not place a stumbling block before the blind." What did you think this passage of Leviticus was all about?

"I read in a commentary," a bearded gentleman replied, "that if a vegetable vendor, for example, covers the rotten vegetables he displays with good ones, he transgresses this law."

— Excellent! the teacher said. That law covers an area as vast as the world, from a vegetable stand in the marketplace to Madison Avenue in New York. The media, too, are culpable if they try to cover up manifestations of human rottenness with the rosy apples of "freedom" and "civil rights." They then violate the law "Thou shall not place a stumbling block before the blind."

— At the point at which we regard the whole area where the line is supposed to be drawn as a dark spot, we have already learned that, according to Holy Writ, the sagacity of the righteous is rewarded by the Creator with a quality of supernatural illumination, as it is written, "A light is sown before the righteous." Implied in this sacred maxim is the idea that most people, even well-meaning people, walk in darkness when it comes to the great questions of existence. The entire opinion-shaping area is, in fact, covered with darkness. We are, for example, completely in the dark when it comes to deciding whether some perverse books that could exercise great influence over human behavior, particularly the conduct of life of many young people, should be placed behind the inviolable barrier of "art for art's sake." Lafcadio, the hero of André Gide's *Caves du Vatican* pushes someone off a train in Italy for no other reason than to prove to himself that he is absolutely capable of committing any act whatsover, however motiveless and senseless. Since the book by the French Nobel Prize winner was regarded as "art for art's sake," it would not bother anybody, if under its influence, a young person actually pushed someone off a train in motion.

The Day on Which It Doesn't Say
And God Saw It Was Good

— Now, in the first chapter of Genesis, the creation of every day, except the second, ends with the refrain "And God saw it was good." When it comes to the last day, however, on which man was created, the words "And God saw it was good" are not there. For man was not created good. He was created to create himself. If he makes no effort at self-creation, he is naturally inclined toward evil. If the artistically perfect description of a gratuitous act in a book of fiction whereby a young man pushes somebody off a train just for the heck of it, as they say, can cause — as it does, alas! — other young men to try and do likewise, the deed described in the book of fiction, as Simone Weil remarked, can no longer be regarded as fiction, but must be seen as fact. Such a fiction-fact work creates a climate zone of opinion that makes it possible for young persons walking in a darkness of soul and eclipse of inner light to stumble and fall on the many stumbling blocks put in their way by the celebrated masters of "art for art's sake." While nobody dares as yet to claim the privilege of art for art's sake in support of crime, there is a general "liberal" outcry against any attempt to prevent artistic stumbling blocks from being placed before the blind. "That's censorship!" they cry. "And you cannot censor thoughts!" But I am concerned about thoughts that create a climate zone for criminal acts. In the Bible, thoughts and acts are often interchangeable. Thoughts are depicted as criminal if they create a clmate for criminal acts.

And the Evil Man Said in His Heart: There Is No God

The teacher quoted from Psalms 14:1: — The evil man (*naval*) said in his heart, there is no God. . . . They are corrupt, they have done abominable works, there is none that doeth good."

— Why, the teacher asked, should a man who says in his heart "There is no God" be regarded as "evil"? (*Naval* is not "a fool," as it is usually translated, but "a wicked man on account of his uprooted ness.") He did not propagate it; he said it only in his heart. Why, then, call him *naval*? The answer lies in the second part of the passage: He may say it only in his heart, but in the climate zone of opinion generated just by believing this, dreadful acts begin to happen: "They are corrupt . . . they have done abominable works . . . there is none that doeth good." But was the man who said it in his heart not "honest"? Was he not "sincere"? We have dealt with the question of what constitutes sincerity and honesty before, but let us return to it. *Naval*, by saying what he said in his heart, was honest with himself — he really meant it; he believed in what he thought. Yet he generated corruption and abominations, because there is an evil in the world that is doubly evil on account of its honesty.

The Place of Judgment That Wickedness Was There

The teacher quoted from the third chapter of Ecclesiastes: — "And moreover I saw under the sun the place of judgment that wickedness was there, and the place of righteousness that iniquity was there."

—Here Ecclesiastes denounces the special kind of wickedness that grows out of judgment or "justice." He prophetically denounces, if you will, a state of the world such as ours today, in which human injustice leads some people to embrace inhuman justice and be very sincere about it. A freed American hostage said of his political abductors in Iran that they were "sincere, dedicated people who believed in what they were doing." He did not realize that there can be no honesty without a dimension of truth. Had he understood this, he would have known that it was precisely his captors' "honesty" that made their deeds and opinions doubly abominable.

Who Should Draw the Line?

—Most people walk in darkness when it comes to the great questions of existence, began the teacher the next day. But there are some people, very few, who are endowed by the Creator with a quality of supernatural illumination, as it is written, "A light is sown for the righteous." Since the ability to see in the dark is given to the righteous, they alone can draw the line.

"But who are the righteous?" someone asked rather loudly.

The teacher wished to approach this question indirectly. He read from the first chapter of Hosea:

For the Land Will Go Awhoring
Before the Lord

The beginning of the word of the Lord by Hosea.... And the Lord said to Hosea: Go take unto thee a wife of whoredom and children of whoredom for the land hath committed whoredom departing from the Lord.... So he went and took Gomer, the daughter of Diblaim; which conceived and bore him a son.... And the Lord said unto him: Call his name Jezreel, for yet a little while and I will visit the blood of Jezreel upon the house of Jehu, and will cause to cease the kingdom of the house of Israel.... And it shall come to pass on that day that I shall break the bow of Israel in the valley of Jezreel.... And she conceived again and bore a daughter. And God said unto him: Call her Lo-Ruhama [the unpitied one]; for I will no more have mercy upon the house of Israel.

—Now what is this amazing account, replete with actual names, all about? the teacher asked. Imagine: A prophet of God is told by Him on High to marry a whore and give birth to whorish offspring and call them dreadful names because the land "hath gone awhoring" before the Lord. Logically, it should have been the opposite: If the land had gone awhoring before the Lord, the prophet should have been ordered to run away, to escape the perversity, to hide. What is the idea behind a divine order to a prophet, the epitome of the perfect man of honor and grace, that he marry a woman whose life represents nothing but dishonor and disgrace?

Happy Is He Who Can Grasp the Hand of the Guilty

— Many are the interpretations of this amazing biblical story, as numerous as the languages and dialects into which the Bible has been translated. But there is one Hasidic interpretation that seems to contain the element of the "eternally contemporary" that we should always look for in scripture. Hasidism, as we all know, believed that the master, the zaddik, the man with the enlightened soul, in order to reach great heights, must also be capable of descending, and sometimes must actually descend, to great depths, even if those depths are the unsavory dwelling place of sinful souls and even of the evil inclination itself.

— It is told that the Baal Shem Tov, saintly founder of the Hasidic movement, once remarked to a zaddik who was overdoing his sermons of chastisement: "What do you know about chastising? You yourself have remained unacquainted with sin all the days of your life, and you have nothing in common with the people around you—how should you know what their sinning is?" Hasidism did not think much of a zaddik who isolated himself from the people and looked down on the lowly of spirit and the transgressors in their ignorance. Going in the footsteps of the Kabbalah, Hasidism believed that every man has a spark of holiness, which craves the great flame, and also that the "shells,"—the *Kelipoth*—that imprison the sparks can be released only through the proximity of the zaddik, who must descend to the shells in order to release the sparks. In Kabbalah it is called "ascent that requires descent." The zaddik's concern for his disciples implies involvement even in their sins. The zaddik puts himself in the place of the sinner in such a manner that he considers himself to be the sinner, and the sin that he sees and craves to remove is his own sin as well. That is what the holy Zohar meant when it said "Happy is he who can grasp the hand of the guilty."

— In line with these basic tenets of Hasidism, Ariel Halevi continued, Rabbi Yakob Yosef of Polnoye, a disciple of Israel Baal Shem Tov, interpreted the first chapter of Hosea — and this is a truly revolutionary interpretation — to mean that the prophet, by divine order, had to undergo the consummate pain of being wedded to a harlot before he could truly comprehend the harlotry of a society that went "awhoring before the Lord."

The Days of Old and the Years
of Every Generation

— To return to the question "Who are the righteous?": The answer is in Deuteronomy 32. Moses, before he dies, tells his people the secret of righteousness: "Remember the days of old; understand the years of every generation; ask they father and he will show thee, thy elders and will tell thee." To know the old, understand the new, and find out, through learning, that the truth was discovered long ago is the biblical prescription for, and definition of, the righteous man. I mentioned before, the teacher continued, that the truly righteous man is ultimately endowed by Providence with a special ability to see things in the darkness. According to Samuel 1, the original name of the prophet was in fact "The Seer."

The Eternally Contemporary
of the Hosea Story

There was a question from the audience as to what lesson, what moral, one might draw from the amazing Hosea story for our day and age.

— The story, replied the teacher, is a timeless denunciation of unrelatedness. So-called spiritual leaders who are totally unrelated to the real lives and circumstances of recognizable human beings, yet keep on delivering sermons about love, justice, mercy, and easy grace, are, in the words of Harvey Cox, "religious pornographers. This is true," the teacher read, "in a very literal sense. The pornography of sex and violence qualifies as pornography because it presents sex and violence unrelated to the concrete lives and circumstances of recognizable human beings. It is faceless." —This unrelatedness, the teacher went on, is even more faceless, impersonal, and, hence, "pornographic" when it comes to self-styled revolutionaries and to revolutionary phraseology. A term like "justice," when invoked by those revolutionaries, has as much to do with actual human beings and actual human suffering as the word "God" has to do with it when invoked by "spiritual leaders." There is no relatedness whatsoever in either case. "Spiritual leaders" have made God irrelevant to life as social revolutionaries have made justice irrelevant to truth.

Justice and Truth in the Bible

"But justice *is* truth!" someone exclaimed.

—No, it is not, the teacher countered. Justice by itself can in fact be a murderous untruth.

"What do you mean 'by itself'?"

The teacher quoted from a talk delivered in New York by a well-known intellectual, a darling of the radical establishment in the United States. —She startled her listeners by declaring, "We were so taken by our fight for justice that we didn't see the truth." What truth was it that she and her associates did not see? It was the truth that some of the most ardent fighters for "justice"—terrorists, "revolutionaries," kidnappers—are murderers at heart, motivated more by hatred than by social pain. Of course, these young men and women "sincerely" believe in the justice of their cause, but it was a totally unrelated, faceless, and heartless justice that, in its divorce from truth, is the perversion most typical of our times. It is this very typicality that explains to us the real and lasting meaning of an enigmatic passage in the nineteenth psalm: "The judgments of the Lord are true and righteous *together*." This one word "together," *yachdav,* incorrectly translated "altogether," is an eye-opener. God's judgments (or justice) are *truth* "because they are righteous *together*." Justice, in other words, can be regarded as righteous *only* when it goes *together* with truth. What follows is that a justice that blinds one to truth can be conducive to murder.

11

Thou Shall Not See
Thy Neighbor In His Disgrace

To Embellish the Poor

A passage in the nineteenth chapter of Leviticus was the subject of the first question that was put to the teacher the next time the class met. "After the sentence dealing with the sin of placing a 'stumbling block before the blind,'" someone commented "there is one that says, 'Thou shall not respect the person of the poor nor honor the person of the mighty; but in righteousness thou shall judge thy neighbor.' What I find difficult to understand," the man said, "is why the danger of respecting the person of the poor on trial is placed, in this law, on the same level as honoring the person of the mighty on trial. It seems to me, there is no symmetry in here."

The teacher replied. —I draw your attention to another biblical maxim following the law prohibiting bribes, which says, "Thou shall not embellish the poor man in his dispute." The juxtaposition suggests that arbitrarily, unjustifiably, and, so to speak, "ideologically" to embellish the poor is in the same category as accepting bribes from the rich, and what is more, has the same effect, namely, it may blind one to justice as truth. Now, how do these admonitions apply to our own day and age? In our time, the murderer can be rehabilitated as long as he claims a political excuse. Quite a few people love to play the role of martyrs while doing the work of executioners, political executioners. They almost invariably have their liberal defenders, who dramatize the underdog status of the criminal so as to underplay the crime

120

itself. But to do so is "embellishing the poor," the biblical word for the underdog, in his dispute, and the Bible regards this as a crime. Why? Because when it is not a man's guilt or innocence but his status that determines the verdict, this is a bribery in reverse: judges bribed not by money, but by misery, emotionally bribed to overlook the severity of a crime just because it has a social excuse.

"In the United States," someone remarked wryly, "we have a name for it: 'Bleeding hearts.'"

— Exactly! the teacher exclaimed. "Bleeding hearts," ideologically bleeding hearts, hearts practicing selective compassion. Selective compassion, in fact, *is* bribery, for there is a kind of bribery that can be worse than that effected by wealth, and that is the bribery of selective compassion, a compassion accorded to those who *use* their underdog status to get away with murder. Thus the danger of "respecting" the person of the poor, that is to say, of being carried away by his underdog status to a point of overlooking, if not actually *embellishing*, his crime is the same as honoring the person of the mighty on account of his being the overdog. The teacher paused before he went on.

— But this passage has another meaning, too. First let me mention that the sages tell us that the nineteenth chapter of Leviticus, titled *Kedoshin*, "Holy," contains the essence of the entire Law. Every word in it is pregnant with meanings that only the Absolute Spirit could have vested in them for all eternity. Something was said here about a certain lack of symmetry between the first and the second parts of the passage we have just discussed. And this is right, of course, for at first sight there does not really seem to be any symmetry there. But what about another lack of symmetry in the same passage? "Thou shall not respect the person of the poor nor honor the person of the mighty." Should it not have said the person of the *rich*?

The Significance of Greatness

— The Hebrew word in that passage, which is translated for some reason as "mighty," is *gadol*, the teacher went on. *Gadol* is not "mighty" in Hebrew, but "great," or "big." And there is a meaning to it, an acute historiosophic meaning for today. In writing about Hitler, Simone Weil said, in essence, that Hitler, under regular circumstances, could not really be punished. There was one thing, she said in

1942, that Hitler desired above anything else, and he would have it whether he won the war or lost it: a secure place in history. He could be killed, tortured, humiliated—history would always be there to shield his "spirit" from all the ravages of suffering and death. And not only that. What we would inflict on him if he lost was bound to be a "historic death," so to speak. It could, in fact, be history. Just as for him who has reached the perfect love of God, whatever happens is good as coming from God, so for this anti-God and idolizer of history: Everything connected with making history must be good. Hitler, moreover, Simone Weil argues, had in fact a very considerable advantage: While the pure love of God, when it inhabits the center of the soul, leaves one's sensitivity exposed to injury—for it cannot possibly form an armor—idolatry *is* an armor. As such it totally prevents pain from entering the soul. Whatever Hitler was made to suffer, she wrote, would only enhance his feelings of superiority. But, above all, it would not stop some solitary, publicity-seeking little dreamers in the future, whether German or otherwise, from seeing in Hitler a superb figure worthy of emulation, and from desperately seeking a similar destiny.

—The only punishment, Simone Weil argues, capable of really punishing Hitler and deterring little boys thirsting for greatness from following his example would be such a total transformation of the meaning attached to greatness that he should be automatically excluded from it. One could not exclude Hitler from the title to greatness without a total transformation among our contemporaries of the idea and significance of greatness. To be able to contribute to such a transformation, she maintains, one must "this very moment," as she put it, commence Hitler's punishment inside one's own self by radically modifying the scope of the sentiment attached to greatness. To this, the teacher went on, let me add a clarifying thought: If one says, for example, as many do—as so many *Jews* do!—"Yes, of course, he was evil, that Hitler, but he was a great man," one assures that madman not only a place in history, but a successor or successors. I cherish a line by Marcus Aurelius with reference to Alexander the Great and Julius Caesar: "If they are not *just*, nothing forces me to imitate them." Similarly, nothing compels us to admire them except, perhaps, the dreadfully sovereign impact of force, of power, which actually thrives on making a mockery of justice.

—Now, said the teacher after a pause for breath, we may better understand the biblical admonition against honoring the person of the *great*, an admonition that is followed by an actual pinpointing of the criteria we must use if we are to determine the right notions of greatness as truth. "Thou shall not respect the person of the poor nor honor the person of the great, but with justice thou shall judge thy neighbor." Divorce greatness from justness, from truth, and Hitler's dream is partly fulfilled.

Thou Shall Not Stand on Thy Brother's Blood

The teacher was asked how this famous biblical admonition applied to interpersonal relations. "We all know," the man said, "that in international relations everybody stands on everybody else's blood, and nobody cares. We know it even better as Jews and Israelis. But what kind of personal message does this admonition carry?"

—Aside from the obvious interpretations, the teacher replied, the sages of the Mishna in the "Chapters of the Fathers," where lies more wisdom than in all of Greek philosophy, warn us in what seems to be a logical derivative of the biblical admonition "not to see your neighbor in his disgrace." To me, the teacher went on, this variation on the grand biblical theme seems so important and so timely that I do not hesitate to ask you what, among the things that we are witnessing almost daily in our lives, would constitute, in your view, a violation of a law that says "Thou shall not see thy neighbor in his disgrace"?

Thou Shall Not See Thy Neighbor In His Disgrace

An American in the class remarked, "What comes to mind is the increasing role played by the media in seeing, and showing to others, fallen people in their disgrace. I think of the case of a former U.S. attorney general who was tried and convicted of complicity in the Watergate cover-up. I watched the disgraced man on television as he arrived in court and left it to enter his car, and I saw dozens of pressmen and television cameramen along with noisy groups of abusive demonstrators waiting for the man like vultures for a corpse. Such barbarous joy, such morbid eagerness—the media people couldn't wait to see their neighbor in his disgrace. I wondered, was there no law anywhere prohibiting this sort of moral bloodshed?"

— There is indeed such a law, said the teacher. To see one's neighbor in his disgrace is a violation of the biblical law that says "And thou shall not stand on thy brother's blood." We stand on our brother's blood if we add to his disgrace by deliberately being there when we should not, as we add to his torment by *not* being there when we should. In either case it is insensitivity and indifference. Perhaps the most vital contemporary lesson to be drawn from that biblical admonition is an unwritten yet implied commandment, "Thou shall not be indifferent!" Let me read a few lines of Charles Peguy, the French poet-philosopher, a man of sensitivity and spirituality, on this matter of indifference:

Infinite Cowardice Everywhere

> He who allows things to be done is like him who orders them to be done. It is all one. It goes together. And he who allows things to be done, just like him who orders them to be done, it is altogether like him who *does* them. Because he who does, shows courage, at least, in doing. He who commits a crime, has at least the courage to commit it. And when you allow the crime to be committed, you have the same crime, and cowardice to boot; cowardice on top of it all.
> There is infinite cowardice everywhere.

On Love

It was the end of a class. The teacher said he would tell a Hasidic story about love, love as the opposite of indifference even more than it is of hatred. — Rabbi Moshe Leib of Sasov told the following story: "What love is all about I learned from a peasant in an inn. The peasant was sitting with another peasant, drinking. For a long while he was silent, but then, moved by the liquor, he asked his friend, 'Tell me, Vaska, do you love me?' 'You know I do!' Vaska replied as he placed his arm around his friend's shoulders. 'You are sure, Vaska?' the man persisted. 'Trust me,' Vaska replied. 'I do love you!' 'If you really love me, Vaska,' the man said, 'then tell me what's ailing me?' And he wept.

—"Now I know," Rabbi Leib of Sasov concluded his story, "to love someone is to know what ails him!"

He Who Hates Gifts Shall Live

Nobody suspected that a seemingly casual question raised at the next class would lead back to love. The passage in question appears in the fifteenth chapter of Proverbs and says, "He who hates gifts shall live." Someone remarked that unless there is something in this passage that went beyond the obvious, it does not make much sense. "Why *hate* gifts?" asked this student. "And in what way does the hatred of gifts ensure life? What gifts are we talking about? A poor man would starve to death but for the gifts he receives!"

The teacher nodded in gratitude. — It is indeed a puzzling passage, he began quietly, whose meaning cannot possibly lie in what seems to be obvious about it. But the whole point about the Bible is that its meaning so often lies in what is *not* obvious about it. Well, then, what is the meaning here? As strange as it may sound, this brief, simple passage is about love. The world, in Rabbi Eliyahu Dessler's interpretation of that passage, is divided between givers and takers. Love is giving. The lovers are givers. Thus the meaning of "shall live" at the end of the passage is simply that the *giver* — he or she who knows love as *giving — lives,* that is to say, knows life to its fullest. "He who hates gifts," which means he who shuns taking and craves giving, "shall live."

12

The Tower of Babel

The Tower of Babel

In answer to a question at an earlier class, about the meaning of the biblical myth of the Tower of Babel, Ariel Halevi read to us from the biblical text in Genesis 11 dealing with the Tower of Babel:

> And the whole earth was of one language and of one speech . . . .
> And it came to pass as they journeyed from the East that they
> found a plain in the land of Shinear; and they dwelled there . . . .
> And they said to one another: Go to, let us make brick and burn
> them thoroughly; and they had brick for stone and slime they had
> for mortar. . . . And they said: Go to, let us build a city and a tower
> whose top may reach unto heaven, and let us make us a name lest
> we be scattered upon the face of the earth. . . . And the Lord came
> down to see the city and the tower which the children of men have
> built. . . . And he said: Behold, the people is one, and they have all
> one language, and this they begin to do; and now nothing will be
> restrained from them which they have imagined to do.

—I would like to say something first, he began, about what someone here called a myth, "the myth of the Tower of Babel." Let me
quote again Denis de Rougemont on the subject of myth: "If someone
tells me, the devil is only a myth, therefore he does not exist—a
rationalistic formula—I answer: The devil *is* a myth, therefore he
does exist and is unceasingly active. . . . For a myth is a story which
describes and illustrates, through dramatic form, certain profound
structures of reality." Let us look at some profound structures of
contemporary reality that the myth of the Tower of Babel describes
and illustrates.

—The generation of the tower, or as the sages call it "the generation of Confusion," was one of conformity and sameness, as it is written, "of one language and of one speech." One speech underlines the meaning of one language: Linguistic sameness was used as a means to assure the sameness of thought. The Bible tells us that it was not a generation of thought but of thoughtless action—visible, demonstrable action. In the terrible boredom generated by the sameness of speech and thought, those people decided to build a tower "whose top may reach unto heaven." Why a tower of such colossal dimensions? Because as sameness breeds decline, which it always does, people acquire an irresistible need for what the late Professor Pitirim Sorokin called "quantitative colossalism." The emptier the sameness and the "samer" the emptiness from within, the greater the need for something to fill external spaces, for superstructures. Oswald Spengler speaks of this phenomenon, which he calls agglomeration, as the one that preceded the fall of the Roman Empire. The masses took over from the elite, and soon the rule of the masses, which is always one of sameness, of dullness, of banality, began to preside over the decline and decay of the empire. The physically colossal, we should remember, is the god of the commonplace, the ultimate expression of "one language and one thought," of a language used for the furtherance of action at the expense of thought. Our own era exemplifies this situation.

One Vision

The teacher now spoke of William Blake and his terrible vision about a "one-vision" culture. —Blake, he said, a Bible-intoxicated visionary, actually spoke of a coming age that would see "a Babylon builded in the waste, founded in human desolation." Theodore Roszak says in *The Edge of the Wasteland:*

> Blake, the isolated and unheeded prophet of our age and himself an avid student of the Gnostic tradition, saw more deeply than anyone into the tragic irony. For him industrial society was "Babylon builded in the waste, founded in human desolation." And yet what a marvel it was, and what a religious zeal fired its builders! They were not merely raising up a new social order, they were remaking the universe at large, imprisoning heaven and eternity in

the chains of their social needs. It was what the process historians would later call the "secularization" of Western culture; Blake wrote never a word about it that was not touched with awe and horror . . . . The architect of that industrial colossus, Blake identified as "Mighty Urizen," the god of mad rationality and purposeless power whose other name (in the mythology of Blake's visionary epics) was Satan. For mankind beneath the surface of this deity, "obscure, shadowy, void, solitary," Blake could foresee only the death of nature and of the soul. He called Urizen's affliction *"single vision"*; touched by its passion, man becomes

> . . . *Self exiled from the face of light and the*
> *shine of morning,*
> *In the dark world, a narrow house! He wanders*
> *up and down seeking for rest and finding none.*

—It is "single vision" that characterizes the builders of the Tower of Babel. Blake saw the decline of vision as the beginning of the end of poetic genius—not to be confused with, but rather to be juxtaposed to, scientific and rational genius. As spiritual villains Blake singles out such gigantic figures as Bacon, Newton, Locke, Rousseau, Gibbon, Voltaire—the noblest spirits of the Enlightenment and natural religion. He suspected, and rightly so, that with them begins the denaturing of visionary imagination and its confinement to the single vision of "quantitative colossalism."

"Yes, the superstructure, the supermarket, the superbowl, the superpower, the superspectacle, the—" remarked a participant.

—Yes, but also something else: the intoxication with the visible, the provable, the showable, the assessable; the emergence of an action-culture devoid of thought, but packed with explosives. The "myth" of the Tower of Babel, my friends, thus tells us a contemporary story.

How to Read the Bible

"Are we to read biblical stories as an account of something that has actually come to pass at a certain point in time or as a divinely conceived allegory purposely invoked as a vehicle for prophecy?" asked someone in the class.

—The Bible must never be read as history *alone* or as prophecy *alone*, answered the teacher, but rather as *prophetic history leading up to historic prophecy.* Using the metaphor of flowers for prophecy and of earthquake for catastrophe, we can say that the Bible is an account of flowers growing out of earthquakes — earthquakes that are bound to recur because of one vision — people cannot possibly see flowers growing out of an earthquake. In the Bible the reality of the earthquake is *organic* to the validity and the finality of the flowers. Nothing in the Bible exists in a vacuum, least of all the flowers that grow out of an earthquake. As soon as the earthquake cracks the ground of reality, the flower springs up in the crack. The earthly time sense is, as it were, in abeyance. Immediate future, demonstrable present, and distant future are equally the "flowers." I mean not only the prophecy invoked by prophets of God, but the narrative of the Bible as a whole. The accidents of period and place would make no sense, or would be irrelevant, without the emphasis on and the understanding of what is of eternal value in those "accidents." Let me give you one example. Do you remember that amazing passage in Deuteronomy where Moses mentions, as one of the supreme attributes of God, that "He doesn't take bribes?"

"I could never understand it," someone said, speaking for everyone present.

The Attempts to Bribe God

— This seemingly incredible passage says, in essence, the teacher explained, that since nothing, absolutely nothing exists in a vacuum, a religion that is comfortable with its existence in a vacuum — and religion has degenerated into this form today — should be regarded as an attempt to bribe God.

"How so? someone asked.

The teacher explained. — The Bible will not permit religion to exist in a vacuum, to create a no-man's land between man's attitude to God and his attitude to man. Unless a person's worship of God is matched by just deeds toward other people, then rituals, ceremonies, and sacrifices are abhorrent to God. Like bribes, they stifle, as the remarkable translator of *Four Prophets,* J. B. Phillips, observed, the moral and social conscience of the so-called observant by all the *business* of religion. The business of religion is, in fact, an attempt to *bribe God.* That is what Moses meant when he said that you cannot bribe God:

You are actually trying to bribe Him through externalized rituals and observances if you do not please him through your deeds. This fear of a religion practiced in a vacuum moves all the prophets—all the Bible—to vehement indignation.

Nothing Will Be Restrained from Them

Returning to the Tower of Babel, the teacher asked what passage, if any, in the biblical account of the Tower of Babel struck the class as familiar? Someone pointed out the disturbing passage, "And now nothing will be restrained from them which they have imagined to do." "Doesn't this suggest divine jealousy?"

—No, the teacher replied, it suggests divine abhorrence of human arrogance, to start with. The very idea of a tower reaching unto heaven was arrogance incarnate. But that is not all. In addition to all the reasons for the building of the tower we mentioned before, there was the familiar reason of hunger for fame, as it is written, "Let us make us a name." As in our own day, quantitative colossalism went hand in hand with a need for celebrity. People today, as then, go for the super. Now, regarding that passage which suggests divine jealousy, what does the passage say? It says that the mysterious builders of the tower reached such a stage of rational self-sufficiency, of "mad rationality" in Blake's words, that they were convinced they could do anything they imagined, an idea, as we know, that greatly displeased Him on High. Not divine jealousy but divine abhorrence caused this reaction. The sages say that it is of the arrogant man—not of the sinner or the criminal, mind you, but of the arrogant man—that the Lord says: "He and I cannot live in one world." The builders of the ancient Tower of Babel imagined themselves capable of doing anything they desired. Now what exactly were they capable of doing that caused such divine displeasure? I want to read to you the words of an eminent scientist about the state of science today and what it regards itself as capable of doing. Emmanuel Mesthene has said,

> We have now, or know how to acquire, the technical capability *to do very nearly anything we want.* Can we transplant hearts, control personality, order the weather that suits us, travel to Mars or Venus? Of course we can, if not now or in five years to ten years, then certainly in twenty-five, in fifty or in one hundred.

—Is this not just what the builders of the Tower of Babel had in mind? "And now nothing will be restrained from them which they have imagined to do."

"Are you saying that self-sufficient reason leading up to a morally neutral science is a modern, one-vision version of the Tower of Babel?" asked a hearer.

—I believe this is implied in the Bible, the teacher replied.

"You are implying then," someone asked, "that we are approaching the end of days?"

A Story About Napoleon

The teacher left the question hanging and told a story instead. —In the month of December 1798, General Bonaparte, the future Emperor Napoleon, arrived at the head of his army at Suez. After having toured the city and the port, he decided to visit the so-called fountains of Moses. At eight o'clock in the morning, when the tide was low, he crossed the Red Sea into Asia Minor. After visiting the springs and talking with some Arab chiefs, he started to return. Darkness had fallen and the tide was rising. Napoleon was advised to camp out for the night on the shore, but he refused; he called his Arab guide and ordered him to lead the way. The guide, greatly troubled by the responsibility, took the wrong road down to the shore, losing a quarter of an hour of precious time. When they were no more than halfway to the shore, the fast-rising tide began to lap at the horse's feet. The little troop fell into disorder. General Caffarelli, whose wooden leg made it difficult for him to keep a firm seat in the saddle, called for help. His outcry, interpreted as a signal of acute distress, compounded the confusion. The riders went off in different directions. Only Napoleon, imperturbable and alone, followed the alarmed guide. As the waters continued to rise, the horse took fright and refused to proceed.

—Alexander Dumas, in his memorable account of the exploit, describes the situation that arose as very grave. The least further delay was dangerous. One of Napoleon's escorts, a regular Hercules of a fellow, rushed back to the scene, jumped into the water, and carried the general on his shoulders, holding onto the tail of the Arab's horse. A few minutes later, the water was up to his armpits and the powerful man began to lose his balance. The sea was still rising rapidly, and the destiny of the world, in Dumas's words, might have been altered by the death of a single man carried like a baby in the arms of a big fellow who happened to be his guard. Suddenly the Arab guide emitted a cry of relief: He had reached the opposite shore. The escort fell to his knees. Now that his general was safe, he was overcome by emotion and forced down by exhaustion. The little troop came back to Suez without the loss of a single man. Only Bonaparte's horse was drowned.

—Seventeen years later, Napoleon was taken as a prisoner of the British aboard the *Northumberland* to the island of St. Helena. In the course of that trip, the former emperor of the French told of his Red Sea experience to Las Casas, who wrote it down in his *memorial*. And what Las Cases wrote was that during an interval of leisure in Egypt, the commanding general took advantage of the low tide to cross the Red Sea on dry land. On the way back, Bonaparte was overtaken by night and got lost in the rising tide. The danger was so great that he very nearly perished, like Pharaoh of old. Napoleon's comment to this story, which could have ended tragically, was, "It would have given the Christian preachers a splendid text to use against me."

In this remarkable rendition, the teacher commented, Napoleon actually echoed the exact biblical account. He confirmed, if confirmation was needed, the existence of the kind of fact that is sometimes at base of a religious story, or to be more exact, of a religious *myth*.

What Is a Miracle?

Someone asked the teacher whether this interpretation of the splitting of the Red Sea as natural history does not infringe on the miraculousness of the event? The teacher replied: —The commentators, Maimonides in particular, dwell on this question as on the nature of miracles in general, and their answer is this: A miracle, in most cases, is indeed eternity breaking through time, including time understood as nature. However, is it any less of a miracle if the Omnipotent and Omniscient One sees to it that a historic event "coincides" with a natural one? The great Franz Rosenzweig writes that nothing in fact is miraculous about a miracle except that it takes place *when* it does. The east wind, he says, has probably swept bare the ford of the Red Sea hundreds of times, and will do so again hundreds of times. But that it did it at a moment when the people in their distress set foot in the sea—*that* is the miracle!

And the Earth Was Corrupt Before the Lord

There was a question from the audience about the flood, as mentioned in Genesis, and the generation of the flood. "We know it was an evil generation, but what was the nature of the evil to merit no less a devastation than the flood?" asked the listener.

The teacher read to us the relevant passage: — "And the earth was corrupt before the Lord and the earth was filled with violence." The word "earth" is mentioned twice in the same brief passage, while the words "before the Lord" do not seem to be in the right place, commented the teacher. It should have been either "And the earth was corrupt and filled with violence before the Lord," or, "And the earth was corrupt and filled with violence." But the insertion of the words "before the Lord" between two similar descriptions of the earth's "fallenness" tells an important story.

— But let me first ask you something, the teacher continued. Does a state in which the earth is full of corruption necessarily imply that the corrupt individuals who inhabit it are unaware that they are corrupt? Would you say that as long as one knows he is corrupt, there is still hope for him?

"Obviously," came the answer.

— But is it not a hopeless kind of evil when one is so corrupt that he does not know he is corrupt? the teacher pressed.

"Certainly."

—Evil, in other words, the teacher continued, is redeemable so long as it is regarded as such by the evil-doers themselves. But when evil is no longer evil in man's eyes, or in society's eyes, but only in God's eyes, only *before the Lord*—

—Understand this well, he went on. There is corruption and there is violence. The heart gets corrupt long before it begets violence. External violence is preceded by corruption from within, a corruption of the heart that was known only to the corrupt themselves and to the all-knowing, all-seeing God. Now imagine the measure and extent of corruption when the corrupt person no longer sees it in himself, and the only One Who sees it, Who knows it, is God. Then the end of all flesh is at hand.

This subtle interpretation became clearer later, when the teacher was asked how "before the Lord" applied to the state of the world today.

He replied: — We live in a generation that is trying in the name of the biological interpretation of man to obliterate our notions of sin and guilt. But the idea of modern psychology, particularly Freudian, that the sense of guilt is abnormal and entirely and necessarily due to repressions planted by civilization is not only, as Reinhold Niebuhr pointed out, a consequence of a too superficial view of the complexities of the relationship between spirit and nature. It is also a cause for an inner corruption so unknown to itself that it regards its spread — its epidemic spread — as progress. We live in an era in which people are trying more to unlearn than to learn things and to find psychological excuses for moral atrocities. But once man does away with sin and guilt, he no longer can tell right from wrong. Thus the "before God" in the biblical passage tells us that the generation of the flood did not know feelings of sin and guilt. Hence it was inevitable then, as it may be today, that what started out as corruption "before the Lord" ended as an earth filled with violence.

— I read an article recently in an American magazine where the author, a psychiatrist, tried to defend incest. Dismissing all moral and religious grounds as scientifically invalid, the psychiatrist was concerned only with the question of how incest can be psychologically legitimated. Dialectically speaking, I would say that since nothing like "before God" existed for that psychiatrist, his corruption, of which he was totally unaware, was precisely and *only* "before God."

And Noah Walked Before God

The teacher said that the biblical passage "and Noah walked before God" was not clear. — It is usually translated "and Noah walked *with* God." The problem lies with the Hebrew word *et*, he explained, which can mean "with," "and," "before," "the," and so forth. The words of the Hebrew tongue in the Bible, as Martin Luther rightly observed centuries ago, have a peculiar energy of their own. It is impossible to convey so much so briefly, Luther said, in any other language. To render them intelligibly we must not attempt to give word for word, but only to aim at the sense and the idea. Now, of Noah it is said that he was a righteous man in his time and that he walked before God. The sages adduce from the qualification implied by the words "in his time" that Noah, though he was a righteous man, was righteous not in an absolute but only in a relative sense, relative to his times. Abraham's righteousness, by contradistinction, was absolute and for all times. We are also told by the sages some of the reasons for the relative nature of Noah's righteousness as compared with Abraham's. As an example: When God tells Abraham that He is soon to destroy Sodom and Gomorrah, Abraham makes the first and most moving attempt by man to question God's ways. He pleads for the doomed cities until he exhausts all the arguments in their favor. Noah, however, when told about the flood and the imminent destruction "of all flesh," takes the dreadful news in stride. He makes no attempt whatsoever to plead for mercy or even to register a protest. And it is here, my friends, in Noah's disinclination to get involved with the fate of men, that his lesser nature comes to the fore. Contrary to the generation of the flood, which was corrupt "before God," Noah, *uncorrupt*, walked "before God," but *only* before God, not before men! He was no leader of men, nor did he try to save them. His righteousness was thus only relative to his time. The truly righteous man is fully aware that there can be no walking "before God" without walking before men, that is to say, for men. As Hillel said in his famous advice to the man who wanted to learn the whole Law "on one foot," "'Love thy neighor as thyself,' this is the whole Law; the rest is commentary; go and study."

13

Troubles Have Enlarged
My Heart

The Daughters of Job

The teacher raised the question of the daughters of Job as soon as the class had gathered for its next session. — At the conclusion of the book of Job, he said, the Bible tells us that Job's later years were even more blessed than his earlier. The Bible tells us little about the nature of those blessings, except in the case of his daughters, born to him in his latter years. "And in the entire land," it says, "there were no maidens found more fair than the daughters of Job." Now, it seems extraordinarily strange that after all Job's trials and tribulations, after his loss of family, property, health, years, hope — in fact, of everything except his soul — that the Bible is specific *only* about the nature of one compensation: the beauty of his daughters! The passage that describes it is hauntingly beautiful. But in what way do fair daughters, even the fairest, make up for the afflictions of Job? And not only that, but in what way does the quality of fairness, of beauty, of feminine beauty to be exact, address itself to Job's suffering? To his wounded soul?

"If I may interrupt," someone remarked, "it's almost a Greek question, or a Greek situation. The Greeks always saw the connection between the tragic and the beautiful."

— That is true, the teacher agreed. The Greeks, as Nietzsche said, resorted to the beautiful out of fear of the dreadful. But that is not quite the same thing. In Job's case there is no *effort* to resort to the beautiful out of fear of the dreadful. The beautiful appears almost as *organic* to the dreadful, or perhaps dreadful is the wrong word. I would rather

136

evoke the metaphor of earthquake and flowers again: In Job's case, the flowers, as symbolized by the fair maidens, are not so much consolation for the earthquake as its transformation. The Bible is trying to tell us, in words of visionary poesy, that the beauty bestowed on the daughters of Job did not signify a break with their father's tragic past, but a newly found, marvelously creative ability to let that past *mold the nature of their fairness*. The beauty of the daughters of Job did not come to compensate for tragedy but, to the contrary, as Abraham Kariv observes in truth, the consciousness of tragedy nourished, refined, and distilled their beauty to a point of perfection. The teacher lowered his voice to invoke the biblical sentence again: "And in the entire land no maidens were found more fair than the daughters of Job." But like anything in scripture, this ancient story takes a stand on a burning contemporary issue. Can you guess what I am driving at?

"At the escape from pain, I assume?" someone suggested.

— Precisely, the teacher nodded. A generation like ours, full of pain, yet escaping it, denying it, subverting it, distorting it as if it were a shame. That is what I am driving at. Our inability to understand the necessity of tragedy blurs our sense of beauty.

The Wonderful Crisis of Middle Age

— In a book written several years ago, the American writer Eda LeShan tells about a newspaper interview with a well-known American couple who happened to be close friends of hers. What a perfect, totally untroubled life, Miss Le Shan writes, was described in that interview! Such sharing, such happiness, such richness and completeness of living, such joy: the model marriage, the perfect family life, beautiful people living the gorgeous life people expect them to live. But, Miss Le Shan says, "I knew those people, I knew their problems, their courageous struggle to overcome difficulties, to grow, to change, to become more real to each other, to find their own selves in a deeper, more meaningful way. The truth about them," she writes, "is far more beautiful than that perfect story, the perfect happiness." The truth is full of such poignant humanity, Miss LeShan says, that she feels sorry for the thousands of readers who devour such stories and really believe it is possible to be perfectly happy. "By now," she writes, "we know that the books and movies we grew up on don't tell the truth about life, that they are lying to us. But people tend to believe what they read in newspapers and magazines. But we should not!" she cries out. "We must see things in their right perspective and never allow ourselves to become depressed by the thought: *They* made it, *they* conquered the tragic part, why can't *we*? The truth of the matter is, "she writes, "that nobody gets off so easily. It's an impossible goal, because the two halves, the tragic and the happy, are equally necessary and real."

The teacher added that in a utilitarian, commodity-oriented society very few people realize that tragedy is not only an unavoidable but an indispensable ingredient of life. Tragedy, if we know how to treat it, makes us grow; it enlarges our heart.

Troubles Have Enlarged My Heart

The teacher quoted from Psalm 25: — "Troubles have enlarged my heart; O lead me out of my affliction." This means, the teacher explained, that since the purpose of trouble is to enlarge man's heart, the leading out of affliction had been achieved. But nowhere, he added, has the refining nature of trouble been explained so cryptically, yet so powerfully, as in that hymnlike psalm, the twenty-third, which starts with the words, "The Lord is my Shepherd, I shall not want."

Thy Rod and Thy Staff, They Comfort Me

—Surely we must have been bothered, the teacher said, by the question of how a rod, a whipping rod, can be placed on the same sustaining and consoling level as a staff. For the understanding of the lived life, we must know what is meant by such an equation. The example I shall give was first invoked by a luminary of the Lithuanian Mussar movement, Rabbi Yitzhak Blazer, in a High Holiday sermon that dealt with the meaning of a prayer based on a passage in the hundred and third psalm, "Like a father who is merciful to his children, show mercy upon us, O Lord!" Rabbi Yitzhak shocked the congregation of learned men with a prefatory statement to the effect that for the prayer for divine mercy to be like that of a father toward his children *terrified* him. He explained his terror with the following example:

—A man walks home at night and encounters a drunkard, noisily swaying in front of him. So what does he do? He steps aside as fast as he can so as to avoid a collision, and walks on.

— If, however, a man is walking home at night and encounters a noisily swaying drunkard whose face seems familiar, someone he had known in years past, he will make sure not only that he avoids a collision, but, even more importantly, that he isn't noticed by his former friend whom circumstances have obviously forced to embrace such a life of wretchedness.

— Now, suppose that the man who is walking home late at night comes across a noisily swaying drunkard in whom he recognizes a dear friend of more recent vintage. What will he do then? He will, most likely, stop and try to talk sense to his troubled friend. 'Come on! Let's go! I'll take you home! Let's go! Please!'

— But suppose a man, walking home at night, comes across a noisy, swaying drunkard in whom he recognizes his brother. What then? In such a case he will not only try to talk to him, but shout at him, shake him, and finally try to take him home even by force.

— Now imagine a situation in which a man, walking home late at night, runs into a noisy, swaying drunkard in whom he recognizes his son, and not just a son, but one in whom he had placed great hopes. "If this happens," Rabbi Yitzhak cried out, "if this happens, the loving merciful father would hardly be merciful in his love if, after trying in vain to talk sense to his wayward son, he didn't try to bring him back to his senses by resorting to the rod. Do you understand now," Rabbi Yitzhak cried out in a tear-choked voice "why this prayer makes me shudder? The *more* we are His children — His wayward children, alas, who were supposed to be *less* wayward than the others — the more — " And the saintly man broke down crying.

— Now, my friends, the teacher went on after a pause, I would like to add a different twist to the example. Suppose the son, the wayward son, the drunkard in the night, is brought back to his senses, is sobered up, and, in a moment of sorrow and heartbreak, falls on his father's neck and cries. What then? Such a reaction would invariably signal a turning point in the life of the wayward son. I am not speaking here of what such an eruption may do to the father. "I must have done something dreadful if my father had to beat me up like that!" is what the son, in his metamorphosis, must have thought. When such a thought occurs, when such a change happens, the rod, my friends, is automatically promoted to the level of a staff; it sustains and consoles.   "But who can reach such a state?" someone cried out.

— Very few, the teacher replied. — But those who cannot reach it should at least realize that it exists. If we could only realize that the mess we make of our lives — the frustration, the despair, the alienation — signify, above all, a failure of courage, as Otto Rank pointed out! It takes real courage to understand that genuine pain is not the same as dull despair.

De Profundis

"What's the difference?" someone inquired.

— The son, in our elaboration of Blazer's story, the teacher replied, would not have cried out of dull despair, but only out of genuine pain. That is the difference. After a pause he said, You are familiar, I am sure, with Oscar Wilde's "De Profundis." Do you know where Wilde wrote it?

"In prison," someone responded.

— Precisely, the teacher confirmed. There were three periods in Wilde's life: the period of dizzying success, the period of dull despair, and the period of genuine pain. The enduring things he wrote, like "De Profundis" and the "Ballad of Reading Gaol," belong to the third period. During the period of dull despair, when he had just been thrown into prison, he said to himself, as he reveals in "De Profundis," "What an end, what a dreadful end!" Then, slowly, as the rod assumed the nature of a staff, he began experiencing genuine pain. Then the outcry, as he tells us, was different: "What a beginning, what a great beginning!" And there is something else he wrote in prison that stays with me, the teacher went on. It was something like this: "And there is nothing wrong when a heart breaks; a heart is made in order to break. The problem begins when it is no longer capable of breaking, when it turns into stone." A Hasidic master summed it up in one memorable sentence: "There is nothing more *whole* than a *broken* heart." But that is something we know only *de profundis*, out of the depths.

Min Hametzar

Someone in the audience remarked that something about the passage in the one hundred eighteenth psalm where the phrase *min ham-*

etzar, "out of the depths," was first mentioned puzzled him. "It says 'Out of the depths' — or out of distress — 'I called upon the Lord; He answered me in a large place.' Something here doesn't make sense. The passage clearly implies that when man calls on God in distress, or out of the depths — for which, of course, there is another word — *mi-ma'amakin* — he gets the answer somewhere else, or that in order to get the answer to his cry, man must first be somewhere else — 'in a large place.' That's how it sounds, at least," he concluded.

— To the contrary, the teacher answered. What this passage implies is that *in order to be* somewhere else, that is to say, "in a large place," we must *first* absorb the answer.

"What exactly do you mean by 'the answer'?" someone queried.

— Let us first see, the teacher replied, what is meant by the question or the statement. *Min hametzar*, in its exact translation, is "out of constriction," of "tightness," of "narrowness of space" — out of a strait jacket, so to speak. The psalmist says that sin that is, as explained on another occasion, its own punishment is an enslaving, constricting, imprisoning sensation. Atonement for sin is presented by the psalmist here as on other occasions not as pietistic but as a therapeutic formula. The resolution of sin is not just atonement, but freedom. Thus the opposite of sin, of imprisonment in oneself, is *merhavia*, "a very large place." More than a century ago, the teacher went on, Rabbi Samson Rafael Hirsh explained that the word *merhavia*, like "*hallelujah*," would denote one single concept, namely, divine "breadth," liberation from every sensation of constricting anxiety. The "very vast place" thus becomes an enlargement of reality, a blessed relief that only faith can provide and that causes, in Hirsh's words, anyone confined to the narrow straits of oppression to sense that God is near.

I Am the Lord

Someone reminded the teacher that on previous occasions he had quoted the famous answer that Hillel the Sage gave to the strange fellow who desired to learn the whole Law "on one foot": "Love thy neighbor as thyself. The rest is commentary; go and study."

— In fact, interrupted the teacher, Hillel quoted not the biblical admonition, "And thou shall love thy neighbor as thyself," but an explanatory variation: "What is hateful to you do not do unto your neighbor."It is very important to understand the difference. The original biblical admonition may lead the uninitiated to confusion. "Love thy neighbor as thyself?" Suppose one's love of oneself is a sick love? Suppose it is a degenerate, dissolute kind of love in which he finds himself adrift and powerless to stop the process of his own deterioration? There are things a person can do to himself that are actually hateful to him, things he knows to be wrong, but he cannot help doing them time and again because his courage fails him, or his will power deserts him. Take smoking as an example: We all know people who literally hate themselves for being unable to stop—though they say in their embarrassment that they don't want to—but they are helpless to do anything about it. Hillel had such and much greater failures of courage in mind when he said, in essence, "Don't do unto another the hateful things—hateful even to you—that you do to yourself."

The questioner continued on his original tack. "Why does the Bible invoke God's name at the conclusion of admonitions, or laws, of a distinctly social and ethical nature, like 'thou shall love thy neighbor as thyself'—laws and admonitions, in other words, to whose validity people could subscribe regardless of whether they believe in God? Almost all the ethical 'Thou shalt not's' in Leviticus 19 end with the stern reminder 'I am the Lord!' I see why a warning like 'I am the Lord!' should follow purely religious laws like the law against idolatry or against the desecration of the Sabbath. But what does 'I am the Lord!' mean when it follows a law against talebearing, or against the mistreatment of workers? Isn't a social conscience enough to prevent people from doing such things?"

—Metaethics, which is what biblical ethics is all about, the teacher replied, means two things: one, that a social conscience is not enough to prevent us from doing bad things, and two, that the things we do, both good and bad, have cosmic reverberations. If one is a talebearer, for example, or an exploiter of the underdog, the worker, one's sin is not only social or moral, but cosmic, for one weakens "the Rock that begat" him. This startling yet basic tenet of Kabbalah, Rabbi Hain of Volozhin stresses, recurs very frequently in the Zohar, as in the phrase, "The sins of man cause imperfections above." It follows that the very idea of autonomous ethics must be regarded as a denial of the

Torah. Before I go on, let me read to you from the biblical text in question, Leviticus 19:

> And thou shall not go up and down as a talebearer among thy people, neither shall thou stand on the blood of thy brother; I am the Lord.
> Thou shall not avenge, nor bear any grudge against the children of thy people, but thou shall love thy neighbor as thyself; I am the Lord.
> Thou shall not defraud thy neighbor, neither rob him . . . . The wages of him that is hired shall not abide with thee all night until morning . . . . Thou shall not curse the deaf nor put a stumbling block before the blind, but shall fear thy God; I am the Lord.
> Thou shall rise up before the hoary head and honor the face of the old man and fear thy God; I am the Lord.
> And if a stranger sojourn with thee in thy land, you shall not vex him, but the stranger that dwelleth with you shall be unto you as one born among you, and you shall love him as yourself, for you were strangers in the land of Egypt; I am the Lord your God.

— Now, a clear understanding of what "autonomous ethics" is all about is essential to understand the prophetic nature of these biblical admonitions and their applicability to our contemporary reality.

Autonomous Ethics

The teacher explained: — With the exception of a few powerful, dissenting voices, the nineteenth century was almost unanimous in its belief that the ascent of science was a guarantee of the moral improvement of man. As the sworn rationalists gleefully kept destroying man's belief in God, they kept proclaiming their belief in man. Man, on the one hand, was depicted as an advanced outgrowth of the monkey, but, on the other hand, was proclaimed as a creature who can "rationally" work out his own salvation. Vladimir Soloviev, the great Russian philosopher, expressed the incompatibility of scientific optimism about man with man's proclaimed biological inferiority in a marvelously ironic phrase: "Man," Soloviev said, "is a descendent of the monkeys; he can *therefore* be relied upon to bring about a period of happiness and progress to mankind." But that was an isolated voice. More typical was Swinburne's famous anthem to man, quoted before: "Glory to man in the highest, / The maker and master of things."

There was a growing conviction that science could be relied on to provide a secure rational foundation for all of our ethical and moral standards. The philosophical roots of this conviction can be traced to Greek philosophy, which holds to the fundamental idea that ethics — the principles of right and wrong, good and bad — can be deduced by man's own reason from the nature of things, including the nature of man. God — or the gods — played only an incidental part in Greek thought. The Greeks believed in the supremacy of reason, and their entire philosophy is based on the conviction that reason, and reason alone, teaches man his duties and responsibilities, among which are certain duties he owes to his gods. Religion in Greek thought is thus relegated to a minor subdivision of ethics. Greek philosophy thus relied on human reason to derive moral and ethical principles from the nature of things, rather than from God, as the Hebrews believe. An ethics thus divorced from God is autonomous.

— Now, I do not have to tell you about the spiritual and physical destruction the idea of autonomous ethics has brought to mankind. Once ethics are autonomous, anything can happen, including racist or Bolshevist notions of ethics in which the state replaces God and becomes the source and arbiter of what is right and wrong. And I do not want anybody to tell me that God-centered ethics did not prove of much use either, or that he knows religious people who are unethical and irreligious ones who are ethical. So do I. But this is to overlook the essence of the history of the great monotheistic religions as expressed in the simple piety of countless millions down the ages who, submitting themselves to the discipline of the God-derived moral law, lived lives of humble love, prayerful hope, and subdued expectations from life. Morally speaking, my friends, the shtetl Jew of Eastern Europe was without peer in the history of communal morality. Poverty-stricken, oppressed, hated, mocked, woefully lacking in aesthetics, the shtetl Jew reached heights of ethical and moral purity that made crime in his midst unthinkable and social indifference impossible. Nobody starved in the poor shtetl, and nobody was denied the opportunity to acquire knowledge, a much more sought-after and much more respected commodity than money. I will never forget what the late Nobel Prize winner Zalman Waxman said about the shtetl: "In the Eastern European little shtetl where I was born," he said, "the material poverty was beyond description and the spiritual richness beyond imagination."

—Now, how did this come to pass? Why did poverty and oppression, which usually breed crime, breed, in the mud of the shtetl, purity of heart as a mass phenomenon? The answer, my friends, is in the Bible: Believing, as the shtetl Jews did, that ethical behavior is God-centered, they took God as their measure. And because they took God as their measure, they had to make sure—to mention just one tiny example dealing with measures—that even weights and measures used in local Jewish groceries were exact enough, honest enough to measure themselves against the Ultimate Measure of all things. The history of the shtetl is crowned with stories about saintly men who would go at least once a week from store to store to examine weights and measures. Our entire history bears witness before God and man that ethics become a way of life—not a fossilized thought, but a way of life—only when they are God-derived. Do you understand now why an ethical admonition like "And thou shall not be a talebearer among your brethren" would have been incomplete and ineffective without "I am the Lord!"? Only *if* "I am the Lord" will you refrain from being a talebearer among your brethren! If I am not the Lord, so to speak, if you deny me, all your ethical vows never to be a talebearer are null and void. Without God there are no ethics. That is precisely what Dostoevsky had in mind when he said, "If there is no God, murder is permissible." Abraham, as we must always remember, said it more than four millennia earlier: "There is no fear of God in this land, and whoever finds me may slay me."

14

The Ways of the Lord
Which the Wicked Tread

What Is Man?

What is man that Thou art mindful of him, and the son of man
that Thou dost care for him? Yet, Thou hast made him a little less
than God, and dost crown him with glory and honor.

The question of the meaning of these memorable lines in the eighth
psalm was raised by a young man who introduced himself as a
newcomer. "How is one to equate the two parts of the same great
psalm?" was the question. "On the one hand there is the bitter question
'What is man?' to which the answer that begs itself is 'Nothing!' But, on
the other hand, there is the enigmatic yet reassuring statement 'Thou
has made him a little less than the angels,' as one translation has it, or 'a
little less than God,' as it appears in most translations. But if the latter,
how can one equate such an exalted state with the first desperate cry?
Isn't there a contradiction here?"

—I am grateful for the occasion to explain these famous lines, said
the teacher, for the psalm lends itself to various interpretations. First, a
line by Rav Kook: "The more man knows his value . . . the greater his
value." "Value" and "merit" are here interchangeable: If man merits it,
his value is infinite; if he does not, he is nothing. In *Bereshith Rabbah*
the sages of old put it this way: "If man merits it, he is told [by Him on
High]: You take precedence over the angels; if not, he is told: A mos-
quito takes precedence over you." Now, the main topic of the eighth

146

psalm is man as a *relation*. The term "man as a relation," the teacher explained, belongs to Kierkegaard. The self, Kierkegaard says, acquires a new quality in the fact that it is the self directly in the sight of God. This self is no longer the merely human self but what he would call, he said, hoping not to be misunderstood, the theological self — the self directly in the sight of God. And what an infinite reality this self acquires by being before God! Let me repeat his vivid image: A herdsman who is a self only in the sight of cows is as base as is the ruler who is a self in the sight of slaves — for in both cases the scale or measure is lacking. The child who hitherto had only his parents to measure himself by becomes a self when he is a man by getting, let us say, the state as a measure. But what an infinite accent, Kierkegaard cries out, falls on the self by getting God as a measure!

The "Without" and the "Within"

— Now, the teacher went on, the kind of relation that exists between the herdsman and his cows, for example, or the master and his slaves, or even the citizen and the state or society is a relation to something *outside* oneself — to a "without," as opposed to a "within." Though the relation between person and state or society involves a degree of within, since it demands the shaping of reactions and opinions of a more advanced nature, even these reactions and opinions are shaped primarily by the without. I am not talking about the ideal society or the ideal state run by philosophers — a Greek dream or prophetic vision. I mean the state and society as we have come to know them: disturbingly concrete, yet alienatingly abstract withouts. What kind of relation is experienced by the self who is, in Kierkegaard's words, directly in the sight of God, the self who gets God as a measure? Will it not be, above all, a relation to a within? In his famous conclusion to *The Critique of Practical Reason*, Immanuel Kant makes the observation that "two things fill the mind with ever new and increasing admiration and awe the oftener and the more steadily we reflect upon them: the starry heavens above and the moral law within." The moral law, which bears testimony to the godly in us, can reside only in the within, for it is only felt, not seen. By contradistinction, the stars, visible to the eyes, belong to the without, though they too can fill the poetic soul with wonder and awe. So we have here two types of relation: a relation to the without, which stands for the physical universe as symbolized by the stars, and a relation to the within, which stands for the spiritual universe as represented by the moral law. Now, suppose a person sees himself only in relation to the without, to the physical universe alone, what would he think of himself?

"It depends." was the answer. "If by 'without' you really mean the physical universe, that is to say, man's seeing himself against the background of the whole physical universe, then the answer is 'Nothing,' for he sees himself as a nothing by comparison. If, however, by 'without' you mean the state, the party, the society, the 'Joneses,' the small, visible world from without, a person who sees himself against this limited background may very well regard himself as a demigod. We all know such people, don't we?"

"Yes," another person agreed. "These are people whose standards are determined by status, not by values; who know everything about the standard of living and nothing about the quality of life. I knew a good man back in the States who suffered a mental breakdown, from which he never fully recovered, because he had to lower his living standards."

The Waters and the Mirror

— There is a passage in Proverbs, Ariel Halevi said, that has therapeutic implications for this situation. I read somewhere that to lower one's standards may be a cure for some forms of neurosis, stress, and depression, and in Proverbs we read, "As in water, face answereth to face, so the heart of man to man." The question immediately arises, if the purpose of the passage was to stress the need for man to see himself as he really is, why use the metaphor of water and not of a mirror? Surely in a mirror one can see himself more clearly than in water? Hasidic literature provides a meaningful answer. Man cannot possibly see his reflection in water unless he *bends down,* which is not the case with a mirror. In a mirror you may even look up to yourself, while there is no way on earth to see yourself in flowing waters without "lowering" yourself, so to speak. The biblical passage suggests, then, that if you can see yourself as in waters, by lowering yourself in your own eyes, you will reach a state of sincerity and unpretentiousness that will make it possible for other hearts in a similar state to respond to yours.

—Now, a few minutes ago someone observed here that the more limited the background against which we see ourselves, the more likely we are to show our arrogance. If society is "god" and someone is a so-called social lion, he is at least a demigod. In such a situation this person is hardly likely to think of himself as a "nothing," for if society is everything, he is at least a something—a something in his own eyes and in the eyes of those like him. If, however, the background against which secular man sees himself is enlarged to encompass the whole physical world, the feeling of insignificance that is bound to seize him in a thinking mood can be overpowering. Yet, would you say that he would feel nothing if he acquired a spiritual ability to see himself in relation to the great "within"?

"But, sir!" someone exclaimed, "aren't we told time and again in the Bible, in prayers, in theology, that not for a moment must we forget that we are nothing but dust?"

The teacher replied with a quote from Walt Whitman: — "For dust thou art and to dust return has not been spoken of the soul." And this brings us back, he went on, to the meaning of the eighth psalm, which consists of two lines it draws, the line of dust and the line of soul. Helmut Thielicke, the German theologian, in his excellent book *Nihilism*, defines the difference between these two lines as follows: One line is that of the physical universe. The fact that the human self is a point on this line means that it is an insignificant quantity. What is even the whole earth compared to the planetary system, and what is this planetary system compared with cosmic space measured in light years? Within this tiny earth-point man himself is almost an unimaginable trifle, a nothing. One look at the cosmos, Thielicke writes, shatters man to pieces insofar as he is a quantity.

—The other line, the teacher went on, is represented by the intelligible world as conceived by an expanding, spiritual "within": Since man in that intelligible world is the bearer of the moral law, he suddenly becomes a qualitative magnitude of absolute uniqueness. He can no longer be described quantitatively, as a mere component of the universe, as a functional self. To the contrary, in this exalted state he is capable, as Thielicke puts it, of opposing the whole cosmos. For the tremendous cosmic quantities, the planets, the fixed star systems, all move according to immutable mathematical laws; they are unfree. Man, however, is free, and in his freedom and free will he can create or destroy worlds. And that is what the great eighth psalm is all about. It says, in essence, that man is a *relation*: In relation to the physical universe he is nothing, but he is everything in relation to the moral law within.

I Am, Notwithstanding

— There is a Hasidic story, the teacher concluded, about Rabbi Aaron of Karlin, who was asked what he had learned from his master, the Great Maggid. "Nothing at all," he replied. Pressed to explain what he meant, he said, "The nothing-at-all is what I learned, that is to say, I learned the meaning of nothingness. I learned that I am nothing at all, and that *I Am*, notwithstanding!"

In Vain

There was a pause, and then came a question about the twenty-fourth psalm, specifically the passage that only he will ascend the mountain of the Lord who "has clean hands and a pure heart; who has not carried his soul unto vanity nor sworn deceitfully." "Now," was the question, "doesn't the Hebrew word for vanity used in that psalm, *lashav*, actually mean 'in vain'? What exactly does "in vain" mean?"

The teacher asked whether anyone had read about the suicide of a young man in Haifa, who left behind a note that said he could not "go on living in vain." The word used for "in vain" was precisely *lashav*.

The student said, "Now my question assumes a frightening relevance. *Lashav*—'in vain'—may well be the saddest word in the Bible—"

— The saddest word in human life, the teacher suggested, and then, —Where else does this word appear?

"'And thou shall not carry the name of the Lord thy God in vain'" someone replied.

— So here we have it, the teacher said. The sin of carrying the name of God in vain is almost as great as that of carrying the name of man in vain, that is to say, of man's carrying his own name—"man"—his own life—his own soul—in vain. The psalm tells us, in His name, I have given you a soul: Don't carry it *in vain*, don't waste it, don't misuse it, don't handle it indelicately; it is fragile; it requires special care, special love, special treatment. It is My soul — *nafshi* — which I entrust to you. Take care! That is what He says. In view of this discussion, how would you describe, in contemporary terms, the state or type of man who carries his soul in vain?

— That state, he replied, is the sadly muted feeling that strikes many middle-aged men and women after all the so-called itches are over, the proverbial seven-year itch or the less proverbial twenty-year itch, and so forth. Many experience in the wake of those itches the realization that something vital is missing in their lives, or, worse, that there is suddenly something in their lives that is terribly present, a sense of futility, of no expectation, of no source of inspiration, in short, of *in vain*, as expressed, for example, in one typical bitter question that comes to mind: "Is this all there is to it?"

Someone added another observation. "The question 'what am I breaking my neck for?' which many American males would ask themselves at about forty or fifty may be the root of the sense of futility and meaninglessness, of a life lived 'in vain' or of an oncoming fear of 'in vain' to which very few are likely to admit."

Is This All There Is To It?

— Let me offer some comments on the equation "Is this all there is to it?" with "in vain," responded the teacher. This question, or "what the heck am I breaking my neck for," bespeaks a sense that what we once thought would be sufficient to completely fill our lives, be it the marital or the material, has not proved sufficient at all. A question like "Is this all there is to it?" — to life — cannot possibly be raised when one knows a priori that the material or the marital is definitely *not* all there is to it. The question is most likely to trouble people who have believed that all there was to life was confined exclusively to the social, material, or sensual realms. Life under such conditions becomes a matter of *outer* pursuits, like the "pursuit of happiness."

"You are not suggesting," an American in the audience asked. "that the 'pursuit of happiness' should be relegated to the realm of the 'in vain,' are you?"

— I certainly am! the teacher exclaimed. The Bible took a stand on the subject of this pursuit a few millennia before America's Declaration of Independence.

Happiness and Mercy

The teacher asked what the Hebrew word *tuv* stood for in scripture. The reply was that in the first chapter of Isaiah *tuv* stands for material good, as it is written, "If you be willing and obedient, ye shall eat the good of the land."

— It also appears, said the teacher, in the twenty-third psalm, which starts with the words "The Lord is my Shepherd" and ends with "Surely, goodness (*tuv*) and mercy will pursue me all the days of my life." Thus, in one instance, *tuv* stands for earthly good; in another, for goodness as a quality of virtue. The combination of the two, goodness of body and soul, is happiness. But does it say about this goodness, which is the essence of happiness, that we should pursue *it*, or that it should pursue *us*?

— What things, then, according to the Bible, are for *us* to pursue?

Justice, Justice Thou Shall Pursue

"Justice," someone replied, "as it is written, 'Justice, justice thou shall pursue.'"

— Correct, the teacher said. Justice is for *us* to pursue; happiness can only pursue *us*. The pursuit of happiness, as commonly understood, may, in fact, destroy all chances of ever attaining it. The very idea that happiness is something we must pursue with a view of attaining it makes happiness a silent partner to our existential stupidity. James Thomas Merton says somewhere that a life without problems may literally be more hopeless than one that always verges on despair — and how right he was!

Giving Birth to Confusion

— There is an ancient prayer, said the teacher, recited daily, which uses another word for the same "in vain" — *larik*. That prayer expresses the hope and supplication that He may place in our hearts His love and reverence so that we may serve Him with a whole heart; that we may not labor in vain (*larik*) "nor give birth to ruin" (*labehalah*), "ruin" being the common translation of *labehalah*. But this translation is incorrect. The Hebrew word *labehalah* is not "unto ruin" but "unto confusion." The passage, moreover, clearly speaks not merely of giving birth to confusion, that is to say, of being confused and contributing toward the spread of confusion in the world, but, quite literally, of bringing confused children into the world. To put it differently, this remarkable passage says that if we live in vain — *larik*, purposelessly, aimlessly, rootlessly — we bring children as sacrifices to our confusion.

"What a fearful reality this describes!" someone exclaimed. "I myself know quite a few families back in California of whose sons and daughters it can be safely said that they were born *labehalah*. What are the Jesus freaks, Jews for Jesus, Hari-Krishna addicts, Moonies, and so forth, if not children born *labehalah*?"

The Fathers Have Eaten Unripe Fruit

"Doesn't Isaiah say, 'The fathers have eaten unripe fruit and the teeth of the children are set at an edge'?" someone asked.

— Yes, the teacher said. Vinegar, a common metaphor in ancient times, would have been more convincing here if the whole idea were limited to the consequences, namely, the children's teeth that are set on edge. But the idea of "unripe fruit" is nothing short of prophetic: What better word to describe all those unripe ideas that the fathers, regarding these fruits as ripe, modern, fashionable, progressive, tried to transmit to their children? Unripe progressivism, unripe liberalism, unripe scientism, unripe modernism, and, above all, unripe rationalism — do you think for one moment that the fathers would have eaten those fruits themselves had they thought them unripe? But they thought, in their immaturity, that in order to be "mature," "ripe," "modern," "progressive," one must first cut off one's roots to the past. The only thing they knew, in fact, about all those unripe ideas was that they demanded, as a condition for acceptance, the cutting off of roots in the past.

"Yet," someone remarked, "many fathers and mothers experience the pain of their own teeth being set on edge while actually *continuing* to eat the unripe fruit! How is one to explain it?"

You Have Touched Upon a Wound

— You have touched upon a wound, a social wound, the teacher replied, ransacked, as it were, by the same society that inflicts it. The "in vain" is a self-inflicted pain that people experience without know-ing what it is. The pain of "in vain" is so great, in fact, that people who feel it but cannot trace it to its cause walk around with a scream inside them. When you think you are not supposed to feel a certain pain, to feel it is a kind of heresy, something to be ashamed of, like a social disease. The "beautiful people" of the gossip columns may be the very ones plagued by this feeling of "in vain." The synthetic society around us has subjected itself to the tyranny of masks, and under those masks there are screams trying desperately to stay buried. These people, whether they realize it or not, are not so much afraid of suffer-ing as of suffering "in vain." I venture to say, moreover, that they would not mind suffering for something *not in vain* if they only knew what it was. Unable to discover the meaning of the "not in vain," they live on with the stifled scream of "in vain" inside them. And the sound of that inner scream — the scream of "in vain" — is the reason noises, wild, barbarous noises, play such an important role in amusement and entertainment. People young and old are simply trying to subject themselves to noises that may outscream for a while those screams from within.

Someone spoke out. "I am from California myself. California was once described by somebody as 'a Guernica with a tan.' Everybody is aware of the tan, but how many are aware of the Guernica?"

— When nobody is aware of the Guernica, the teacher replied, the Guernica is bound to become a scream. That is the state in which one can say of oneself, "I am both wound and knife."

Where Is Abel Thy Brother?

A question was now put to the teacher concerning Cain and Abel. "What bothers me about the story, as related in scripture, is the an-swer that Cain gives to God's question 'Cain, where is Abel your broth-er?' The answer Cain gives seems to be no answer at all. In the very same sentence, Cain uses first a lie, and then an ironically rhetorical counter-question: 'Am I my brother's keeper?' What I want to under-stand is this: Didn't Cain know, when he gave those answers, that God knows the truth?"

— This question is of great importance, the teacher replied, for it helps us understand the biblical concept of sin. Here we see the first murderer refusing to testify against himself before God. Before a human judge, of course, such behavior is a privilege of the defendant. But how can one understand such a refusal to testify before the all-knowing, all-seeing God? The answer, according to an excellent comment by Ernst Simon, is that the Bible is trying to tell us what sin does to the sinner: In extreme cases it simply strikes him with temporary insanity. Crime and madness are interrelated. The crime itself maddens the criminal as much as the spirit of madness induces someone to commit a crime. The maddened criminal screams—like the people of Sodom and Gomorrah, like Hitler in his speeches. "No man commits a sin," say the sages of the Talmud, "unless he is possessed of a spirit of madness." Cain, stricken with temporary insanity, thus takes leave to the Supreme Judge as if He were a judge of flesh and blood. Ernst Simon says that the biblical mood confirms the platonic maxim that only an ethically sound person is able to grasp the truth. Thus Cain, like Adam his father, became ill with sin and began to lie. What surprises me, the teacher commented, is that in connection with this vital premise people, even learned people like Dr. Simon, would rather quote Plato than mention the fact that an entire movement in Judaism was based on the living, practiced idea that, as Rabbi Israel Salanter put it, "if your deeds are right, so are your opinions." The Mussar movement of Lithuania made this truth its foundation. In the Bible—long before Plato—this truth was first pronounced in the sixteenth chapter of Proverbs.

Ethics a Mystical Process

—"Commit thy works unto the Lord, and thy thoughts shall be *rightened*," the teacher quoted. Then he explained: —The Hebrew word *yikonu* means both "established" and "rightened." "Rightened," much more than "established," implies a process. What kind of process? A mystical one! This remarkable passage speaks of a process by which, in Leo Baeck's apt definition of Hebrew metaethicism, every commandment of the Law suggests a mystery and every mystery a commandment. That is why any opposition between mysticism and ethics has no place in the Bible or in religious Hebrew thought in general. No experience without tasks and no tasks without experience. Life dwells only, in Leo Baeck's words again, where both are present. In Judaism, all ethics has its mysticism and all mysticism its ethics. This applies to the whole vast area of its ideas. For Jewish mysticism, the commandments, welling up out of God, are energies of the will: Floods of mystery full of commandments and floods of commandments full of mystery issue from God, and the deed that fulfills God's commandment opens up a gate through which these floods surge into man's day. Ethics is here rooted in the profundity of a living eperience of the godly. Ethics in Judaism is thus an ethics of revelation. It is not in vain that in the Hebrew language of the Middle Ages the same word is used to designate a mystical absorption and an ethical disposition. He who wholeheartedly follows the commandments can also experience the tidings of the divine truth.

Which He Lived

— Baeck's vitally Hebraic thought that life dwells only where both commandment and mystery are present reminds me of an observation the Gaon of Vilna made in connection with the number of years lived by two of the greatest men in the Bible — that they really *lived* those years: Adam and Abraham, the first man and the first Hebrew. Instead of the usual "and he died at the age of" or "the number of his years was," when it comes to Adam and Abraham it says, "And the number of the years *which they lived*" — *asher hai*. The totally atypical addition suggests an extraordinary fullness of life, a life, or lives, lived to the full. If the lives of the first man and the first Hebrew were not full, whose life can ever be?

The Ways of the Lord
Which the Wicked Tread

"For the ways of the Lord are just, and the righteous shall walk in them, but the transgressor shall stumble and fall therein."

This passage in Hosea 14 was the subject of a question from the audience. "The passage," the questioner said, "was always a mystery to me: Doesn't it imply the impossible thought that the wicked, too, walk the ways of the Lord?"

— It does, the teacher replied, and that is what is so eternally contemporary about this seemingly baffling passage. Justness, which is the way of the Lord, is trodden not only by the truly and wholly just, but by the dangerously and wickedly unjust. We recognize the dangerously half-just who walk, up to a point, the ways of the Lord, by the half-truths which they make into fetishes. We all know that most of the ills and woes that beset our society and strain it to a breaking point are partly, at least, the result of an unprecedented effort to right wrongs. Both good people and some of the bad ones want to right wrongs, but while the good know that to right wrongs is not enough unless you know what good is, the bad, who know how to hate what is wrong at the expense of knowing what is right, are bound to stumble and fall — morally speaking — on the same road on which they walked, up to a point, along with the good.

— The same is true of "morality." Morality is the road of the just, as we all know, yet there is hardly an evil regime in the world that does not use the excuse of the "morality" of freedom to commit the greatest immorality of all: the suppression of freedom. The same is true of "honesty." We have discussed it on other occasions, but it bears repeating. There is something terrible about an honesty that is only a half-truth, for what it does is not to make one unmask oneself to reveal the real man, but to unleash the beast in him. Robespierre, an executioner of the first rank, was called "The Incorruptible." And he was, alas! In a book by Eugenia Ginzburg about Soviet concentration camps, the author, who later killed herself, tells of a German lady in charge of the camps in Siberia, an ascetic, unsmiling, chaste, incorruptible woman who was the scourge of the inmates precisely *on account* of her incorruptibility. At least from the "corruptible" ones you could still get an extra piece of bread in return for an illegal ruble! "Honesty," "justice," "morality," "peace," are certainly descriptive of God's ways walked by the righteous. But divorce them from God Himself, from the fullness of truth and the experience of compassion, and those very same roads become moral stumbling blocks for the unrighteous who have walked them for a while.

The Day of the Honest Judge

The teacher said he wanted to end the meeting with one more commentary. — In regard to the biblical passage in Genesis "And Lot sat at the gate of the city," he said, Rashi says it was a day on which Lot sat in judgment at the gates of Sodom. And on that very day, the Bible tells us, the angels of the Lord also came to announce to Lot, Abraham's nephew, that the wicked city was doomed. Why the fate of Sodom was sealed precisely on a day when Lot, an honest man, was dispensing judgment is explained by a wonderful homiletic twist. Up to the day when honest Lot sat in judgment, Sodom avoided destruction by divine wrath through bribery: The only way for the few innocent people of Sodom, or the many who passed through and were constantly dragged to corrupt judges — the only way for them to escape punishment was through bribing these judges. Bribery was used to prevent the injustice that was the law of the land from being perpetrated against the innocent. This prevention of injustice by means of bribery was then the sole *moral* reason for Sodom's continued existence! But then came the day when the judge was an honest man who shunned bribes and stuck to the letter of the immoral law simply because it was the law of the land, which he could not violate. And thus on that day, the day of the honest judge, the destruction of Sodom became inevitable and imminent.

15

The Ripeness of Evil

And Nabal Said

At the outset of the next class a question was raised again concerning the meaning of the passage in the fourteenth psalm: "And Nabal said in his heart: There is no God." "Now," a young man asked, "we all know what *nabal* means in coloquial Hebrew: an evil, mean person. I am also aware that the King James translation of the word is 'fool.' On another occasion you said that *nabal* did not mean a fool, that biblical Hebrew had many names for fools and *nabal* was not one of them. Now, there must have been many good people in the concentration camps who, in their total despair, cried out in their hearts 'There is no god!' yet remained good to the bitter end. How would that biblical passage stand up before such 'godless' martyrs?"

—Let me first say, the teacher replied, that *nabal* is not a fool or a knave or a wicked man, but "a withered man." How would you say in Hebrew "the flowers have withered," for example?

"*Haperahim nablu,*" someone replied.

—Yes, the teacher said. *Nabal* is thus the prototype of the withered man, the man without roots, according to Rabbi Samson Rafael Hirsh's translation of the word *nabal* as "withered." It denotes the disappearance of moral strength and spiritual values even if those withered people continue to speak of "ethics." The withered man can easily be an exponent of autonomous ethics. The "cut-flower culture" says "there is no God" and yet can retain for a while — but only for a while — the original beauty and fragrance of those flowers. The vitality of this culture, however, is at best a one-generation proposition. After that, the roots begin to rot along with the flowers. If the flowers are permitted to stay in the vase, or, rather, forced to stay on by all kinds of artificial means, they begin to emit a bad odor. The withered man, rationally self-sufficient, a *nabal*, says in his heart, "There is no God."

In His Heart

—Miguel de Unamuno, continued the teacher, was a great Spaniard with an almost desperately passionate need for God. De Unamuno said that the reason it is a wicked man who says in his heart, "There is no God" is that he says it in his *heart!* Had he said it in his mind, had he come to this conclusion out of cold, rationalistic considerations, the Bible would have never have called him wicked. But to have a heart that is completely at peace with the idea that there is no God—such a heart is wicked!

And They Sought Many Inventions

"For God created man upright, but they sought many inventions." "What is the meaning" was the question, "of 'And they sought many inventions?' What kind of inventions is Ecclesiastes talking about, and in what way do inventions interfere with man's uprightness?"

—I think, in this context, said the teacher, of Karl Jaspers' observation that the inner resistance to or suspicion of empirical knowledge and technology is ageless.

—The ancients looked on scientists as wizards and aides to the devil. In our time, we hear that Karl Bosch, the originator, with Fritz Haber, of the nitrogen synthesis for military use in World War I, without which Germany would have been defeated much earlier, was greatly troubled in his old age by the thought of what he had done. We read how profoundly shaken Otto Hahn was at the news of Hiroshima and Nagasaki, as if he had committed the act of destroying them. He had nothing to do with the bomb, but as a scientist he was in the unique position of having made the particular discovery that started it. The same was true of Einstein and Oppenheimer. But while some of the truly great men of science were often terrified at the thought of where their inventions might lead, lesser spirits, when compelled to choose between moral considerations and the delight of innovation, not only chose the second, but were convinced that the second made the first superfluous. Innovation for no real reason, yet in the name of rational self-sufficiency, thus became the enemy of tradition. The machine told the spirit, "There is no place for you in my realm, you only bother me." Is there any wonder, Ecclesiastes says, that man was rendered less upright by seeking "many inventions?" He was also rendered less wise and, as incredible as it may sound, *less cultured.* According to Ortega y Gasset, a great Spaniard, there were more cultured men in the Europe of 1750 than today. Now, I want to tell you a story.

The Old Gardener and
the Disciple of Confucius

— There is an ancient story, the teacher said, about a discussion between a disciple of Confucius and an old gardener. The gardener was watering his plot, fetching the water in a bucket, which he carried with great effort up and down the steps that were hewed into the wall of his well. Noticing this, the disciple of Confucius approached the old gardener and told him about an invention called a draw-well that made it possible to bring up lots of water very quickly and with much less toil. But the idea of adopting the easy, effective means moved the gardener to indignation. "Sir," he told the disciple, "I know about this invention, and I don't plan to use it." "But why?" the disciple asked in amazement; to which the old gardener replied, "Because where there are wicked inventions, there are wicked uses, and where there are wicked uses, there are wicked hearts. If one's heart is wicked, he has soiled the purity of his soul. I would be ashamed of using this invention." This, the teacher commented, may be an extreme illustration of the danger to the soul that is contained in seeking many inventions. But what is so bitterly right and relevant about the fable is the scorn with which it treats sacrosanct "progress." As it has turned out, progress today is nothing but an improvement, in the political field, of man's capacity to deceive, and, in another field, dreadful proof of his incapacity to understand that an improvement of inventions, or of standard of living, has very little to do with the quality of life. "And they sought many inventions" is to me, the teacher concluded, the first prophetic warning against rational self-sufficiency. Nietzsche's "last men," whom he describes as "contemptible," say, "We invented happiness!"

Lean Not Unto Thy Own Understanding

A question was put to the teacher whether scripture, warning so relentlessly against folly, takes a stand against the folly of relying on one's reason. The teacher answered in the affirmative. — You find the answer, he said, in the third chapter of Proverbs: "Trust in the Lord with all your heart, *And lean not unto thy own understanding.*" Here, faith and reason or understanding are pitted against each other. There is no disparagement of reason here, only a warning against treating it as an autonomous entity in man, as a final judge. Somewhere there is the wonderful line "I have often enough made a fool of myself when I let my reason guide me."

"But isn't it true," someone asked, "that faith without reason can be as bad as reason without faith?"

— Absolutely, the teacher replied. But as there are two kinds of reason, there are two kinds of faith: the faith that never clashed with reason but superseded it from the beginning—this can be called naive faith; and the difficult faith that is, as Kierkegaard called it, "a leap" into a different realm, an escape from the straitjacket of reason into learned self-transcendence. In such a supreme state of tested faith, which only very few can attain, one reaches the highest rung of being by feeling like a child again.

As a Weaned Child

— The saintly Hafetz Hayim, the teacher went on, refused to get together with one of the greatest Kabbalists of his time, Rabbi Moshe Elyashiv, whom he treated, from a distance, almost reverentially. You see, having transcended reason—though he remained a marvelously reasonable man—he simply hesitated to get involved with any speculative discipline dealing with the nature of God, even one as divine as the Kabbalah, which might rob him of his "naiveté." He quoted in support of his stand that soothing passage in the one hundred thirty-first psalm, "My soul within me is even as a weaned child."

— Let me tell you a story about this so-called naive faith; it deals with something else, as well. The story emanates from sixteenth-century Safed.

The Man Who Baked Bread for God

There lived in Safed, amid the largest and most significant group of Kabbalists ever assembled in one small place, that "awesome man of God," as he is called to this very day, the father of practical Kabbalah, Isaac Luria, the holy Ari, of blessed memory. In one of those turbulent days—it was not too long after the expulsion from Spain—a refugee from persecutions in a faraway land arrived in Safed with his family. He was not a learned man, but very pious, very good, and very, very simple. On his first Sabbath in Safed, he heard a local rabbi preach in the synagogue on the subject of *showbread*, which was offered regularly in the Temple on the Sabbath. The rabbi's deep grief over the cessation of that sacred rite with the destruction of the Temple made a great impression on the refugee, particularly since the rabbi sounded as if all this had happened very recently. Coming home, he told his wife to bake two loaves of bread made out of the purest and finest flour, for he intended, he said, to offer them to God every Friday. His wife, sure he was doing the right thing now that they were in the Holy Land, baked special loaves of bread every Friday, and the man took them to the synagogue, where he would place them, after prayers, before the Holy Ark and withdraw. On Saturday mornings he would be first in the synagogue so as to check whether his offering was accepted, and there was no end to his joy when he found the loaves of bread gone. His prayers on such Sabbath days were cheerfully and tearfully ecstatic. Very few people have ever felt closer to God than that simple man who baked bread for the Creator, and who did not know that the poor Synagogue beadle, who thought the man left those loaves for charity, took them for himself.

—After a while, however, even the beadle began to suspect that there was something more to the bread than charity, and he told the story to the rabbi. The next Friday, when the rabbi, hiding behind a curtain, saw the man place the loaves of bread before the Holy Ark, he materialized before the man and asked what he was doing. The man told him he had been doing it for some time now and that God must have been very pleased with his offering for He was taking it up

to heaven. Shocked and indignant, the rabbi insulted the man.
"Fool!" he shouted. "Is God a man that He should eat and drink? Ignorant! Blasphemer!" The rabbi's reprimanding shouts alarmed the
beadle, who soon told the disconsolate man where his loaves of bread
had gone. The same Sabbath, after sunset, a messenger came to sum-
mon the rabbi to the holy Ari. "Prepare yourself to die," the Ari told
the horrified rabbi. "Since the destruction of the Temple nothing has
caused more pleasure in heaven than that poor man's bread offerings.
That you stopped him from continuing this rite is bad enough, but
your shaming him in such a manner is unforgivable." The rabbi, so
the story goes, passed away a few days later.

A long silence followed. Then someone, an elderly man, reminded
the teacher that he had said there was something else to the story be-
side the sacredness of naive faith. The teacher nodded. — What I
wanted to add, Ariel Halevi said, is that the story is actually mentioned in the book where I first read it as an elucidation of the biblical
story of Tamar.

Tamar

— Tamar was the daughter-in-law of Jacob's fourth son, Judah.
When her husband died childless, she married, according to the
claim of levirate marriage, Judah's second son, who soon passed on as
well without offspring. Judah's third son refused to marry Tamar, but
she remained in or around Judah's house, a tragic figure, lamenting
her fate. Her greatest desire was to bring a child to the family of Judah, and when this was denied her, she conceived the idea of seducing
Judah by playing the prostitute. Veiling her face and voice, she placed
herself on the road he habitually traveled and induced him to make
love to her. We must remember that giving herself to Judah after having been rejected for good by the third son, was not regarded as sinful.
But as Tamar got pregnant, and evil tongues spread the word that the
child she was bearing was conceived in harlotry, Tamar, so as not to
shame Judah in public — he, after all, had gone to her as to a prostitute — refused to identify him as the father even when she heard that
Judah, on learning of her pregnancy, cried out, "Burn her!" Tamar
held on to her secret to the end, and only as a last resort did she identify herself to Judah by some unmistakable signs. The Bible makes

sure that we are aware of Tamar's offspring, many generations later: the house of Jesse and David. Why did Tamar deserve such illustrious descendants? Because, the sages say, of her refusal to shame Judah in public. They adduced from the Tamar story the maxim "A man should rather throw himself into a fiery furnace than humiliate his neighbor in public."

And Thou Shall Not Spare a Soul

"How does a Divine order like 'And thou shall not spare a soul!' fit into a Bible that seems so considerate of human life?" came a new question. "The book of Joshua bristles with such orders. In the process of conquering the promised land, Joshua is directed by God to destroy his enemies not only lock, stock, and barrel, but man, woman, and child. How can we attribute such unmerciful decrees to a merciful God Who regards shaming someone in public as tantamount to bloodshed?"

— The acquired knowledge of how to read the Bible does not guarantee an unveiling of its mysteries. It does guarantee the emergence of an unshakable feeling that what remains mysterious, even more than what is revealed, reveals enough to whet our appetite for the hidden, but never enough to satisfy it. The question of "And thou shall not spare a soul" belongs in this category: It is a mystery, yet there is a clue provided centuries earlier. This clue is contained in the covenant that was made with Abraham. Look at Genesis 15:12.

The Ripeness of Evil

And when the sun was about to set, a deep sleep fell upon Abraham; and, lo, a horror of great darkness fell upon him.

And He said unto Abraham: Know of surety that thy seed shall be a stranger in a land that is not theirs, and shall serve them; and they shall afflict them four hundred years.

And also that nation whom they serve will I judge; and afterwards shall they come out with great substance.

And thou shalt go to thy fathers in peace, and shall be buried in a good old age.

But in the fourth generation they shall come hither again; for the iniquity of the Amorites is not yet full.

And it came to pass that when the sun went down, and it was

dark, behold, a smoking furnace and a burning lamp that passed between those pieces.

The same day, the Lord made a covenant with Abraham, saying: Unto thy seed have I given this land, from the river of Egypt until the great river, the river Ephratus.

The teacher went on after a pause. — In the passages we just read, mention is made of a nation that Joshua was ordered, centuries later, to destroy.

"The Amorites," someone said.

— The Amorites, the teacher nodded. Do we know anything about the nature of those Amorites? he asked. What of the words "For the iniquity of the Amorites is not yet full"?

— Is it not strange, the teacher went on, that the reason the promised land was not given right away to Abraham was that four centuries had to pass — centuries that included the Egyptian exile — before the iniquity of the Amorites was "full"? What does "full" mean?

— These few lines in the Bible, the teacher continued, tell an amazing story: the story of evil that has, so to speak, to mature and ripen before it falls, under the weight of its own rottenness, from the tree of life. When this happens, when evil has "matured" enough to fall, not only heaven can no longer take it, but earth as well.

"Meaning what?" someone asked.

— Meaning, the teacher replied, what the Bible tells us much later about the abominations of the Amorites and the other nations who inhabited the promised land. It was not only that the Israelites were promised that land, but the land, the earth, had to reach a state of inability to take the others any longer.

And the Earth Vomited Out Its Inhabitants

— I am thinking, the teacher explained, of a biblical passage, often repeated, that the nations that inhabited the land of Canaan were defeated more by their own abominations than by the Israelites. The Israelites, victorious in battle, are warned time and again by Him on High not to imitate the abominations of the nations they have defeated lest "the earth vomit them out" as it had their enemies. The very notion of the earth getting nauseated with evil and vomiting out its inhabitants suggests a universe that knows us, not one into which we are thrown and, in Sartre's words, "knows us not." *The biblical universe is endowned with awareness.* When Cain kills Abel, his brother, God tells the first murderer that he is cursed "from the earth which hath opened her mouth to receive thy brother's blood from thy hands." The curse came from a defiled earth even more than from an angered heaven. Must there not have been something truly horrendous—unimaginably horrendous—about the abominations of the Moloch-worshiping Amorites if the earth had to "vomit them out"?

"Granted," someone exclaimed. "But does *anything* justify a decree like 'Don't spare a soul'?"

—I do not know the full answer, the teacher replied. But I assume that an abomination that took four hundred years to "mature" tells, on the one hand a story of divine noninterference in processes of maturation, but on the other hand declares that the world is built on moral foundations though it may take centuries before moral judgment is finally revealed.

A man in the audience who identified himself as a former inmate of a concentration camp put to the teacher the following question: "What kind of consolation can such a long-term hope, even a long-term faith, hold out to a man on the threshold of the gas chamber? Do you really think he would feel any better at the thought that in a few centuries morality will triumph?"

It took a while for the teacher to answer. He spoke in a subdued voice. —I was not there, as you know, and I do not know how I would have felt on the threshold of a gas chamber. But I can tell you of one who was there and who not only felt better himself, if that is the word for it, at the thought that the world is built on moral foundations, but made others, standing, like him, on the threshold of extinction, feel better, too. I am speaking of the saintly Rabbi Menahem Ziemba of Praga.

The World Is Built On Moral Foundations

—It would be useful, the teacher went on, in the context of our classes to acquaint ourselves with this modern saint and contemporary biblical figure. Though he was not the Rabbi of Warsaw, Europe's largest Jewish community, the community in its affliction looked up to him as to its guiding light. In January 1943 it became clear in the

Warsaw Ghetto that the thousands of Jews sent almost daily to the *Umschlagplatz* for deportation were actually being sent to their death. Up to that point the Jews in the ghetto had refused to believe the rumors about gas chambers and were careful not to antagonize the German authorities by refusing to supply contingents of Jews for deportation to concentration camps, described by the Nazis as work-camps with bread and soup for all. When it became clear what those work camps were all about, an urgent meeting was convened in the Warsaw archives at which A. G. Friedenson, the chairman, explained the dilemma: to resist or not to resist deportation orders. "The very atmosphere," he said, "is saturated with some explosive that may be hurled at us any moment with a terrible force. What are we to do?"

— Rabbi Menahem Ziemba, gentle, meek, and physically frail from childhood, rose to speak like a prophet of old. He first asserted that the world is built on moral foundations and that, in the long run, it will go ill with the evildoer and well with the just. His verdict, based on the Law, whether to resist deportation orders, was clear and unequivocal: Resist! "We are prohibited by our Law from betraying others, nor may we deliver ourselves into the hands of the arch-enemy. . . . Our much-vaunted prudence," the saintly man warned, "not to be identified with genuine wisdom and true understanding, has blurred our vision and turned out to be more devastating than folly and stupidity." Here Rabbi Menahem paraphrased a comment of the sages on the sin of Korah of old who rose against Moses' authority: "Korah of old," he paraphrased, "accentuated his innate aptitude for prudence to such an extent that it spelled his ultimate doom." Having pronounced his verdict along with his denunciation of foolish prudence, Rabbi Menahem then spoke of *Kiddush Hashem*. I shall explain to you how Rabbi Menahem Ziemba perceived and defined the concept of *Kiddush Hashem*, self-immolation for the sanctification of the divine name.

Kiddush Hashem

— To Rabbi Menahem, the teacher continued with quiet emotion, the meaning of the sublime ideal of *Kiddush Hashem* changed with the temper of the age, the need of the times, and the nature of the enemy. It was not to be evoked as a fixed formula or a stereotyped and

changeless concept but was born anew with every act of self-fulfillment as self-transcendence. *Kiddush Hashem* is an act of wedding the
temporal with the eternal; it is, in the words of a medieval mystic and
moralist, the reaching out to the highest point of eternity in the flux of
temporality. Out of the pitch darkness of the hour comes a voice that
discloses the ineffable in man. It helps bear the heaviest burden and
leaves in its wake neither frustration nor regret.

—Turning to the dilemma they faced at that awesome moment,
Rabbi Menahem went on to say that *Kiddush Hashem* was the ultimate means properly to regard the enemy as they had come to know
him, namely, as something so utterly defiled that his bullet was pre-
ferable to his touch. It was Rabbi Menahem Ziemba, the teacher went
on, who long before the Warsaw Ghetto uprising decreed that just to
look at Hitler's picture was defiling, like touching a loathsome reptile.
"Keep yourself from anything that even appears ugly," he would say,
and ugly to him meant, above all, morally ugly. Precisely the loathsome vulgarity of the utterly soulless enemy demanded the most urgent and most powerful manifestations of the life of the soul as *embodied* in the grand act of *Kiddush Hashem*. Thus he told that assembly of the doomed that the soul of man, ever in need of consecration,
must arise now *in body* to assert the dignity of the human personality
and the moral supremacy of the Jew. "In the face of an enemy," Rabbi
Menahem declared, "whose ruthlessness knows no bounds, the Law
demands that we fight to the very end with unequaled determination
and valor for the sanctification of God's name."

—This verdict, the teacher went on, put an end the stormy discussion on what course to take. It was clear what the great man meant:
Kiddush Hashem was more than a free offering of the select few; it
was the paramount duty and *halacha p'sukah*—clear legal decision—
based on a verdict by Maimonides dating back to the year 1161 in Cai-
ro, and was incumbent on the entire community.

Balm in Gilead

—The story of the life and death of Rabbi Menahem Ziemba,
added the teacher, would not be complete without another detail that
could point toward an answer to the question as to what solace there
can be, when facing death, in the thought that the world is built on
moral foundations.

— On the morning of April 19, 1943, a few days before the Warsaw Ghetto erupted, Rabbi Menahem and two of his younger colleagues, David Shapiro and Samson Stockheimer, were secretly summoned before the higher echelons of the church authorities. The three sages were told that the hierarchy of the Catholic Church had decided to save their lives provided they agreed to leave the ghetto within twenty-four hours. The three men were given an hour to decide, but less than an hour had passed when the youngest of the group, Rabbi Shapiro, arose to announce the decision. He said essentially this: "We, the teachers of our people, cannot abandon our brethren on their last mile. Though we cannot help them any longer materially, we are commissioned by Him on High to be near them. This act of grace will serve as a 'balm in Gilead' to strengthen them in their courage and lift their broken spirits. We have no choice but to reject the offer with thanks but no regrets."

— Rabbi Menahem Ziemba was killed by a Nazi bullet while crossing the street on the fifth day of Passover of 1943. A few days earlier, he had officiated at the Seder in his bunker. Some members of the resistance movement were present at the ceremony. His last words to them were those that the Pharaoh of old had said to his minions according to the Psalms: "Come, let us cut them off from being a people so that the name of Israel may be remembered no more." There was singing at the Seder. The anthem of Jewish faith, *Ani-Ma'amin*, the song of unshakable belief in the coming of the Messiah, rose from the bunker like a battle cry. Rabbi Stockheimer was killed two days before VE day in the Schwartzfeld camps. Rabbi David Shapiro, who took active part in the ghetto uprising, survived.

— The next time we meet, concluded Ariel Halevi, we shall discuss an apropos passage in Jeremiah 45: "Behold," God tells the prophet, "What I have built I am breaking down, and what I have planted, I am plucking up. . . . And do you seek great things for yourself? Seek them not, for behold! I am bringing evil upon all flesh, but I shall give you your soul as a prize of war in all the places to which you may go."

16

And I Shall Give You Your Soul as a Prize of War

And I Shall Give You Your Soul as a Prize of War

The teacher opened the next class with some remarks about the meaning of two of the words in the passage. —*Nafsheha* (from *nefesh*, "your soul") is usually translated to mean "your life," and though the two words "soul" and "life" stand for the same thing, in this context soul stands for more than merely physical life. *Shalal* is usually translated "prey" — "And I shall give you your soul as *shalal*." However, in the biblical idiom, it stands for war booty, or prize of war. Therefore the correct translation of the concluding lines of that passage in Jeremiah would be "And I shall give you your soul as a prize of war."

— Actually, the teacher went on, there are two questions that come to mind on reading this passage: One, what kind of great things has this most tragic of prophets sought for himself that seeking them no more will entitle him to get his soul as a prize of war? Two, what does life, or the keeping of one's soul, as a prize of war mean under circumstances of total destruction? How can a soul saved from a holocaust regard itself as rewarded? Is "rewarded" the right word for such a state?

— Rabbi Menahem Ziemba, the teacher said, did reach the state that was promised to Jeremiah: an increase of soul going hand-in-hand with a decrease of hope. The afflicted man, whose soul is expanding as his hopes diminish is, then, in a higher sense, given his soul as a prize of war. Dietrich Bonhoeffer, whom we have mentioned before, was, in his own words, increasingly unable "to get away from Jeremiah 45." "My thoughts and feelings," Bonhoeffer writes in a letter from prison of December 1943, "seem to be getting more and more like those of the Old Testament." In a letter of February 1944, about a year before his death by hanging, Bonhoeffer gives his own explanation of Jeremiah 45.

If We Can Save Our Souls Unscathed

—I will read some passages from Bonhoeffer's letters, said the teacher.

> We have grown up with the experience of our parents and grand-parents that a man can and must plan, develop, and shape his own life, and that life has a purpose about which man must make up his mind, and which he must then pursue with all his strength. But we have learned from experience that we cannot plan even for the coming day, that what we have built up is being destroyed over-night, and that our life, in contrast to that of our parents, has become formless, or even fragmentary. In spite of that, I can say that I have no wish to live in any other time but our own, though it is so inconsiderate of our outward well-being. We read more clearly than ever before that the world lies under the wrath and grace of God. . . . We read in Jeremiah 45: "Thus says the Lord: Behold, what I have built I am breaking down, and what I planted, I am plucking up, and do you seek great things for yourself? Seek them not; for, behold, I am bringing evil upon all flesh, but I shall give you your soul as a prize of war in all the places to which you may go." If we can save our souls unscathed from the wreckage of our material possessions, let us be satisfied with that. If the Creator destroys his own handiwork, what right have we to lament the destruction of ours? It will be the task of our generation not "to seek great things," but to save and preserve our souls out of the chaos, and to realize that it is the only thing we can carry as a prize from the burning building. "Keep your heart with all vigilance; for from it flows the spring of life" (Prov. 4:23). We shall have to keep our lives rather than to shape them, to hold out rather than march forward."

Ask Your Father and He Will Tell You

A young woman remarked how moving it was to hear Bonhoeffer refer to the experience of his parents that life had a purpose. "Isn't this experience gone now?" she asked. "I sometimes think of those mighty words in Deuteronomy 32 you quoted to us not too long ago: 'Remember the days of old, consider the years of many generations; ask you father and he will tell you, your elders and they will show you.' I don't think there's really much fathers can tell us now. Am I wrong?"

— Though we discussed this subject in connection with the passage in Isaiah "The fathers have eaten unripe fruit and the teeth of the children are set at an edge," replied the teacher, the invocation of that passage in Deuteronomy is very timely. It deals with the meaning of knowledge and with the crucial question whether education can be divorced from tradition. It has been said by certain radical progressives that the hunger for the past simply because it is past is reactionary. Much has also been said about the need to *unlearn* the teachings of the past. Walter Benjamin, a former Marxist who became a thinker of great spiritual insight, had something to say on the subject that can serve as a comment to the same passage in Deuteronomy. He called it "transmittance." But before I cite Walter Benjamin, let me mention a biblical passage that is the very opposite of transmittance: the Law, as pronounced in Deuteronomy 21, about "a rebellious and obstinate son."

— There is one word in that passage, the teacher went on, that may explain the severity of the punishment imposed on such a son. The word is *moreh*. *Moreh* is the Hebrew word used for "rebellious" in this passage. But *moreh* spelled the same way also means "teacher." Thus the Sifri interprets it to mean that the sin of the rebellious son consists mostly in "his teaching himself to do the wrong things." To me, however, it seems that the very term *moreh* implies even more strongly his teaching *others*. This is a familiar contemporary phenomenon: an obstinate and rebellious son who becomes an ideologue, a teacher of his rebelliousness.

Transmittance

The teacher now read from a book he held before him: — The only person who is capable of transmitting knowledge is he who conceives of his own knowledge as having been *transmitted to him*." This, my friends, is not just a thought, but a guide. Walter Benjamin goes on to say that he was convinced that tradition as transmittance—spiritual transmittance—is the medium by which one who is continuously engaged in learning reaches a point at which he suddenly emerges as a teacher, as a *transmitter*. When he reaches that point, something in him begins to overflow and seeks further avenues of transmission. Using the sea as a metaphor for transmitted knowledge, Benjamin says that if we take a wave of the ocean to symbolize man, man has to strive to the utmost to surrender to the great movement of the ocean that swells until it crests and spills over with snow-white foam. This enormous freedom of spilling over represents transmitted education, spilling over from a life lived to its fullest. I would add, the teacher continued, that the person whose learning is a transmittance *from* the past and *into* the future constantly increases his absorptive capacity for thought, indeed his capacity for the most ingenious mental exercises, as he grows older.

"Is sagacity a guarantee against senility?" someone asked.

Full of Sap and Vigor

— The Bible says yes, answered the teacher. Let me again point out that at the end of the ninety-second psalm, it speaks of the righteous and learned man who is "planted in the house of the Lord." "They [such men] will still bear fruit even in old age, they will remain full of sap and vigor forever." Thus, there is not — there cannot be — such a thing as a senile sage! The sages of the Talmud say, "The learned men, the older they get the wiser; the ignoramuses, the older they get, the more stupid." Do you all know the term the sages use for an ignoramus?

Am Ha'aretz

"*Am ha'aretz*," someone said.

— Yes, responded Ariel Halevi. Literally it means "a man of the earth." But it also means a man totally disposed toward the earthly, the tangible, the visible, the material things in life — in short, toward things alone. It means, moreover, a man so much disposed toward the earthly that he has never developed the slightest predilection for the "heavenly." This is the man we have come to know as the ideal product of the technical life order. He is the busy-busy man who knows what to do with his economy and society. He does not realize, however, that when the limited range of socioeconomic problems is the maximum to which his mind can expand, such a mind, in old age, will have shrunk. This shrinkage is evident quite often in senility and also in an inability to handle being alone. Socioeconomic man, the *am ha'aretz*, is in constant need of company, while the sage, in contrast, not only knows how to handle being alone, but would not know what to do without it! Solitude for the sage, for the learned man in general, is a condition for growth.

— If the tragedy of solitude today, of loneliness, of lonely old age, is so great, it is primarily the result of bringing to old age *only* one's socioeconomic self. This is the way to tragedy or senility or both. Old age is increasingly becoming a problem of despair for the aged as well as of exasperation for their children primarily *because ignoramuses know no transmittance!* Abraham Joshua Heschel says somewhere that we have nearly lost the art of conveying to our children our ability to cherish things that cannot be quantified. But worse than that, exclaimed the teacher, we ourselves have lost our ability to cherish those things. And in the absence of this ability we become silly old men when we grow old, or, as Heschel put it, if I remember correctly, "To my child, I am either the embodiment of the spirit or its caricature!"

Nor His Natural Force Abated

— Do you remember how scripture describes Moses at his death? the teacher asked. Once again: "And Moses was a hundred and twenty years when he died: His eye was not dim, nor his natural force abated." Now Moses, years earlier, when he first heard God's voice from the burning bush, described himself to the Lord as a stutterer, as "heavy of speech," that is to say, as one with a speech impediment. "I am not a man of words," he said. Where or how then did such a man come by an eloquence so majestic, a prophecy so oceanic, a language so potent and overpowering, that each time we are exposed to it we gasp as if overcome by mighty waves? Simply this: As he got older, his growing wisdom filled him to overflowing. His mind for many years kept expanding along with his soul—in wisdom the two expand together—to a point where the great lawgiver became an equally great soul restorer, of his own soul to start with.

The Breaking of the Tablets

"Speaking of Moses," someone said, "I was always bothered by the question why Moses had to break the Tablets of the Law on descending Mount Sinai and seeing his people worshiping a golden calf. His wrath was understandable, but why let it out on stone rendered holy by God's word?"

— Rabbi Meir Simha, responded the teacher, the Gaon of Dwinsk, answered the question in a manner that should make us shudder. Rabbi Meir Simha's interpretation sounds like some kind of verdict. Moses, according to the Gaon of Dwinsk, had to break the Tablets of the Law out of fear that the people might start worshiping them.

"Worshiping whom?" someone asked.

— The tablets, the teacher replied.

"What — what's wrong with that?"

— Everything, the teacher replied. The Tablets of the Law are holy only so long as they derive their spiritual sustenance, so to speak, from Absolute Spirit. They are holy not because of *what* is written on them, but because of *Who* wrote it and for whom it was written. If the Spirit behind those tablets is denied, decried, unheeded, the tablets, even with the Ten Commandments on them, become mere pieces of engraved stone. Thus Moses, on descending the mountain and finding the people in a frenzied, idolatrous mood, was seized by the fear that they might dance around the Tablets of the Law as they did around the golden calf, as if the tablets themselves could be worshiped *apart* from God, or worse, *against* God. The fact that those tablets carried the divine signature in the form of the commandments only exacerbated Moses' worst fears: The people, in a wildly idolatrous mood, might worship not only the stone, but what was engraved on it as something totally separate from the Great Engraver and independent of Him. That is what Rabbi Meir Simha says.

"Then are we to deduce from what you have just said that all those worshipers in the many prayer houses ornamented with the Tablets of the Law, who don't believe that those tablets, those commandments, were God-given — " someone began.

— Are idol worshipers? Is that what you want to ask? interpolated the teacher.

"Precisely."

—According to the Gaon of Dwinsk, they are, the teacher replied.
"But that's a frightening thought!" someone exclaimed.

—It is, the teacher agreed, and I would rather not pursue it any
further. Instead, let me tell you a story that Franz Rosenzweig tells
about his master and teacher, Hermann Cohen.

Where is the *Bore Olam*

—When Hermann Cohen was in Marburg, he once expounded the
God idea of his *Ethics* to an old Jew of that city. For a long while the
Jew listened with reverent attention, but when Cohen was through, he
asked, "Yes, but where is the *Bore Olam* [The Creator]?" Cohen had
no answer to this, and tears rose to his eyes.

—You see, the teacher concluded, it is all very nice with those tablets, but where is the *Bore Olam*?

The Graves of Lust

"How is it," someone asked, "that Moses's rage at the sight of the
idol was not as great as his sense of outrage when the Israelites complained to him about how sorely they missed the fleshpots of Egypt—
the fish, the garlic, the onions. For isn't the sin of idolatry infinitely
greater than that of gluttony?"

—Let us discuss this question at our next class, the teacher proposed. But let us now first acquaint ourselves more fully with what
happened at that place in the desert which was later given the unusual
name *Kivroth hata'avah*, "The Graves of Lust."

The teacher read some passages from Numbers 11:

> And the mixed multitude that was amongst them felt a lusting;
> and the children of Israel also wept again, and said, Who shall give
> us fish to eat? But now our soul is dried away; there is nothing at all
> beside this manna before our eyes . . . . Then Moses heard the peo-
> ple weep throughout their families, every man at the door of his
> tent; and the anger of the Lord was kindled greatly. Moses also was
> displeased . . . . And Moses said unto the Lord, Wherefore has
> thou afflicted Thy servant? And wherefore have I not found favor
> in Thy sight that Thou layest the burden of all this people upon
> me?. . . Have I conceived all this people? Have I begotten them
> that Thou shouldest say unto me, Carry them in thy bosom as a

nursing father beareth his sucking child, unto the land which
Thou hast sworn to their fathers? Whence should I have flesh to
give unto all this people, for they weep unto me saying, Give us
flesh that we may eat . . . . I am not able to bear all this people
alone because it is too heavy for me . . . . And if Thou deal thus
with me, kill me, I pray Thee, out of hand, if I have found favor in
Thy sight; and let me not see my wretchedness.

— As you remember, the teacher continued, God, disgusted with
His people, promises them meat. You will eat meat, He tells them in-
dignantly, not one day, not two days, not ten or twenty days, but

even a whole month. Until it comes out at your nostrils, and it be
loathsome unto you . . . . And there went forth a wind from the
Lord, and brought quails from the sea, and let them fall by the
camp . . . . Two cubits high upon the face of the earth . . . . And
the people stood up all that day and all that night and all the next
day and they gathered the quails; he that gathered least, gathered
ten omers; and they spread them all abroad for themselves round
about the camp . . . . And while the flesh was between their teeth,
ere it was chewed, the wrath of the Lord was kindled against the
people, and the Lord smote the people with a very great
plague . . . . And he called the name of that place *Kivroth
hata'avah* because there they buried the people that lusted.

Amnon and Tamar

Someone asked about a biblical story that deals with a case of lust
and rape in high places, or with what happens to love when it degenerates into lust — the story of Tamar, sister of Absalom, the son of David the King. She was raped by her half brother, Amnon.

With some encouragement, the student told the story. "Amnon, as
we are told in the Bible, not only loved Absalom's beautiful sister, but
was literally lovesick. His lovesickness even became visible to the eye,
for he began to lose weight, and his face was fallen. When his closest
friend, Yehonadav, asked him what was wrong, Amnon told him of
his love for Tamar, and sought advice. Yehonadav advised him to
feign sickness and stay in bed till his father, the king, came to visit
him. When this came to pass, Yehonadav said, Amnon should tell the
king that if only Tamar could come and prepare some meat cakes for
him, he would feel better. The king then visited Amnon and complied

with his request. Tamar came to Amnon's lodgings and baked meat cakes for him, but when she was about to serve them, he said no, not in the presence of the servants. 'Let everybody leave!' he commanded, and everybody left. Tamar tried to serve him the meat cakes but he took hold of her. Now let me read from the biblical text:

> He took hold of her and said, Come lie with me, my sister . . . . And she answered him, Nay, my brother, do not force me, for no such thing ought to be done in Israel; do not thou do this folly . . . . And I, whither shall I cause my shame to go? And as far as thee, thou shall be as one of the knaves of Israel. Now, therefore, I pray thee, speak unto the king, for he will not withhold me from thee . . . . But he would not hearken to her voice; being stronger than her, he forced her, and lay with her. . . . Then Amnon hated her exceedingly, so that the hatred wherewith he hated her was greater than the love wherewith he loved her. And Amnon said unto her, Arise, be gone . . . . And she said unto him: Let there be no cause for this great evil in the other that thou didst to me . . . . But he would not hearken unto her . . . . Then he called his servant that ministered unto him, and said: Put now this woman out from me, and bolt the door after her . . . . And she had a garment of divers flowers upon her; for with such robes were the king's daughters that were virgins appareled . . . . Then his servant brought her out and bolted the door after her . . . . And Tamar put ashes on her head, and rent the garment of divers flowers that was on her, and laid her hand on her head and went on, crying.

"It is a frightening story," the student commented, "in which everything, absolutely everything is told, yet something is inexplicable: What exactly happened so suddenly to the lovesick Amnon?"

In his answer the teacher observed first that this story, like many others dealing with human emotions, was so great and so moving because in a few words everything was told and told in a manner that transcended style and detail.

—Heine described the sensation of reading the Bible: In the Bible, he said, no trace of art is evident. Its style is that of a notebook in which the Absolute Spirit, seemingly without the assistance of any individual human being, has jotted down the events of the day with the same factual accuracy with which we list our laundry. One cannot pass judgment on its style; one can only observe its effect on our minds.

Sin as an Anti-Aesthetic Experience

— What happened to Amnon, the teacher went on, is explained in
a remarkable work by the Rav (Rabbi Yosef Dov Soloveitchik of Boston) titled "On Repentance." The Rav draws our attention to the neg-
lected fact that, on many major occasions, scripture describes the
reaction of the people to sins they have committed as one of *mourning*, as it is written, "And the people mourned." What did they
mourn? They mourned their purity, their sanctity, their wholeness. A
man in mourning, as commonly understood, mourns over a dear soul
that *he* has *lost*; the sinner mourns over *his lost soul*. In this kind of
mourning, the Rav stresses, there is always an element of masochism:
The sinner begins to feel a disgust with himself, a loathing of himself,
an aversion, a masochistic self-hatred. The sin itself becomes an
abomination, aesthetically — much more than morally — nauseating.
We suddenly ask ourselves, as we mourn our lost purity, how we could
have done it. "We are amazed at our souls," the Rav quotes the saintly
author of *Haye Adam*. "How was this abomination possible?" We are,
after all, blessed with a sense of beauty, with aesthetic souls, with a
craving for the refined — how could we have defiled ourselves? To illustrate how sin is transmuted into self-disgust, that is to say, how sin
degenerates into its own punishment, the Rav resorts to this very biblical story, that of Amnon and Tamar.

Amnon's Great Hatred

— He makes an observation, continued the teacher, that is of paramount psychological importance. The sinner, he says, is quite often
pursued not so much by the good impulse in himself, which is usually
weak and retreating, but by the much more aggressive, assertive and,
indeed, devious aesthetic sense. The Bible, when telling us the story of
Amnon and Tamar, makes sure that we know she was beautiful. We
also know how totally Amnon was under her spell. A minute before
that horrible sin he committed, Amnon, as we can well imagine, was
utterly convinced that Tamar represented the utmost in beauty, in
grace, in refinement. But then, immediately following the rape, Amnon began to hate her "with a hatred that was greater than the love
with which he loved her." He began to hate her, says the Rav, not be-

cause of sudden remorse and pangs of conscience, but because what he had done became so abominable in his mind, so ugly, so loathsome, that her very beauty, the cause of his intoxication with her, now looked ugly to him. He began to hate himself and because of this self-hatred, he hated her.

— Sin, the Rav amplifies, has a masochistic influence on the sinner. Amnon hates himself and, in his frenzy of sudden self-hatred, he begins to hate the pure, good, innocent "cause" of his degradation, Tamar. He treats her abominably because he is trying, by treating her so, to escape an abomination he perpetrated against her, and, through her, against himself. His sin thus became the beginning of punishment. Once again we realize how the Bible is dotted with statements, albeit veiled, to the effect that evildoers are eventually punished not so much *for* as *by* their sins. Now Maimonides, the Rav says, like Rabenu Behaye and other Jewish philosophers of the Middle Ages, in speaking of "mental sicknesses" has in mind moral deficiencies, that is, sins. The idea, says the Rav, is simple: Exactly as some physical sicknesses constitute a physical pathology, so sin is a symptom of mental pathology. And since sin is a sickness, it also has the traits of a sickness. What are they? Pains. Like physical sickness, the sickness of soul penetrates the consciousness of man by means of pains. We all know, says the Rav, how many tragedies are due to the *belated arrival* of pains.

"In the case of Amnon," said a student, "there was no belated arrival of pains — if pains is the word for it — for his sense of urgency to get rid of Tamar was as obnoxious as what he had done to her. But that's what I am trying to understand: A hatred of the kind that Amnon was suddenly stricken with could conceivably have developed gradually. But whence its immediacy, its suddenness, its irrevocability? What kind of people were these?"

Biblical People

— Biblical people, the teacher replied. Larger than life, as were their passions, their lusts, and their retreats from their lusts. In addition, biblical people did not always have to wait long for their punishments. Punishments in the Bible, be they divine or human, were, quite often, on-the-spot propositions. If biblical punishments were immediate, why would not self-punishments of biblical figures also be? Have you noticed, as you read through scripture, that the Absolute Spirit, in biblical times, has actually invited us to test his immediacy?

"What do you mean by 'immediacy'?" someone asked.

— Take *shemitah*, as one striking example, the teacher explained. There are many others. But according to the Mosaic Law, the earth, as you know, must rest every seventh year; animals must rest like humans, every seventh day, and the earth must not be made to work every seventh year. This is the year of *shemitah*. But how can the earth rest, not be tilled or planted, without causing people to die of hunger? Here is where the immediacy of the divine enters. It is a phenomenon confined to the biblical era. The Transcendent becomes, as it were, imminent: If you faithfully undertake to refrain from touching the earth in the seventh year, the year of *shemitah*, says God, the harvest of the sixth year will be enough to make up for the two. This seems to me to be a case of divine immediacy, that is to say, provable, on-the-spot reward for being one with the divine Law.

"Then could the experience of the Godly at the summit of the biblical era be defined as 'provable'?" someone asked.

— Yes, the teacher exclaimed. But so could the experience of the Satanic!

About the Immortality of the Soul

"To tell the truth," someone said, "I was always bothered by the question of why scripture enters into descriptions of divine awards mostly in terms of material blessings in town and field and fails to mention the immortality of the soul as the ultimate reward for the upright life. I could never understand it."

— It does not fail to mention it, the teacher responded, but it is careful, for some reason, not to spell it out. Let me tell you how Nachmanides answers this question, in an interpretation I myself regard as nothing short of astounding.

— Nachmanides says that the Torah emphasizes the material, this-worldly aspects of reward and punishment precisely *because* we would not ordinarily assume them to be natural consequences of our obedience or disobedience to the divine Law. He raises the question whether there is any natural connection between observance of the Law and the blessing in offspring, harvest, and daily bread and replies that all these are what he calls *nissim nistarim*, invisible miracles, performed by God acting through the apparent laws of nature. By contrast, Nachmanides maintains, the immortality of the soul is a *natural* consequence of man's compliance with the divine will! Since both the soul, he says, and the Law are of divine origin, it is natural that the soul, once it attains a state of oneness with the word of God, is as deathless as the word itself. Since it is obvious, Nachmanides argues, that man's clinging to God in his lifetime imbues him with a light that is not of this world, his spiritual bliss in afterlife becomes logically consequential, almost "natural." This, in fact, is the essence of Rabbi Haim Volozhiner's concept of reward and punishment. Rabbi Haim, the great disciple of the Gaon of Vilna, rejects almost as blasphemy the idea that an almighty and all-merciful God actually avenges himself on his sinful creatures when it is too late for them to do anything about their misdeeds, that is to say, in afterlife. No, Rabbi Haim says, that is not what hell and heaven are all about. Hell or heaven begins right here, when we are alive, and we carry the hell or heaven we have built for ourselves by our deeds into eternity. The atheist Jean-Paul Sartre provides the best dramatization of Rabbi Haim's all-embracing concept of sin as its own punishment through perpetuation in the beyond in his play *No Exit*. Goethe, in his conversations with Eckermann, spoke in a similar vein on the question of immortality of the soul. "The belief in the continuity of our existence," Goethe says, "I derive out of the nature and intensity of my creativity. If I act well and relentlessly to the last moment of my life, nature is obliged, as it were, to prepare for me another form of existence if the former one is no longer in a position to contain my spirit." To this, an excited Eckermann remarked, "Who will not want to act creatively and positively till the very end if he sees in the very act of his creativity a guarantee for life eternal?"

17

The Reduced Man

Back to the Graves of Lust

The teacher opened the next class by recapitulating what had transpired, according to scripture, at a place in the desert later called "The Graves of Lust." —Superficially, he said, this is the story of people who were oddly overwhelmed by an irresistible desire for meat. It would seem to have been a relatively minor infraction, appearing even more minor in comparison with the sin of idolatry that preceded it. The protests of the Israelites against their meatless menus, moreover, were rather subdued. They complained, they cried, they demanded— nothing more. Yet this seemingly harmless demand aroused God's wrath more than outright iniquities, more even than the outrage of the golden calf. Moses himself was so embittered by the demand that he asked to die on the spot. What constituted the sin that warranted such harsh retribution?

—The Rav, the teacher went on, makes a distinction between idolatry and paganism. Idolatry, he says, actually signifies worship, ritual and cultic performances, specific acts to propitiate deities presumed to reside within the idols or to be represented by them. But paganism involves a cultural system, a manner of living. Our sages are convinced that idol worship inevitably leads to paganism, that worship influences a society's way of life, yet paganism can persist even after idol worship has been discarded. The later Greeks and Romans, having cast aside idol worship, still lived as pagans, with a pagan life-style and value system. In our day, with idol worship no longer in existence, paganism is still rampant. The pagan worships deities that represent forces in

184

nature. The deities are themselves without moral norms and make no demands on man beyond specific acts of propitiation. For man to lustily partake in nature, to uphold his nature as synonymous with existential fulfillment, is therefore an act of identifying with pagan gods. Man, in such a state, actually sees himself as coextensive with nature and craves unlimited indulgence. While in Judaism, man's divine image manifests itself in his self-control, in his overcoming nature, in paganism man *is* nature and, hence, what is possible is permissible, and to acknowledge restraints on human appetites is to interfere with human freedom.

— The Torah, according to the Rav, detested the pagan way of life even more than it hated idol worship. The latter is short-lived. It eventually collapses. One can teach, persuade, and enlighten against its validity. Yet paganism has a tremendous hold on people long after actual idol worship has been discarded. The sin of the golden calf, the Rav stresses, was idol worship; the *Kivroth hata'avah* episode, however, was paganism. It revealed that even without idol worship, paganism still exercised its hold on the people, a vestigial remnant of their long stay in Egypt. The Torah describes the gathering of the quails as an insatiable accumulation of property and the gratification of hungry senses, characteristics of paganism. "And the people stood up all that day and all the night and all the next day and they gathered the quails; he that gathered least, gathered ten omers; and they spread them all abroad for themselves round about the camp." We have here, the Rav says, desire gone berserk, a craving without any restraint.

— The text, says the Rav, speaks only of the unlimited gathering of quails. Our sages, however, tell us that it was a rebellion against all inhibitions. It expressed itself also in a repudiation of the sexual code that had just recently been prescribed on Mount Sinai. On the verse in that same chapter, "And they journeyed from God's mountain," the sages add, "What does God's mountain [symbolically] signify?" Rabbi Hama, son of Hanina, explained that they turned away from the restrictive discipline that Sinai had imposed on them. Their complaint "Who shall give us flesh?" was merely a pretext, according to Rashi, for flesh is here a euphemism for the sensual. The sentence "We remember the fish which we did eat in Egypt" refers, according to the sages, to sexual immorality, the licentiousness the Torah now restricted. "Moses heard the people weep among their families." The people were wailing, Rashi says, because of "family" matters, because the intermarriage of blood relatives was now forbidden to them. The oral tradition, as expressed by our sages, thus understood *Kivroth hata'avah*—"The Graves of Lust"—as an orgy of the senses, an idolization of unrestricted indulgence. It was what the Greeks meant by *hedone*, or what is meant today by "hedonism."

— One can argue effectively against idol worship but what does one do, the Rav asks, with paganism, which is morally nihilistic? In view of this remarkable juxtaposition of idolatry with paganism, the teacher concluded, we not only understand Moses' total exasperation with his people and the divine wrath that was poured out against them; we also understand the nature of the spiritual plague that is devouring technological society today. To equate nature with freedom, as is the grand fashion today in life, in literature, in the arts, is paganism. If our present-day civilization goes under, as it is so desperately trying to, could there be a more appropriate inscription on its gravestone than "The Graves of Lust"?

The Righteous Eateth to the Satisfying of His Soul

The next question sounded as if it had been triggered by the foregoing discussion. "How would you explain," asked someone, "that passage at the end of Proverbs 13 that says, 'The righteous eateth to the satisfying of his soul; but the belly of the wicked shall want'? The truth seems to be the opposite: The wicked person is much more likely to eat to the satisfying of his soul than the righteous. The righteous person, in fact, quite often goes hungry. Isn't that so?"

— It is, the teacher replied, and I am glad you brought up this passage immediately following our explanation of *Kivroth hata'avah*. Let me ask you, does the Bible, in Proverbs 13, dealing with the two different kinds of men, use the same term to denote the part of the body that determines satiety?

Someone replied that while the word that is used for the wicked is "belly," in the case of the righteous, the word that is used is *nefesh*, soul.

— Exactly! the teacher exclaimed. *Nefesh* is the lowest form of soul.

Above the *nefesh* is the *ruah* and above this is the supersoul, *neshamah*. The enjoyment of food belongs, one must assume, to the realm of the *nefesh*. The righteous man, however, having other delights besides the physical, the delights of the *ruah* and the *neshamah*, does not need very much to satisfy his *nefesh*. The wicked man, by contrast, who has only one delight — the material — and has subjugated his whole *nefesh* to the belly, never has enough. His belly becomes his *nefesh*, and when the belly replaces the *nefesh*, man knows no other cravings but the physical and the material. Can one ever satisfy such cravings? The physical man's idea of never having enough often spoils all joy of having it.

Heavenly and Earthly Pleasures

— Reb Mendel of Kotzk, as a young man, made a pilgrimage to see his rebbe in a distant town. He went on foot, in wintertime, a bundle slung over his back. Suddenly, a sumptuous carriage, drawn by four horses, stopped at his side. It belonged to the rich man of Reb Mendel's town, who recognized the pious young man and offered to take him along since they were going in the same direction. Sitting in the upholstered carriage was a genuine pleasure. Reb Mendel was given blankets to cover his knees and was even offered a drink, which he did not refuse. The rich man, at the same time, was enjoying himself on piece after piece of roast goose and sip after sip of the finest vodka. Suddenly Reb Mendel turned to his host with a strange question: "Tell me, please, what are your earthly pleasures?" The rich man looked at Reb Mendel in astonishment. "What a question! Can't you see? The carriage and the horses, the goose and the vodka, the blankets and the coachman — do you mean to say that all this is not enough for a fellow like you?" "You don't seem to understand," teased Reb Mendel. "These are your *heavenly* pleasures; this is the *acme* of your pleasures, but where your earthly, your worldly pleasures are, that's what I want to know!"

I and Thou

— I want to implant in your memory that remarkable maxim by Reb Mendel of Kotzk about the meaning of man: "As long as I am I

because I am I and you are you because you are you, then I am I and
you are you; but if I am I because you are you, and you are you because I am I, then I am not I and you are not you!"

The Reduced Man

Someone in the audience raised a question about the meaning of
the ninth passage in the second chapter of Isaiah. It is usually translated, he said, as follows: "And the mean man boweth down and the
great man humbleth himself; therefore forgive them not." "Why
should a man be regarded as 'mean' if he 'boweth down,'" asked the
student, "and why is it a sin if the great man 'humbleth himself'?
Then, immediately afterwards, Isaiah appeals to God not to forgive
them for sins that don't appear to be sins at all! And we are even more
at a loss to understand the nature of these sins in view of the eleventh
passage of that same chapter, which says that God will punish those
sinners with that which, according to all accepted interpretations,
they have *already* used to punish themselves: 'The lofty looks of man
shall be humbled and the haughtiness of man shall be bowed down,
and the Lord alone shall be exalted on that day.' But if the 'mean man
boweth down,' as mentioned in the ninth passage, and 'the great man
humbleth himself,' then what on earth is the difference between what
these supposedly sinful men do to themselves and what God Almighty
promises to do to them by way of punishment? What kind of people is
that chapter trying to depict?"

Before explaining why he found this question extremely relevant,
the teacher made an extended, general comment about translations
of the Bible. — To do justice to the prophetic stance of scripture, he
noted, a sense of prophecy was needed *even to translate it*. Except for
Onkelos's translation of the Bible into Aramaic, there is no translation, except, perhaps, for the Septuagint, that does not distort it in
one way or another. Nor could it be otherwise, the teacher explained.
There are many prophecies that reach out toward the end of days, so
that their meaning could not have been grasped in terms of the human predicament as experienced, say, during the reign of King
James. Thus it came to pass that prophecies dealing with circumstances that were not identifiable in historical terms a few hundred years
ago were translated in a manner that unwittingly made a mockery of

their meaning, and the puzzling passages in Isaiah are typical of this situation.

— What kind of people is this chapter trying to depict? the teacher repeated the question. First note how Isaiah describes the social conditions that gave or will give rise — in prophecy, we must remember, past, present, and future are often laid out on the same plateau — to these people: It is a state of triumphant materiality, of the worship of externality, of intoxication with the visible, the provable, the showable, as it is written, "Their land also is full of silver and gold, neither is there any end to their treasures; their land is also full of horses; neither is there any end to their chariots . . . . Their land also is full of idols; *they worship the work of their own hands,* that which their own fingers have made." Immediately afterwards, the teacher continued, comes the description of the type of man who is bound to emerge as a direct result of such a state of intoxication with matter: *the reduced man.*

— Let me explain, the teacher proceeded. We live in an era of reductionism. Reductionist science, which for a couple of centuries hammered away at the idea that man is "nothing but" his biological components, did not realize that such a man would be a *reduced* man, a "nothing but-nick," to use an expression of Viktor Frankl. And it is not only specialization that brought about this state — specialization is inevitable in a technological life order — but *totalization*: the idea that there is something akin to universality about the *totality* of specialization. What is dangerous, Dr. Frankl writes, is the attempt of a man who is an expert, say, in the field of biology, to understand and explain human beings *exclusively* in terms of biology. At the moment at which totality is claimed for the part, Dr. Frankl argues, biology becomes biologism, psychology becomes psychologism, and sociology becomes sociologism. In other words, at that moment, science is reduced to ideology. Dr. Frankl tells us in his *Will to a Meaning* that he once came across a quotation defining man as "*nothing but* a complex biochemical mechanism powered by a combustion system which energizes computers with prodigious storage facilities for retaining encoded information." To this Dr. Frankl observed that as a neurologist he would approve of using the computer as a model, say, for the activity of the central nervous system. Thus in a certain sense the statement is valid: Man *is* a computer. However, at the same time,

he is infinitely more than a computer! The statement is fatally errone-
ous insofar as it defines man as *nothing but* a computer. He is also
defined as "nothing but" a bundle of nerves, "nothing but" a pleasure
principle, "nothing but" a branch on the monkey tree, "nothing but"
an instinctual reaction, and the like. Where is man after all these
"nothing but's"? Let me tell you a joke about this, he said.

The Cat and the Butter

— Two Jews, he began, who were neighbors, came to the rabbi with
a grave problem. His neighbor's cat, one of them claimed, had
sneaked into his kitchen and eaten up five pounds of butter. The
other denied the charge. "Maybe half an ounce, an ounce, but five
pounds!" "Five pounds!" the first man insisted. "All right," said the
rabbi, "bring me the cat." They brought him the cat. "Now," the rabbi said, "bring me a pair of scales." They brought him the scales. The
rabbi placed the cat on one scale and a five-pound weight on the
other, and to everybody's surprise, the cat weighed exactly five pounds.
"Now," the rabbi exclaimed, "we have the butter, but where on earth
is the cat?"

The class roared. — Times are so critical, Ariel Halevi said almost
apologetically, the subject at hand so serious, that we forget to laugh.
But we shouldn't, really. Can you recall a passage in Psalms in which
the man who sours everything is equated with him who wrongs everybody?

Of Him Who Clouds Happiness

— The passage in question, the teacher said, appears in the seventy-
first psalm: "O my God, let me escape the might of the lawless, the
hand of the wrongdoer and of him who clouds happiness." Now, the
teacher went on, this passage is mistranslated in the King James version, as in almost every other, where the word *hometz* — "sour" or
"sourer" — is interpreted as "cruel man." But that is incorrect. The
man who sours everything may possess a streak of cruelty, but he cannot be described as a cruel man. Samson Rafael Hirsh, a wonderful
interpreter of the Psalms, thinks the word *hometz* means "he who
clouds happiness," which is true, of course, because the man who

sours everything is, by definition, a killjoy. But it seems to me, the teacher went on, that in all faithfulness to the biblical text, which we must guard like the apple of our eye, the meaning of the two biblical words that describe the two kinds of people one should beware of, *Meavel vehometz*, is, as I have suggested, "the man who wrongs everybody and the man who sours everything." Now to return to the reduced man.

And Man Grew Small

—The kind of man about whom Isaiah speaks immediately after setting forth the conditions that were conducive to his emergence is neither one who "boweth down" nor one who "humbleth himself." The whole passage is mistranslated and misunderstood. Isaiah speaks in this passage of the man *who reduced himself*; about the man who grew small, who diminished himself on account of his self-sufficiency and inert self-satisfaction. He speaks of the man who grew so unbearably arrogant, so insufferably haughty in the limitedness of his self-sufficiency that there can be no forgiveness for him. "Therefore, forgive them not!" the prophet cries out.

There was a pause before the teacher continued. —Nietzsche, for whom I have a boundless admiration in spite of the wild flights of his genius, called our time "niggardly." "It isn't your sins," he said, "that cry unto heaven; it's your niggardliness—it's your niggardliness even in sin that cries unto heaven." And Kierkegaard says something similar: "Let others complain that our times are sinful; I say they are *paltry!*" The psychosocial arrogance of modern man, which manages to go hand in hand with his biological "nothing-but-ness," may well invite his doom, since it makes his diminution inevitable. This, my friends, is what the second chapter of Isaiah is all about. "And the small man," it says, "grew low, and the big man grew small; therefore forgive them not." Only in this way can we understand the later statement that "the lofty looks of man shall be humbled and the haughtiness of men shall be bowed down."

Lest Thou Diminish Me

—"O Lord, correct me, but with judgment; not in Thine anger, *lest thou diminish me*," read the teacher from Jeremiah 10.

— I am aware, he said, that according to the usual translation, *pen-tamiteini*, means "lest Thou bring me to nothing." But *tamiteini* literally means "diminish me." The most tragic of prophets pleads here not to be diminished by affliction. Affliction, like inert self-satisfaction, uproots the soul and closes for it the gates of perception. In the very valley of the shadow of death, Jeremiah prayed that he might not stop growing!

At Evening Time There Shall Be Light

The teacher went on with a comment on the words of Zechariah. Here, he said, the prophet says to progress, "You are a lie!" Even without prophecy we would have known it by now, but prophecy knew it long before all the silly humanists treated progress as a deity. According to prophecy, history does not "progress" toward a better world. To the contrary, history will fulfill itself when the world, going from bad to worse, enters a period of darkness that will signal the birth of a supernatural light. It is not that the sun of history is progressively on the rise, but — and this is the heart of the prophetic message of redemption — when the sun of history is about to set, "At evening time there will be light."

— The prophet Amos, the teacher continued, spoke of the first stage: a sad, confused stage of soul that will create a sense of spiritual homelessness among an increasing number of people, particularly the young. The prophet Zefania speaks of the second stage. It will, on the one hand, spell an end to the muddled language that prevails in the world of international relations, and, on the other hand, will introduce a sense of ultimate clarity about the nature of the sought-after word, as it is written, "And I shall bestow upon the nations a *clear* language that they may call together upon the name of the Lord." *Clarity*, then, is the promise of the second stage. The third and final stage is that envisioned by Isaiah: wisdom filling the earth like waters that fill the sea. This wondrous prophecy speaks of a new ocean, perhaps an eternalized "oceanic feeling," that will flood the consciousness of man and endow him with a sense of limitlessness. To the two foundations of the world, the liquid and the solid, there will be added an equally *provable* spiritual dimension. And I say "provable" advisedly. There is a line in the Bible that suggests that on the summit of spiritual awareness, the spiritual, by a process of divine dialectics, becomes provable without losing its quality of infinity. I am referring to one line in the second book of Moses, which describes how a whole people experienced a state of the highest spiritual awareness on perceiving the voice of the Lord thundering down from Mount Sinai. "And the entire people," it says, "*saw* the voice." How can one *see* a voice? But when wisdom, divine wisdom, fills the earth, even for a moment, one can *see* voices and *hear* colors.

— And not even a whole word is required for this staggering vision, but merely a point, a period.

A Point

— The full stop, the period, according to the Gaon of Vilna, conveys something very important about King David. David, as we all know, sins with Bathsheba. Immediately afterward, Nathan the prophet comes to the king armed with the angry word of God. Parenthetically I want to add, the teacher said, that while in eighteenth-century France statesmen told kings "You are gods," three thousand years ago prophets told kings in Israel "You are sinners!" The prophet unmercifully chastises the king, and David replies, simply, "I have sinned against God!" These few words were apparently sufficient, for the seemingly implacable prophet told David, "The Lord also has put away thy sin." How is this possible? The Gaon of Vilna replies that the answer lies in one point, one full stop in the midst of an empty space between words. Open your Bibles, the teacher said, and turn to 2 Samuel 12, passage 13.

The class soon pinpointed not only the passage, but the point. It stands there alone between David's few words to Nathan, "I have sinned," and Nathan's reply, "The Lord also has put away thy sin."

— And it means, the teacher explained, according to the Gaon, that David, after having said "I have sinned," could not continue. He broke down. Long pause. A full stop. Only then did the prophet speak of forgiveness.

18

There Can Be No Depth Without the Way to the Depth

The Witch of Endor

The teacher opened his next lecture by saying that he wanted to talk to the class about the Witch of Endor. — It is one of those stories, he said, that have haunted me since childhood. When I was ten years old or so, I came across a ballad about the Witch of Endor written by the Hebrew poet Saul Chernikhovsky, and I still remember the opening lines: "In the dead of the night, with no arrow or sling/ On a light horse to Endor came Saul the King."

— We all remember the sad story: The unhappy king abandoned by God, besieged by the Philistines, tries to establish a contact with the Supernatural so as to find out what is in store for him. Since there was no way for him to do it through prophecy - the prophet Samuel was dead and the priests had been killed by the embittered king — he tries to do it through witchcraft. Israel's first king, who had burned witches at the stake, now goes to a witch for help. He asks her to conjure up for him the soul of his first mentor and anointer, the prophet Samuel. Though the king comes in disguise, she hesitates. "You know," she tells him, "what Saul has done to those that have familiar spirits. Why then do you lay a snare for my life?" Saul swears by God that no punishment will come to her on account of that sin, and the woman asks him who she is to conjure up. "Bring me up Samuel," Saul says. The woman, the Bible tells us, brings him up not only in voice, but in image, and on seeing him she cries with a loud voice saying, "Why did you deceive me? You are Saul!" The king tells her not to fear and asks her what she sees. "A godlike man," she replies, "covered with a mantle." Perceiving that it is Samuel, Saul stoops with his face to the ground. Samuel asks him why he has disquietened him to bring him up, and Saul replies that he is sore distressed. "The Philistines make war against me and God is departed from me, and answers me no more . . . . I called upon thee that thou mayest make known unto me what I shall do?" Samuel's reply is clear: "Tomorrow shall thou and thy sons be with me."

—This, you will all agree, the teacher continued, is a tragic and mystifying story dealing with the immortality of the soul as seen from a most unexpected angle, namely, from the angle of why one should not indulge in speculations about it. Is it not amazing, the teacher asked, that the only story—and I say *story*, not *statement*—dealing with the hereafter as a state of consciousness of the departed soul is told in the Bible in a manner that involved a transgression?

"It is even more amazing," someone interjected, "that the prophet Samuel's soul, as the Bible tells us, was conjured up *by way of* a transgression!"

—You have touched on the heart of the matter! the teacher exclaimed. And I can answer it only sketchily, for I do not know the full answer.

Ob and *Yideoni*

The teacher spent the rest of the evening clarifying the meaning of sorcery, as opposed to prophecy, in biblical times. *Ob* and *Yideoni* were the biblical names for the worshiped powers of sorcery, whose spread was almost epidemic. The prohibition of sorcery and witchcraft was a result of the dangerous spiritual seductiveness inherent in the magical—black-magical—ability of the practitioners of sorcery to contact the hereafter without purity of soul—not only without purity, but with the active help of *impurity*. Yet this is the whole point, the teacher explained: Man in a state of total moral impurity, in a state of *tum'ah*, "defilement," attracts the powers of the Satanic to the same degree that total purity attracts the powers of the Divine. But since the first is easier to achieve than the second—for there has been, since the Fall, a definite tilt toward evil in the world—there is the danger that this tilt will be aggravated by *evil drawing strength from the supernatural*. The teacher suggested that the class acquaint itself with the history and impact of sorcery and black magic in medieval Germany and with the way this black supernaturalism helped shape Hitler's mind and bring him to power. He mentioned the fact that Jornandes, during the sixth century, insisted that the Huns, ancestors of present-day Germans, were begot by demons who, in his words, coupled like incubi with the evil witches of barbarism. The teacher also drew attention to the fact that most tyrants, even Marxists tyrants, were known to be superstitious. Even people who are professed nonbelievers would hesitate to proceed on a road that had just been crossed by a black cat. Most people are superstitious. Black magic is not superstition, the teacher said, but superstition makes people easy prey for black magic. The Bible tells of a worker of black magic, Balaam, whose power of prophecy was so great that the sages say that he could see, and foresee, by looking into "the black mirror" of sorcery, the same things that Moses could see by looking into the "bright mirror" of prophecy. Sorcery, the sages say in a most daring statement on the subject, "challenges the authority of the '*Yeshivah shel ma'alah*,' the Council of the Most High."

"It sounds like duality," someone said diffidently.

— *Complementarity*, the teacher explained. The law of complementarity, according to Kabbalah, embraces the natural and the supernatural world.

God Also Has Set the One Over Against the Other

— Have you ever given any thought to the meaning of the seventh chapter of Ecclesiastes? the teacher asked. He went on without waiting for an answer. It means that there is a law of complementarity, which is the basis of creation and the foundation of man as a creature endowed with free will. Even science — and I stress the "even" — has recently come around to this view. In biblical thought, however, this law extends even to the hereafter.

"Meaning what?" someone asked.

— Let me ask *you* something, the teacher replied. What do the biblical words *sheol* and *shahat* mean to you?

"Two different words for the grave," was the answer.

— But there is another word for "grave," *kever*. What is the difference between *sheol, shahat,* and *kever?* the teacher asked.

Someone replied that the first two were rarely if ever used in the Bible to describe the final resting place of righteous people.

— Right, the teacher said. Both *sheol* and *shahat* seem to mean a place not of final rest, but of hellish restlessness. In the forty-ninth chapter of Psalms, there are references to both *shahat* and *sheol* as something much worse than the grave: The first says, "And he will live on in eternity and will not see *shahat*; the second, "But God will redeem my soul from the power of *sheol* when He takes me to Himself, *selah.*" *Sheol* and *shahat* both stand in scripture for a netherworld that is given over, at least temporarily, to the very same power of evil the person has served in his lifetime. The Kabbalah, we should remember, refers to Satan not just as "the adversary," "the seducer," or "the evil one," but the *Sitrah ahara*, literally, "the other side" — the dark side of Divinity.

Vayitzer

— I mentioned before, the teacher continued after a pause, that a single point in scripture, a full stop, may tell a whole story. Now let me tell you something about the story told by a single *letter* in the Bible: the letter *yod*. The Maharal of Prague speaks about it with regard to a comment by the sages on the word *vayitzer* — "and He created." The word is spelled with two *yods* when it comes to the creation of man, but is spelled with only one when it speaks of the creation of animals. The Maharal discloses the reason: The double *yod* stands for the two *yetzer's* — urges — in man, the good and the evil. In an animal, however, which has no freedom of choice, no free will, there is only one *yod*, that is to say, one urge, the instinctual, and nothing else.

Complementarity

The teacher opened a new subject. — Nothing, he said, is more foreign to my way of thinking than the apologetic attitude of some "religionists," as I call them, toward science. I am referring to statements that can still be heard here and there to the effect that science can be, after all, quite comfortable with God, as if God's comfort with a morally neutral science were a foregone conclusion. Whenever there is a collision between science and religion, said the teacher, science must prove itself, not religion. To illustrate, here is a story about an encounter between the late David Ben Gurion, then prime minister of Israel, and the saintly Hazon Ish of B'nei Brak.

The Two Wagons

— One day, the teacher said, David Ben Gurion came to see the Hazon Ish in B'nei Brak. The prime minister wanted to discuss with the universally recognized Torah authority the question of religion and state in Israel. The state was only about a dozen years old or so, but it already found itself on a collision course with some basic laws of the Torah. What to do? Ben Gurion, a secular man with an uncanny flair for the Bible, put the question to the Hazon Ish, and elicited the following answer: According to the Law, the saintly old man told the prime minister, when two wagons, one heavy laden, the other lightweight, are traveling in opposite directions on a narrow road and refuse to give way to each other, the one with the minimal load has to give way to that which is fully loaded. "If you will agree, as I assume," said the Hazon Ish, "that the load carried by my wagon is infinitely heavier than yours, you know the answer." Two maxims always come to my mind when that load is discussed, the teacher went on. I hope they will come to yours, too, in similar circumstances. One is by Goethe: "The truth was discovered long ago." The other is by Elie Benamozegh: "Antiquity is the most infallible sign of truth." Both these thoughts imply the idea that there is a road, a way of the spirit, rugged, dangerous, yet unmistakable and indispensable, that leads from eternity to here, and that knows no short cuts. In the same sense the Hazon Ish used the metaphor of the road.

There Can Be No Depth Without
the Way to the Depth

— I have just read something memorable by Paul Tillich, the teacher went on, about "the way." Something very tragic, he says, happens in all periods of man's spiritual life: Truths, deep and powerful, discovered by the greatest geniuses at the price of great suffering, become shallow and superficial when used in daily discussion. How is that possible, Paul Tillich asks. It is possible, he says, because *"there can be no depth without the way to the depth."* Truth without the way to truth is dead. Tillich offers the example of the student who knows the content of the hundred most important books of world history, but whose spiritual life remains as shallow as it ever was. He juxtaposes the well-read student with the intelligent worker who performs a mechanical task day by day, who suddenly asks himself: "What does it *mean*, what I am doing? What does it mean for my life? What *is* the *meaning* of my life?" Because he asks these questions, Tillich states in truth, the man is on the way—on the *way*, the teacher repeated emphatically, into depth, whereas the other fellow, the student, dwells on the surface of things, among petrified bodies, conjured up by some spiritual earthquake of the past.

He Will Set the Teeth of the Nations at an Edge

—You remember, I am sure, the teacher said, the word that Isaiah uses to describe the sensation of "teeth set at an edge": "The fathers have eaten unripe fruit and the teeth of the children are set at an edge"?

"*Tikhena*," someone answered. "And the teeth of the children '*tikhena*.'"

—Right, the teacher said. To translate this one Hebrew word into English, you need *six* words: "will be set at an edge." Now tell me this: Has it occurred to you that a variation of the same word appears in Jacob's blessing to Judah?

"'*Yikhat*'?" a student asked incredulously.

—*Yikhat*, the teacher nodded.

"Meaning what?" someone asked.

—Meaning our entire history, the teacher replied. There are an infinite number of translations and interpretations of this amazing prophecy pronounced by the patriarch whose life prefigures, as it were, Jewish history. But all I will tell you now is this: Since the key to the passage is the word *yikhat*, and since *yikhat* is a word that means

setting teeth at an edge, the blessing that Jacob bestowed on Judah before he died should be read like this: "Till the coming of Shilo"—another word, as we all know, for the Messiah—"he [Judah] will set the
teeth of the nations at an edge." When I visited the United Nations,
the teacher noted, it was during a heated debate over Israel. Watch-
ing the faces of the vast majority of its members, I knew exactly—no, I
saw exactly the fulfillment of Jacob's prophecy about Judah: Those
faces were faces of people whose teeth were set at an edge by Judah's
national existence.

The Animal Soul

The class was about to adjourn for the year when an elderly man
told the teacher that his reference earlier in the class to the biblical
law of complementarity brought to his mind a passage about man and
beast in scripture whose meaning eluded him. This was a passage in
Proverbs 12, he said, that states, "The righteous man knows the soul
(*nefesh*) of his animal, but the mercy of the wicked is cruel." "I am
aware," he said, "that the passage is usually translated 'The righteous
man regardeth the life of his animal,' and so forth. But if that is the
meaning of the first part of the passage, its second half doesn't make
sense. It says that the mercy of the wicked is cruel. Cruel to whom? If
the first part deals simply with noncruelty to animals, the second part,
which must then deal with its opposite, would imply that the wicked
are bound to show cruelty to animals, which is not at all the case, as
we all know. Hitler, for example, was known for his tenderness to
dogs—"
The teacher nodded. —Rabbi Eliyahu Lupian, he said, a latter-
day Mussar sage, interprets this passage to mean not that the righteous knows the soul of his animal, as the literal translation would
suggest, but—listen!—*that the righteous man knows his animal-soul.*
Nefesh behemtoh, "the soul of his animal," is thus translated "of the
animal *in* him." I hardly have to tell you that if the passage is thus
translated, we can easily understand its second part: "But the mercy
of the wicked is cruel." Since the wicked does not realize the extent to
which his animal soul holds sway over him, even his mercies can have
no meaning, for they are deceptive and short-lived.

The Fall of Man

The biblical account of the Fall of Man came up at the last class almost as a summary of what had been learned in the course of the year. The teacher asked what bothered the group most about the story of the Fall of Man as related in the Bible. Someone replied that the serpent, according to the biblical story, did not lie. Why, then, was he cursed? "The woman says unto the serpent that of the fruit of the tree which is in the midst of the garden, 'God hath said, Ye shall not eat, neither shall you touch it, lest ye die.' To which the serpent replies, 'Ye shall not surely die.... For God doth know that in the day ye eat thereof, your eyes shall be opened, and you shall be like gods, knowing good and evil.' So they ate of the fruit of the forbidden tree," the man went on, "but didn't die. The serpent, in other words, was right. Why, then, was he cursed? For telling the truth?"

— I shall tell you, the teacher began, how two great men, one a giant of Hasidism, whom I have quoted before, and the other a great philosopher see this question. This divine account of the Fall of Man is so fraught with mystery that it will never be fully answered, or fully understood. The serpent was cursed, said the Hasidic Seer of Lublin, because it tainted the truth of temptation with a lie and thus distorted the word of God. It is God's will, says the seer, that in the process of temptation, His word, and whatever impels man to act in contradiction to it, shall stand fearlessly and openly face to face. His seal is truth. Thus the first two human beings, Adam and Eve, were originally projections of a divine truth. It is written that the serpent spoke to Eve and said, "And you shall be like gods, knowing good and evil." Did not the first human beings, the seer asks, know good and evil even before this? And he replies: They knew good and evil concerning things which the Holy One desired that they might or might not come to pass. They knew good and evil, more specifically, even as a human being, in his merely and purely human manifestation, knows them. The serpent, however, said that *not until man became like God would he know good and evil!* This clearly is another kind of knowing from the merely human knowing. For it is written in Isaiah, "He Who makes peace and creates evil." If He, Himself, creates it, it cannot be something He desires that it be not. And what is this evil that God creates? the seer asks. The evil that God creates, he replies, is the power — the human power — to *do that which He wishes may not come to pass.*

Did the Serpent Speak the Truth?

The teacher went on: — What the seer says, in essence, is known, and we mentioned it on another occasion: Had He not created this original evil, no one could commit a sin against Him. But he desires His creatures to be able to oppose Him. That is the whole point. He has given His creatures freedom of choice. But the kind of evil the serpent had in mind when he seduced the first humans was another kind of evil than that which Adam and Eve knew. One *can know this other kind of evil only if one creates it.* Consequently, the serpent, in essence, said this: "You will know good and evil like one who creates both; you will know good and evil not merely as something you are to do and something else you are not to do, but as two forms of being that are as contradictory to each other as light to darkness. Did the serpent speak the truth or did he lie to the first humans? the seer asks. God Himself later confirms that the serpent did not lie. Nevertheless, his words were not true, either. The serpent uttered a lying truth. We discussed the meaning of a lying truth before in another context, but it bears repeating. The world we live in is falling apart on account of lying truths. In his short reign as "master of things" man has brought himself and his universe to the brink of destruction. Never in all recorded history, says Will Herberg, has the collapse of the hopes of a civilization taken place so suddenly, almost within one generation. The Seer of Lublin lived long before the collapse we are witnessing today, long before Swinburne's "Hymn to Man." Yet what can be more relevant and revealing than an interpretation of the Fall of Man as his "rise" to independence from God? There is no difference between the serpent's idea of man as the autonomous creator of good and evil and Swinburne's summary of nineteenth-century exaltation of this autonomy.

Knowledge and Death

Now the teacher opened Lev Shestov's *Rome and Jerusalem.* — One of Shestov's basic tenets was a total distrust of autonomous knowledge and self-sufficient reason as expressed in a morally neutral science. The question was raised here, said the teacher, of God's not having kept His word, so to speak, to the first human beings when He warned them that they would die when they ate of the forbidden fruit. Shestov makes the point that *indeed they are dying!* But does it not say "on the day you eat . . . you will surely die"? Yet they did not die on that day, did they? No, they did not. But a day of God is a millennium, as it is written in Psalms: "For a thousand years in Thine eyes are but as yesterday when it is past." So that if the story of the Fall of Man, as we believe, prefigured man's destiny to the end of days, the first human beings who succumbed to the seduction of autonomous knowledge, or self-sufficient reason, against the most stern divine warnings did not have to die on the spot, but brought on themselves a self-pronounced death sentence that they are now slowly executing.

— Now, "God planted in paradise the tree of life and tree of knowledge of good and evil, and He said to man: From every tree of paradise you may eat; however, from the tree of knowledge of good and evil you shall not eat, for on the day you eat thereof you shall surely die."A relationship is thus established, Shestov states, between the fruit of the tree of knowledge and death. God's words here do not mean that man will be punished for having disobeyed, but that knowledge, that is to say, the self-sufficiency of autonomous knowledge, conceals, *within itself,* death. This appears beyond doubt, Shestov argues, if we recall the circumstances in which the Fall took place. The serpent, craftiest of the animals created by God, asks the woman something like this: "Why has God forbidden you to eat of all the fruits of the trees of paradise?" And when the woman replies that God has forbidden them to eat of the fruit of only a single tree that they might not die, the serpent answers: "You shall not die, but God knows that on the day you eat of those fruits, your eyes will be opened and you will be like gods, knowing good and evil." "Your eyes will be opened," says the serpent. "You will die," says God. Thus the metaphysics of knowledge in Genesis is strictly tied to the metaphysics of being, according to Shestov. If God has spoken truly, knowledge — self-sufficient, autonomous knowledge — leads to death. If the serpent has spoken truly, knowledge makes man like God. This, Shestov concludes, was the question posed before the first man, and the one posed before us now.

— Most pious thinkers of the Middle Ages, the teacher went on, could not for a moment admit to the thought that truth was on the side of the serpent. Only the Gnostics dared to declare openly that it was God, not the serpent, Who had "deceived" man. Hegel was not at all embarrassed to say that the serpent had spoken the truth to the first man and that the fruit of the tree of knowledge became the source of philosophy for all time. And this is true, of course, the teacher said, for as long as reason alone remains "the prince and judge of all things," we cannot escape the conclusion that the serpent was right.

— It was Nietzsche, in his merciless treatment of Socratic reason — he even called Socrates "the great deceiver," a title reserved for the serpent — who was one of the first to realize the curse of self-sufficient rational knowledge. Like the first man, both Socrates and Spinoza allowed themselves to be seduced by the promises of the tempter. By doing so, Shestov says, they have actually exchanged the fruits of the tree of life for those of the tree of knowledge. This is to say, the teacher amplified, they have exchanged the things that are not in our power for those we think *are* in our power. Having stretched out his hand toward the tree of rational knowledge, to the exclusion of any other, man has forever lost his freedom, for autonomous reason alone, the father of autonomous knowledge, cannot possibly guarantee that the ability to choose between good and evil, which still flickers in man, will endow him with the *intuitive* and *poetic* knowledge — that is to say, with the *wisdom* — to know what good really is.

"But what, in your view, constitutes a condition for the rise of man?" someone asked.

And I Shall Cleanse Their Blood

— It is one thing, the teacher replied, if by the rise of man we mean his redemption at the end of days, but it is something entirely different if we mean the illumination of the few at *any* time through poetic knowledge. We have said on other occasions that the prophets see redemption at the end of days as a state of interhuman consolation that takes place as a result of a supernatural change in human nature. Paramount among these prophecies is Isaiah's grand vision of the wolf dwelling with the lamb. But there is also a passage at the end of Joel that speaks of the very same thing, though in entirely different terms: "And I shall cleanse their blood that I did not cleanse; for the Lord dwelleth in Zion." The God of the Bible does not cleanse man, as we clearly learn in the divine attributes that Moses enumerates in the hour of his supernal illumination: "And to cleanse He does not cleanse," that is to say, He does not change man. He purifies — yes. But cleansing is man's job in this world. Cleansing belongs to the realm of the *nefesh*, the lowest form of soul, the animal soul, while purifying is an attribute of the *ruah*, or *neshamah*. Since, as the Bible says, "The blood is the *nefesh*," it is the blood that has to be cleansed first by man if the animal soul in him is to be freed from its animality. The cleansing of *that* soul, which was never cleansed before by the Creator, is what the messianic era is all about: "And I will cleanse their blood that I have not cleansed." That is redemption, the teacher concluded.

And I Know My Redeemer Liveth

— This cry of Job at the peak of his misery, the teacher explained, one of the most dramatic in the Bible, is the cry of a soul that knew faith as something that must be learned. I am told that in the ghetto of Slobodka, in Lithuania, a former student of its famous Mussar Yeshiva, who kept his dignity to the bitter end, would move around the barracks that housed the doomed inmates, whispering the passage of the nineteenth chapter of Job "And I know my Redeemer liveth." He whispered it quietly, soothingly, softly, like a man disclosing a sweet secret to a loved one, and I am told by a survivor that whoever saw that man and heard this whisper was ashamed to be afraid.

At War With Every Base Desire

— On the matter of poetic knowledge, a term borrowed from Jacques Maritain, the teacher went on, I will cite a few passages from Shelley. I planned to read them to you long ago; they confirm the universal nature of the intuitive truths of great souls. The very idea expressed by Shelley that the state of mind produced by the most delicate sensibility is at war with every base desire is biblical and serves as the foundation of Mussar:

> We are aware of evanescent visitations of thought and feeling, sometimes associated with place or person, sometimes regarding our own mind alone, and always arising unforeseen and departing unbidden, but elevating and delightful beyond all expression; so that even in the desire and the regret they leave, there cannot but be pleasure, participating, as it does, in the nature of the object. It

is as it were the interpretation of a diviner nature through our own; but its footsteps are those of a wind over the sea, which the coming calm erases, and those traces remain only, as on the wrinkled sand which paves it. Those and corresponding conditions of being are experienced principally by those of the most delicate sensibility and the most enlarged imagination; and the state of mind produced by them *is at war with every base desire.*

Thus for Shelley poetic knowledge is synonymous with the rise of man. The passage tells us something about the Fall of Man, of what may happen even to a temporarily risen man when his mind is no longer "at war with every base desire." I think again of the biblical Balaam.

Balaam

—People often ask, said the teacher, how it is possible that inspired men of letters who have authored important books on the human condition and were always in the forefront of every "just" cause were themselves rotten to the core. The answer is prefigured in the Balaam story.

—Balaam, as we all remember, was, when we first meet him, of grandiose prophetic stature. He had come to curse, but he blessed, and his blessings, both as prophecy and as poetry, have the power and the glory of waterfalls in the mountains. "For from the tops of rocks I see him [Jacob] and from the hills I behold him: Lo, the people shall dwell alone and shall not be reckoned among the nations." This is the generally accepted translation. But there are some who translate that passage differently.

And They Shall Not Pay Heed
unto the Nations

—The Hebrew word *yithashav*, the teacher went on, is usually translated "reckoned among." However, the *Degel Mahane Ephraim* suggests that it may as well stand for "pay heed unto." This is truer to the spirit not only of the prophecy, but of the biblical Hebrew as well. The message takes on a contemporary dimension: "A people that shall dwell alone and pay no heed unto the nations." This reminds me of the accusations of "intransigence" that the State of Israel has often had to face.

— "How goodly are thy tents, O Jacob; thy tabernacles, O Israel!" Balaam exclaims. "Surely there is no sorcery in Jacob, neither is there divination in Israel . . . . In due time it is said unto Jacob and unto Israel what God hath wrought . . . . Let me die the death of the righteous and let my lot be like his." Balaam, as we all remember, cannot resist the temptation to bless the Israelites, as though compelled to do so by what he sees. Moreover, he acknowledges to Balak, his king, that he cannot say things that God has not put in his mouth. Then why later, when Balak and Balaam are back in Moab, does Balaam advise the king to do things that only Satan could have put in his mouth? What has happened to the man "who heard the words of God and knew the knowledge of the Most High?" On the one hand, we see the great prophet of the heathen, of whom the sages say that he was to them what Moses was to the Hebrews, tell Balak that he cannot curse the people whom God blessed. But, on the other hand and in another place, we see him soon afterward advise his king that to defeat the Israelites, he must first undermine them morally. The daughters of Moab, not their armies, are subsequently unleashed against the Israelites as whores, and they succumb. Defeat and disaster soon follow.

— Rabbi Simha Zissel of Kelem, the sage of Lithuanian Mussar, asks how we are to understand the prophetically endowed heathen sage who had just pleaded with Yahweh, in whom he believed, that his death might be a righteous one, and then used his wisdom to plan abominations against the very people whose moral purity had inspired him to bless them in such a grand manner. And Rabbi Simha Zissel replies that the biblical account of the rise and fall of Balaam illustrates what happens to a man whose wisdom is not matched by his deeds. Balaam's deeds were always evil, and he had originally gone to curse the Israelites, as we all know. But then something happened to him. He saw something and he could not curse. What did he see? We have mentioned on another occasion what Rabbi Yohanan ben Zakkai said: He saw that the doors to the tents of the Israelites, to avoid unchaste sights, were not facing each other. This sight alone imbued him with the wisdom and strength to shake off, at least temporarily, the desire to do evil. Exposed as he suddenly was to an environment of purity, the great strange visionary's thoughts and deeds were, for the first time, in harmony with the godly. But this did not last long. Once back in Moab and exposed to its impurities, he began to draw his inspiration not from God, but from Satan. Only Satan could have conceived of the idea — and of the knowledge — that to physically destroy the Israelites they must be defeated morally. Balaam was not less of a visionary when he devised the idea of how to defeat Israel than when he blessed them, but he was a visionary of Satan. The execution of the plan to morally undermine the Israelites was, of course, evil, but the very idea that morally corrupted Israelites are, as such, prone to physical defeat is sacred and prophetic. Balaam, though rotten to the core, could thus use sacred premises to reach abominable conclusions.

The Master and their Disciples

— In conjunction with the Balaam story, said the teacher, I would like to relate a unique commentary to a Talmudic passage on the subject. "Come and see," say the sages of the Talmud, "what the difference is between the disciples of Patriarch Abraham and those of Balaam." Even this prefatory note, the teacher went on, elicited a question from later commentators: Why speak of the difference between the *disciples* of those two great men of old? Why not compare the prototypes themselves? The answer given belongs, in my view, to the category of the eternally contemporary: Both Abraham and Balaam were giants in their day and amid their peoples, and both had divine revelations: Abraham for a lifetime, Balaam for a while, but divine revelations nevertheless! To compare Abraham with Balaam, each in the context of his day and his way, would not be difficult, but such a comparison would not give us a yardstick of greatness that would be valid forever, for the truth of the matter was that both Abraham and Balaam were indeed great men! But to judge truly the ultimate merits and ultimate consequences of their greatness one must look at their disciples, their followers, their adherents. Let us look at some recent examples. Marx, they tell us, was a great man, a humane man. But look at his disciples as, for example, the Marxists now ruling, and slaughtering, Cambodia; the Gulag archipelago; Stalin; and so forth. The same is true of Freud: Freud was a great man, a humane man. No doubt about it. He was also the founder of that school of psychoanalysis usually referred to as "depth psychology." He was certainly a man of depth. But to judge the merits of psychoanalysis today, one must look not at the historical Freud, but at his disciples: No branch of psychology, it seems to me, is more saturated with shallow, hollow, predictable, vulgar clichés, repeated ad nauseam, than that of depth psychology. History thus knows of many great and glorious teachers who, if we judge them by their disciples, we must wish had never been born.

The Book of the Generations of Adam

"In the middle of our last class a question was raised concerning a passage at the beginning of the Bible: 'This is the book of the generations of Adam . . . . In the day that God created Adam, in the likeness of God created He him.' What do we learn from this passage that we haven't known before?" the questioner asked. "Doesn't it say a little earlier 'God created man in His own image; in the image of God created He him'? What new ground does this second passage break?"

— The answer, said the teacher, becomes apparent and relevant in the light of a momentous discussion between two giants of the Mishna, Rabbi Akiba and Ben Azzai, on the question of the existential meaning of two seemingly disparate biblical passages: "This is the book of the generations of Adam," and "Thou shalt love thy neighbor as thyself." Ben Azzai, according to Rav Kook's interpretation, holds that the passage about the generations is the more important of the two because it clearly implies that all the generations of men are bearers of the divine image and, as such, carry within themselves a nucleus of natural morality to be traced to it. Man, in other words, was born with an inclination to do good, and this alone makes him incline to the understanding and realization of God's word in the world. Rabbi Akiba, however, thought that the divine image alone did not guarantee that the generations of men would remain faithful to the spark of goodness that the Almighty implanted in the human heart when He fashioned man unless man realized that the life of the image, that is to say, of the divine in his nature, depends on his deeds — unless he "creates" himself. Rabbi Akiba was saying, then, that even more important than the originally inborn inclination to do good, inherent in the divine image, is the actuality of *doing* it. The divine image in man may, in fact, vanish and die without the learned practice of loving our neighbor, a decisive socioethical act of our own making that reimbues

the image with the Divine in it, or imbues us with the awareness of the
Divine in the image. Not, God forbid, that Ben Azzai belittled deeds,
but he had, it seems, like Rav Kook almost two millennia later, greater faith in the indestructible grandeur of man. It is my feeling, however, the teacher commented, that had Rav Kook, who took Ben Azzai's line, lived in the Auschwitz era, he might have seen this discussion in a different light.

"In a more pessimistic light, you mean?" someone asked. "It seems
as if Rabbi Akiba didn't have much faith in man."

—Yet he was the most towering man of faith in Jewish history! the
teacher countered.

"Can the two go together?"

Rejoice, Young Man, In Thy Youth

—Let me tell you a story about the way a Hasidic master interpreted
a biblical passage where two opposites are presented as capable of going together. We read in the eleventh chapter of Ecclesiastes the following advice given by the wisest of men to the younger generation:
"Rejoice, young man, in thy youth and let thy heart cheer thee in the
days of thy youth, and walk in the ways of thine heart and in the sight
of thine eyes; but know that for all this God will bring thee into judgment." How are we to understand this strange kind of counseling?

—Rabbi David of Kotzk interprets it thus: "Isn't it the highest
rung a man can achieve," he asks, "if he can combine the two things
together? 'Rejoice, young man, in thy youth' and so forth, but
remember that there is judgment for everything." In other words, en-
joy life—yes! But do not forget for a moment that there is a God in
the world!

Bring Man to Judgment
and Call God to Account

The teacher paused before going on:

—"But know," he returned to the same passage, "that for all this
God will bring thee into judgment." But there were also stages in biblical history when faith was so real that it permitted man to call God to
account. We see this in the eighty-ninth psalm, for example, when

David rebukes the Lord God for all the tribulations He has poured on His people. But nowhere is this calling God to account expressed more powerfully than in the book of Job. On the one hand, there is the assertion, "Though He slay me, yet I will trust in Him," but, on the other, the warning, "But I will maintain my own ways before Him." The relation between Job and God is a relation between an I and a Thou, to use Buber's terms. Rav Soloveichik, the great Torah-existentialist, calls it "confrontation." The difference between the Buberian "I-Thou" and the Rav's "confrontation" or "confronted man" is that the first implies a relaxation of tensions while the other is all holy tension—even tension between heaven and earth, which is what the Bible is all about, after all.

The Shaking of the Foundations
and Waiting for God

The teacher read from Isaiah 24 and then from Psalm 130:

> *The foundations of the earth are shaking*
> *Earth breaks to pieces,*
> *Earth is split to pieces,*
> *Earth shakes to pieces,*
> *Earth reels like a drunken man,*
> *Earth rocks like a hammock;*
> *Under the weight of its transgressions earth*
> *   falls down,*
> *To rise no more!*
> *Lift up your eyes to heaven and look upon*
> *   the earth beneath:*
> *For the heavens shall vanish away like smoke;*
> *And the earth shall grow old like a robe;*
> *The world itself shall crumble.*
> *But my righteousness shall be forever,*
> *And my salvation knows no end.*
>
> *I wait for the Lord, my soul doth wait,*
> *   and in his word*
> *Do I hope.*

My soul waiteth for the Lord more than they
*   that watch*
For the morning:
I say, more than they that watch for the
*   morning.*

—There would not necessarily have to be a connection between "the shaking of the foundations" and the "waiting for God." But when a people has been saying for millennia through the mouths of its greatest sages that the world is moving toward an ultimate shaking of its foundations, and the foundations then actually begin to shake, the waiting for God becomes a logical consequence. When I tell people nowadays that the foundations of the world are shaking, they quite often say to me, "They have shaken before; history has known many periods when man thought that the foundations of the world were shaking for good. But no matter how strongly those foundations shook the world has somehow managed to survive." I am not here to tell you, at the conclusion and summation of our year of Bible study, that the world will not survive the present shaking of its foundations. After all, whenever the Bible speaks of the shaking of the foundations, it also announces the proximity of salvation as in that chapter of Isaiah. But a word must be said about the difference between the shaking of the foundations that is taking place now and those that have shaken the world in the past.

—The difference is between "not yet" and "no longer." There may have been a time, in the words of Nicholas Berdyaev, when the image of man, his truly human nature, was *not yet* revealed, some time in the past. But now we face something quite different: The image of man has been shaken and it has begun to disintegrate after it was revealed. This is happening now in all spheres of human endeavor and signifies a total collapse of the humanistic theory of progress. The shaking of the foundations is to a large degree a result of this collapse.

—There was a time, in the long, hopeful periods of "not yet," when we could listen to the prophecies about the shaking of the foundations without feeling and without understanding. There were, in fact, centuries when we did not take them seriously. Today, however, we must take them seriously because a phrase like "earth split to pieces," for example, is no longer a mere vision; it has become physics. Paul Tillich elaborated on it in a sermon titled "The Shaking of the Foundations." We know now, Tillich explains, that in the ground of our earth, and in the ground of everything in the world that has form and structure, destructive forces are bound. When the unruly power of the smallest parts of our material world was restrained by cohesive structure, a place was provided for life to grow and for history to develop. When the foundations of the earth were laid, the key to those bound forces of the ground was God's alone.

—This is not the case any longer. Man has now discovered the key that can unlock the forces of the ground, those forces that were bound when the foundations of the world were laid. He is now, as a result, seized by a tremendous curiosity along with a tremendous anxiety caused by his unlimited capacity to destroy. Lines like "the foundations of the world are shaking" or "earth split in pieces" are no longer poetic metaphors, but hard, bitter realities or horrendous, imminent threats. That is the religious meaning of the age we live in. We had forgotten about such shakings, Tillich writes, and it was science more than anything else that made us forget it—science not as knowledge but as hidden idolatry, which made us believe that we are capable of working out our salvation without God or even against Him—science in this sense.

—False prophets, as Jeremiah called them, cried in his day as they did in the nineteenth century: "Progress! Infinite progress" and "Peace, universal peace! Happiness—happiness for everybody!" But now we know that this lie we lived contributed to the shaking of the foundations. Now we know that whoever says that there still is or can be in the desolate realm of autonomous reason and automatic progress a decent hope in human happiness or even in less troubled days for mankind is either mad or blind. More and more people the world over, young people in particular, are seized by the feeling that there is really nothing any longer to expect in the world. It is becoming apparent that the only kind of waiting one can resort to in the chaos that threatens to engulf us is the waiting for God.

—To us Jews this is not a new experience. Patriarch Jacob, who even more than Abraham and Isaac prefigures Jewish history, cries out on his deathbed, "I wait for Thy deliverance, O Lord!" The psalmist is even more specific when he says, "I wait for the Lord, my soul doth wait and in his word I hope." He implies that this waiting is

not only part of a relation to God, but a promise of steadfastness of
soul in the impossible times that lie ahead. When history goes awry
and the generation of the lie rules over the affairs of men, we experience the waiting for God as a waiting for truth—nay as a waiting
for the vindication of truth as a vindication of God's name in the
world.

—If Thomas Merton, the brilliant Christian thinker, is correct in
saying that the Jews are the eschatological sign of the twentieth century, it would be equally right to assume that Israel, by its very
emergence, has turned this sign into a full-fledged banner. But has
the banner made the waiting for God any less urgent? I am afraid not.
Even more than waiting for God was aroused down the ages by Israel's
persecutors, it is now aroused by her defamers. The intensity of this
defamation, which the emergence of Israel has made worse, endows
the waiting for God with a messianic urgency even stronger than that
engendered by the shaking of the foundations. Our waiting for God is
thus much more intense than that of other nations, because we experience the shaking of the foundations both as human beings and as
Jews. If the others wait for God, in the psalmist's words, as "they that
watch for the morning," our souls, along with the psalmist's, "waiteth
for the Lord" *more* than they that watch for the morning. Thank you
and *shalom* to you all.

Silence followed. Some people began to applaud, but stopped
short: Applause did not seem to fit the serenity of the occasion. Then,
as the teacher turned to go, he was stopped on his way out by a young
man from the class. "Sir," he asked, "would you have a word of advice
to those of us who now intend to continue studying the Bible by ourselves?"

—Study it in a manner that will enable you to see history, prophecy, and personal experience throw light on each other, the teacher
responded. During the Six Day War, a group of Israeli soldiers took
an Arab village on the Golan Heights and found the village deserted.
They came across some artifacts—vases, pottery—in the abandoned
houses and confiscated them. At sunset when they returned to the
camp the officer ordered them to line up in front of him. Without
another word, he pulled a small Bible out of his pocket and read from
the book of Joshua, where the embattled leader of the Israelites pronounces a curse on anyone who loots enemy property. When the offi-

cer had finished, the soldiers wordlessly and almost in unison made a heap of their booty, poured gasoline on it, and set it afire. The thought occurred to me that the soldiers, religious or not, after they had done what they did according to biblical Law, as they stood there around the little campfire at sunset, must have felt toward their officer the kind of gratitude one feels toward a restorer of souls, toward a man who makes it possible, through a simple act, for the soul to experience its own depths.

The Experience of One's Own Depths

—I shall leave you now, the teacher said, with a Hasidic thought on the subject: "When a man is singing," said Rabbi Pinhas of Koretz, "and cannot lift his voice, and another comes and sings with him— another who can lift his voice, then the first will be able to lift his voice, too. This is the secret of the bond between spirit and spirit."

The audience rose together and spontaneously chanted, in hymnic ecstasy, a famous line from the High Holiday prayers:

> *Our Father, our Father, our Lord,*
> *Be lenient with us, we implore;*
> *Our Father, our Lord, be lenient with us*
> *For we have no deeds to report . . .*

Index of Names